Making Sense

Making Sense

Peter Moddel

Ibex Press
Fribourg, Switzerland

Copyright © 2014 by Peter Moddel.
All rights reserved.

Cover Design: Geneviève Romang.

Making Sense—1st ed.
ISBN 978-2-9700967-0-2 (Print edition)
ISBN 978-2-9700967-1-9 (E-book edition)

Contents

Preface   xi
   The Language   xii
   Vocabulary Key   xii
   A Personal Note   xvi
   The Content at a Glance   xvi

Preamble: On Perceiving   1

[1] The Process of Concept Formation   7

PART I: CONSCIOUS AND NONCONSCIOUS MIND ACTIVITY   7
   What Is a Thing?   7
   Denotation   8
   Reaching For and Finding Concepts   10
   Connotation   12
   Beyond Logic   13
   Thinking   14
   An Initial Sketch of the Dual Process of Mind   17
   Mind Activity beyond Consciousness   18
   Describing the Activity of Mind   21
   ~ Interlude: Reality and the Early Renaissance   23
   The Transience of the Perceiving Subject   25
   Feelings into Thoughts   27
   Experiencing Multiplicity and Duration   28
   Conscious Moments and the Noncontinuity of Thought   29
   Conclusions   31

PART II: THE SUBJECTIVE MOMENT OF PERCEPTION   33
   ~ Interlude: Perception Is a Creative Act   33
   The Moment of Integration   35
   The Temporal Present   37
   The Nature of Truth   42
   ~ Interlude: When the Role of Self Is Ignored   44

[2] Sense Perception: Sight and Hearing — 47
Prefacing Remarks — 47

PART I: VISION — 48
Periphery and Fovea Perceived Spatially — 48
Fovea Vision — 49
~ *Interlude: Seeing an Object* — 50
The Intent to See Something — 50
The Disappearing Object of Perception — 51
Visual Periphery Transformations — 53
Limits and Boundaries — 55

PART II: AUDITION — 56
Periphery and Fovea Perceived Temporally — 56
~ *Interlude: Surrealism and the Source of Meaning* — 57
Auditory Periphery — 58
Strange Yet True: Temporal Periphery — 59
What Do Periphery Sounds Sound Like? — 60
Blending *Is* with *Is Not* — 62
Auditory Periphery Is Not Memory — 63

PART III: SENSORY PERCEPTION—A BROADER UNDERSTANDING — 64
Fovea and Periphery in the Creation of Concepts — 64
Intermingling of the Senses in Periphery — 65
To See Without Eyes, to Hear Without Ears — 66
Perceiving the Imperceptible — 67
Periphery as a Subject of Study — 70
Subjectivity and Perception — 71
~ *Interlude: Re-viewing Reality* — 73
Noninterference within Periphery Phenomena — 74
Perceiving Wholes as Wholes: The Ground for Intelligence — 75
Unit Size is Variable — 78
A Narcissistic Effect — 79
~ *Interlude: Narcissus* — 81
Fovea and Periphery in Balance — 81
The Present and How It Happens — 82
Conclusions — 84

[3] Sight and Color Vision — 87

- The Function of Contradiction in Perception — 88
- One-Dimensionality — 88
- The Second Dimension — 89
- Three-Dimensionality and the Visual Experience of Space — 90
- Color Vision — 92
- Spatial Conflict Resolved as Depth; Temporal Conflict Resolved as Color — 95
- The Quality of Depth and the Quality of Color — 96
- Ascent through Different Dimensions — 98
- It Is Subjective, but I Didn't Do It! — 98
- The Surprising Fact of What Constitutes Sight — 99
- ~ *Interlude: Fun with Interference Patterns* — 100
- Conclusions — 101

[4] The Word *Mind* and What It Signifies — 103

PART I: *MIND* AS A NOUN — 104

- A Suggestion to the Reader — 104
- Initial Examples — 104
- Mind and Knowing — 106

PART II: *MIND* AS A VERB — 107

- Set 1: *To Mind*, Signifying Caring — 108
  - With What Do You Mind — 110
  - Minding Interrupted by an Intrusion — 110
  - Minding—Before and After an Intrusion — 111
  - To Be Mindful — 112
  - Summary of Set 1 — 112
- Set 2: *To Mind*, Signifying Being Disturbed — 112
  - Self Awakens to a Disturbance — 113
  - Many Separate *I*'s — 115
  - Query 1: Why Does *To Mind* Signify Aversion? — 116
  - Query 2: Why the Reversal of Subject and Object? — 117
  - Reflections on What Was Found So Far — 119

PART III: PLEASURE AND DISPLEASURE IN MIND ACTIVITY	120
Describing Qualities	120
Two Contrasting Experiences of Mind	120
CONCLUSIONS	123

[5] Intent: What It Is — 125

Intention: A Constant Companion of All That Lives	125
~ *Interlude: Ubiquitous Intent*	126
Preliminary Remarks	127
An Important Caveat about Individual Distinctions	128
Preview of the Trajectory of the Two Chapters on Intent	130
Keeping an Open Mind	131
Subtleties of Intent	133
~ *Interlude: Humility*	138
Intent: Distinct from Thought	139
Intent: Cleansed of Thinking	139
Intent in Objects	142
Intent with No Ascertainable Source	143
Intent and Reality	145
Whose Intent Is It?	147
~ *Interlude: La Gestion Mentale*	148

[6] Intent: How It Functions — 151

~ *Interlude: The Anthill*	152
Taking Form; Losing Randomness	152
Nonmaterial Presence	153
Transmitting Intent	153
Looking for the Unity of Self	154
Formative Influence	155
A Sense That Perceives Integration	157
~ *Interlude: Intent and the Cultivation of Values*	160
Intent versus Entropy	161
A Synopsis: The Intent Circuit	165
The Emerging Vision	167
Where Past Becomes Present and Present Intimates Future	169

	~ Interlude: Romanticism and the Pursuit of Meaning	171
	The "Motor" That Runs the World	172
	A View of Evolution	173
	Thinking and the Action of Intent	174
	Beyond Meaninglessness	176

[7] The Self We Know as "I" — 177

	Understanding Subjectivity	177
	Who Is *I*?	177
	Forming the Concept of *I*	180
	Self as Belonging	182
	~ Interlude: The Song and the Silence	185
	The Disappearing Self	186
	~ Interlude: Cooperation	189
	A Dynamic View of Self	191
	A Pause to Consolidate What Has Emerged So Far	194
	An Impersonal View of Self	195
	From Impersonal to Personal	196
	To Everything a Spirit	196
	~ Interlude: The Reign of Objectivity	197
	Self as Precursor to the World	198
	When We Say *I*	200
	Consciousness and Self-Consciousness	202
	Multiple *I*'s	203
	The First of Two Summaries	204
	A Summary in Dialogue Form	205

[8] Induction Contrasted with Causality — 213

	Conclusions That Will Be Reached in This Chapter	213
	Two Lexical Precisions	214
	Defining Causality and Induction	215
	The Integral Presence That Generates Induction	217
	A Closer Description of Causality and Induction	219
	Induction and Freedom from Determinism	220
	Induction and the Ability to Choose	222

[9] Freedom of Choice 225
Freedom and Intent 225
What It Means That Some-*one* Is Choosing 228
The Contribution of Consciousness 229
Self in Transformation 231
Choosing 232
Promoting a Way of Being 233
~ *Interlude: Direction within the Flux of Events* 234
Values 235
Free to Be Me 236
Character and Uniqueness 237
A Moral Dimension to Self 239

Epilogue: A Personal Viewpoint 243
Index 251

To my teachers

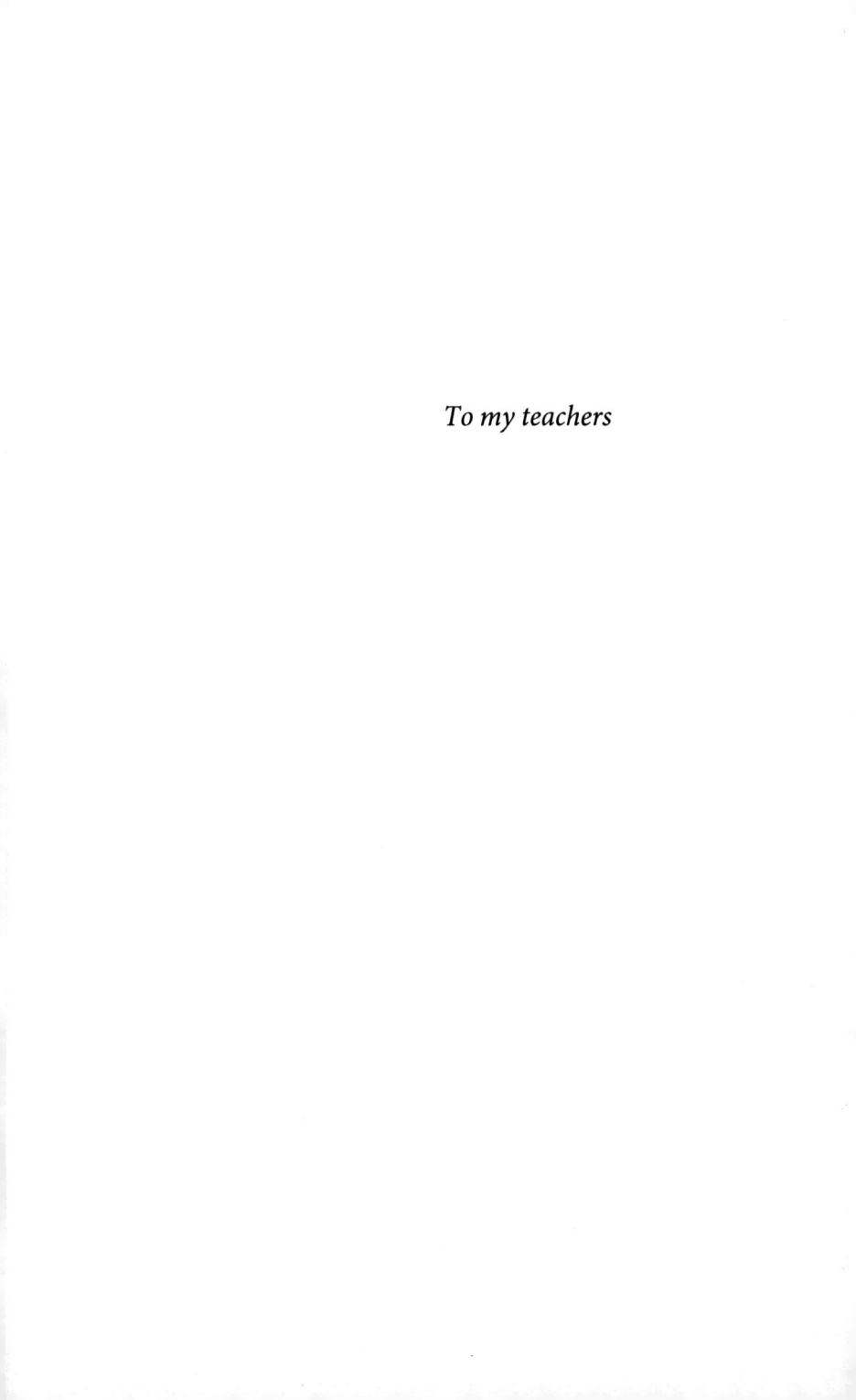

" ... what a thing is is the reason why it is."

—Plotinus (204–270 C.E.)
Enneads VI: 7, 2, 16

Preface

THIS WORK OPENS with a description of the process of thought and what influences it, but the process is considered solely from the subjective perspective of the person thinking. It touches on questions that arise in philosophy, neuroscience, linguistics, pedagogy, and other areas; however, the essential argument is built on experiences we have in common as thinking beings. As such, the presentation is self-contained. Quotes from sources that support or challenge the propositions given here have not been included in the interest of simplifying the presentation and relieving it of excess ballast that, as a rule, becomes gratuitous once the argument is found to be coherent—or incoherent.

This descriptive approach brings into focus a twofold movement of the thinking process. There is the inward movement—centripetal, linear, deductive—guided by the intent of centering on specific units of meaning that become objects of thought. There is a second and complementary movement, frequently overlooked when discussing the thinking process, which is the outward movement away from this focus and into a periphery of ever-shifting proto-information. This movement into multiplicity outpaces the limited linear processing of the conscious mind, which is unable to follow multiple strands at one time. For this reason, the complementary expanding movement of thought remains out of reach of consciousness, that is to say, it is nonconscious or, more precisely, extraconscious. By reflecting on numerous telltale signs of the mind's extended reach into realms out of bounds to rational thought, a coherent description can be assembled of the overall dual movement: the in-breath and the out-breath of the thinking process.

Within the context of this dual process, much else can be described: concept formation, sense perception, the awakening of consciousness, the arising and dissolution of self, the ubiquitous influence of intent, and the possibility of individual independent choice.

The Language

This presentation shuns terminologies, yet precision and brevity are its goals. Though this seems a contradiction, it proves a more direct route. Terminologies require explanations and constant readjustment to any contextual variation, whereas common words have the advantage of saying what they mean. They give an immediate intuitive understanding and minimize the need for explanation. Also, readily available words enable the discussion to remain with what is reciprocal between words and experience. Specific terminologies usually reference a set of ideas that have not fully gelled as a unitary concept and have the effect of distancing the speaker and reader from what is being said. Almost invariably, the ensuing discussion becomes a battle between contrasting positions staked out according to the terms employed: dualist, materialist, and so forth. This presentation ignores such different standpoints, focusing instead on the flow of the emerging understanding—so much so that no position is claimed to be correct, and yet, surprisingly, along this path beliefs that were held as fundamental are released and habitual standpoints are dismissed, leaving this penetrating subject matter light and simple.

Vocabulary Key

Intent and Intention

This work employs the words *intent* and *intention* interchangeably. No specialized meaning is given to the word *intention*; it holds the sense it has in common usage that includes personal engagement towards an outcome. At the beginning of chapter 5, where the topic of intent is breached frontally, definitions are given.

Perception

The word *perception* is employed throughout this work to refer to the act whereby consciousness registers the presence of an object. The object may be perceived as being in the world, or it may be perceived as a thought present in the mind only. To use *perception* in reference to everything that registers in consciousness without attempting to separate concepts from percepts makes the usage clear. In particular, it avoids the pitfall of starting from presuppositions about reality, as happens when one predetermines what is supposedly outside and what is inside the mind. *To perceive* is to recognize some thing whether or not the physical sense organs are involved.

To repeat: *perception* is the presence of an object that arises in consciousness. For this reason the word *perception* is not used to refer to sensations, hunches, and intuitions that produce no specific object. Stated more simply, *perception* does not refer to the content of expanded consciousness (see the next entry).

To understand the act of perception, a finer distinction must be included. It relates to the perceiver's ability to interrupt the act of perception. This factor separates perception in a lucid or wakeful state from perception in a mesmerized state, whether under hypnosis or in a dream state (other than lucid dreaming). Lucid and nonlucid states are both acts of perception because both involve consciousness of an object. The distinction between them comes on another level. The perceiver in the lucid state can break from the thought or observation, while in the mesmerized state this is not possible. Lucid perception is characterized by the ability of the subject to intervene and interrupt the process; this option is not available to the mesmerized perceiver.

This simple distinction creates a helpful path through many an argument about perception and consciousness.

Consciousness

We commonly employ the word *consciousness* to refer to two separate, though related, phenomena. Clarity requires an initial precision on the two contrasting usages of this word.

In its more common usage, the word *consciousness* relates to perception; to be conscious refers to the capacity to perceive. It can be contrasted with the state of being knocked out, oblivious; consciousness is the experience of sensing the presence of some particular thing. In all that follows, this is what is referred to as *consciousness*. Where it is necessary to emphasize that it is distinct from the second meaning described below, it will be called *conceptual consciousness*.

There is a wider sense of gaining understanding, a state of expanded consciousness that includes implicit understanding that never itself becomes the object of thought. It is nonconceptual. We have a vague sense of some presence without otherwise being conscious of any particular thing. For example, in usages such as *I was conscious that something was amiss*, the word *conscious* is employed to refer to a general awareness that includes sensations that do not take the form of specific objects of consciousness, that is, sensations that bypass *conceptual consciousness*. A further example can make this clearer. Subliminal impressions, by definition, do not become conscious; they do not enter the mind as objects of consciousness, and yet, they do affect us. We are conscious of them, true, but conscious in a different sense. What is subliminal registers in our *expanded consciousness*, and this is the expression used in this presentation for this more general, less explicit mode of sensing presence. *Conceptual consciousness* and *expanded consciousness* are separate states, and for the experiencing subject expanded consciousness functions in the absence of conceptual consciousness.

To recapitulate: *consciousness* and *conceptual consciousness* are synonyms, whereas the more generalized sense of being conscious that forms no specific object of consciousness—for example, the sense of being alive—is referred to as *expanded consciousness*.

This fundamental distinction is commonly overlooked.

The Nonconscious

In this study, the word *unconscious* is rarely employed and only as an adjective. *The unconscious*, as a noun, is encumbered by numerous psychological implications, and to avoid these the expression *the nonconscious* has been chosen.

Perception and Consciousness

This entry is interesting for itself, though not taken up directly in this work. Integrating what has been told of perception (lucid versus mesmerized) and of consciousness (conceptual versus expanded) yields two states of consciousness of an object and one state of nonconsciousness:

1A. *Object-consciousness interruptible by the perceiver:* Commonly known as consciousness or lucid perception.
1B. *Object-consciousness uninterruptable by the perceiver:* Commonly understood as dreaming or being mesmerized. Here the perceiver lacks the faculty to intervene in the activity of perception.
2. *Objectless consciousness:* The nonconceptual state of *expanded consciousness* described above.

Mind

No initial definition is given and instead, in chapter 4, the full significance emerges from examples that show how the word *mind* is employed in English. However, a distinction can already be made between two separate activities attributed to the mind: *The Conceptual Mind* and *The Expanded Mind*. The first is the mind's activity that engages consciousness; the second is the activity of the mind that engages expanded consciousness and is ever inaccessible to conceptual consciousness.

The conceptual mind is most commonly referred to as *The Rational Mind*, *The Logical Mind* or *The Analytical Mind* and, in what follows, all these expressions are used to refer this same function. For the non-conscious activity of mind, the expression employed in this work is *The Expanded Mind*.

Awareness

This word has a broader meaning than perception, as defined above. Awareness includes what we sense both through conceptual consciousness and through expanded consciousness.

A Personal Note

Questioning the process of thinking is my way of paying homage to the vast unknown that penetrates our accumulated knowledge. When presenting what we believe we do understand, we generally give little space to what is not understood, and as a result, we tend to forget that it is there. A sense of pride in what has been understood unfurls and tends to hide the presence of the unknown.

Stepping always on sure footholds while ignoring all else gives a very distorted view of nature, society, and the world and produces very real consequences in the way we live, interact, and develop. In what follows, I no doubt parade the same failings, staking claims with vigor, feeding hubris with blind confidence. May this be a warning to the reader! However, my purpose is to call attention to what is unknown and accompanies the known, neither to hide it with explanations nor to temper its strangeness with comforting hypotheses.

The Content at a Glance

— The preamble begins with a concrete example and leads the reader to the questions that prompted this study of intent and meaning.

[1] The first chapter offers a description of the conscious and the nonconscious activity of mind. With an understanding of these two complementary functions, it is possible to describe how, in tandem, they produce concepts and awaken the state we know as consciousness. In this process, intent has a definite function that is described with numerous examples. The examples also serve to bring out the fluctuating presence/absence of the conscious subject, and they clarify how the temporal present we call now is determined.

[2] The second chapter develops these ideas further with regard to the physical senses and the role of periphery in both seeing and hearing.

[3] The third chapter is an analysis of sight and color vision. Adding a new factor—the intent of the conscious subject—to what is known of light and the physical eye allows for a description of how and why colors arise. With this comes a deeper understanding of all perception.

[4] The fourth chapter traces the meaning of the word mind by observing its usage in the English language, and it brings succinct conclusions about mind and its relation to the person who identifies with that mind.
[5] The fifth chapter defines and describes the nature of intent.
[6] The sixth chapter considers the function of intent and includes a presentation on the opposition between entropy and intent. Eventually, the discussion leads past the boundaries of the classical view of reality.
[7] The seventh chapter enters more specifically into how we relate to the person we refer to as me and I. On the basis of first-person experiences and with an understanding of the role of intent, a succinct definition of self is possible.
[8] The eighth chapter presents the background needed to understand the inductive process of intent and shows induction to be distinct from causality.
[9] The ninth and concluding chapter follows naturally from the presentation of self and intent in the previous chapters. It shows how, with an understanding of the function of intent and the reflective role of consciousness, individual freedom of choice is conceivable.
— The epilogue reevaluates the pertinence of the findings contained in this work.

Acknowledgments

My gratitude goes to a number of people who generously assisted me when I needed to find the silence and peace this work required and also many thanks to those who expressed interest and offered helpful comments. I wish also to mention my dear parents whose memory and deep understanding are somehow present between the lines of what I have written.

Preamble: On Perceiving

WHAT DOES ONE NEED TO KNOW in order to be able to perceive an object? For example, if a yellow leaf is lying on the path in front of you, what do you need to know in order to recognize it? While walking in the woods, you notice shadows and light, leaves, branches, trees, fragrances, and birdcalls. A rustle in the undergrowth beside you triggers various thoughts, and the moment you come upon the yellow leaf, you see it and know what it is.

To understand a simple object that comes to your attention, a wealth of information must be present. To distinguish a leaf as separate from the ground requires an understanding of the general form of a leaf and, too, knowledge of the play of light and color that shows it to be a plane surface. The thought *leaf* includes how it feels to the touch, that it is light and pliable; it includes the fact that it grows on a tree and that it fell from a tree. To know a leaf is to know a tree, its shade, the sunlight, the wind, the cycle of seasons, the leaf in different stages of development, and the fact that leaves become sodden and decompose. This is not extra information to be added to what one observes; it is present in the recognition of a leaf as a leaf and gives the particular feeling and sense that is the understanding we bring to the word *leaf*. This implicit understanding goes further. It includes an understanding of plant life and therefore knowledge of other forms of life and the difference between these and rocks and bricks and houses. To sense a leaf as a plant is to know something of life and to know about death. Of course, these are not conscious thoughts but are an understanding contained in the momentary grasp that acknowledges a leaf, for what could *leaf* mean if we did not know these things? And this is only the beginning for, in turn, each of these concepts requires a wealth of background information to hold its particular sense and, as if this were not already vast beyond measure, there are personal meanings too, things that strike a chord because of personal past experiences. Then, too, the act of recognition must also include a sense of direction—where the object is and how one is moving—as well as the attitude that brings this attentiveness. There is something further, unacknowledged no doubt, and it is the fleeting pleasure of forming an image of something, of having some thing—a meaning—enter the conscious mind and occupy it for an instant. (The pleasure of forming an object is independent of the content, which may or may not be pleasurable.)

This vast knowledge hovers somewhere beyond the horizon of what is conscious, and yet, without it, a leaf would not be a leaf and could not mean what it does. Astounding as it may seem, any act of recognition calls for so much undeclared information that it is a wonder we are able to perceive anything at all! Any object that momentarily enters our conscious mind is sustained by a vast network of information that does not break through to consciousness. There is the object we think about consciously, and, too, there is much more that, though it does not become conscious, is necessary to give content to what is recognized.

What enters our conscious mind is, in a sense, the pinnacle of an underlying mass of implicit meaning. Still, beyond this, lies yet a further unreported dimension, for how do these undisclosed meanings spiral inward and unite to produce the item that alights in consciousness? Somehow what never enters our conscious mind flows together to produce the object that enters our conscious mind. What makes that happen? Something gives direction to the nonconscious activity of mind and leads it towards what then become specific thoughts.

To summarize:

A. There is the object we think of (e.g., a leaf).
B. There is all that must be known (tree, life, etc.) to have the meaning we apprehend.
C. There is something (a force field?) that gives direction to level B, guiding all that does not enter consciousness towards the object of which we become conscious.

To state the same in reverse order:

C. There is an influence that gives direction to the mind's activity that is not conscious.
B. There is the rich content of the unconscious mind that stays *below the radar* and does not enter consciousness.
A. There are specific items of understanding that arise in the mind and become our conscious thoughts.

These three levels of activity do not represent some new theory of mind but are experiences we already know well, and for this reason, common words refer to them. All that is done here is to set them out in clear view:

A is the level of conscious activity and thought.

B is the level of mind activity that is not conscious.

C is the level of purposeful activity.

Here are three different levels that represent three different types of activity. These are presented in the first chapter. Understanding that there are these distinct functions brings clarity to how we know what we know, as well as to that which remains unknown and cannot be expressed in these terms.

Level A portrays conscious activity and thought. It holds a dominant role in our society where rational thought, which sets all out in terms of subject and object, has been given the task of explaining all else.

Level B encompasses mind activity that is not conscious. Although largely misunderstood and often mistakenly attributed to psychology, it is simply the fullness of the mind's activity. Conscious thought is essentially linear and, being limited to one-at-a-time processing, lacks rapidity and agility to grasp multiple strands of thought functioning simultaneously. When the mind goes from single-file sequencing to multiprocessing, the conscious mind cannot keep abreast. It is superseded, and the experience is loss of consciousness. The mind continues to function, but conscious thought can do no more than await the fruits of this burgeoning activity that lies beyond its reach. Referring to the oblivious part of the mind as *unconscious* is a case of the disenchanted conscious mind referring to a land it cannot enter, namely, the expanded activity of mind. From the perspective of the full activity of the mind, the view is quite different: the expanded activity is not nonconsciousness but heightened consciousness, because the activity of the mind moves between single consciousness (the state of being conscious) and multiconsciousness (the heightened nonconscious activity of the expanded mind). Throughout this work, the encompassing reach of the mind is referred to as the *expanded mind* or the complementary part of the mind or simply as *out-of-consciousness*. As for *multiconsciousness*, its function is alluded to and aspects of it are described in different contexts, but it does not become a separate subject of study.

> The activity of the mind moves between single consciousness and multiconsciousness.

Level C, purposeful activity, has been given little consideration in our culture and is not generally included in reflections on what we know of the world and ourselves. Without considering the level of purposeful activity, we cannot describe the interconnections that form everything intelligible; nor can we account for the units of meaning we perceive and reference, for instance, with the word *leaf*. The movement towards meaning is purposeful in that it is the tendency to produce an intelligible object. It is what we commonly refer to as intention, and becoming familiar with it leads to the source of our sense of self. I recognize who I am, as well as that I am, because to some degree I sense that I produce acts and thoughts in accordance with my intentions. On the level of intention, we form meaningful relations with all that is, and for this reason an understanding—visceral or intellectual—of what intention involves is instrumental not only to understanding self and subjectivity but to the well-being of all that touches upon our lives. Our understanding of intention is reflected in the society we create and in the relationship we sustain with the natural world.

To enter this field of study, a threshold that has repeatedly proven to be a stumbling block must be passed: the act of concept formation. It seems so simple that a leaf is a leaf, a tune is a tune, a wish is a wish, that each thing is there for itself and we just add words to name it or form images of what it is (names refer to objects; nouns refer to categories of objects). But to assume that names and images do no more than refer to objects is to overlook all that has been told just now of a leaf. It would be to assume the role of innocent observer, witnessing what is. But objects need to be formed. How can there be a meaningful object without an interpreter, without a subject to serve as the focus of the flow that integrates the out-of-conscious impressions that give rise to what becomes known? A tune without *me*, is it a tune or is it just some notes? And a note, is it a note or just a certain frequency of impulses reaching my ears? And a wish without *me*, what can it be? Without that *me*, does anything hold together to become some thing? The leaf, the tune, the wish become what they are together with *me*. But is *me* really me, this me who is just now looking at this page? And whether it is or is not, where is the *me* that I am? Am I part of all that I know as the world, or am I yet something else? In fact, am I anything? Oh, dear! This is all so confusing.

Not at all—it is really quite simple. Confusion results because of unnecessary assumptions that clutter the way to understanding. Release the standard protocol of objectivity and a new field of study opens: the mind. It has been buried beneath scientific prerequisites demanding objectivity that aim to eliminate subjective impressions from everything. But level B, the vast network of hidden knowledge that is the source of meaning in all we recognize, requires a subject, and it requires level C, the purposeful action that leads to the arising of all we observe. Purpose and intent cannot be seen with a microscope, and, I might add, neither with the microscope mentality that looks for what is real in ever-smaller components of what we observe. The study of mind is a discipline with rules of its own that differ from the scientific protocol. As philosophy steps clear of the rules by which science operates and as it regains independence of thought, the presence of meaning, emaciated for so long by prescriptions for objectivity, regains full stature. Meanings alive with meaning rush to fill the existential void we have created. Our participation in an overall tendency to make sense becomes an apparent fact and we find ourselves partaking in the joy of connectivity that makes each of us who we are.

This presentation opens with a description of what happens the moment an intelligible item enters our mind—yours, mine, whomever's, but always someone's because mind is a subjective phenomenon. What comes to mind as a thought might be an observation, an imagination, or the recognition of a sensation and is the presence of something that makes sense. Chapter 1 relates how concepts arise and enter the mind as meaningful units. This more technical part of perceiving and knowing is generally taken to be hidden and inaccessible, and it is exciting to find that it can be described in great detail.

Exposing it in the opening chapter of the book makes for a long chapter, but, in so doing, it sets the path for what follows: an understanding of our personal involvement in all that we know as ourselves and the world.

[1]

The Process of Concept Formation

THIS FIRST CHAPTER is almost a book in itself. It is divided into two main parts.

— The first of these offers an encompassing description of the process by which concepts are formed. It includes a description of the dual functions of mind, one conscious the other nonconscious, and alludes to the influence of intent while leaving a full description of intent for later in the book.
— The second part opens a wider discussion of key aspects outlined in the first part, all of which have to do with the subjective moment in the activity of concept formation that brings a sense of presence.

PART I: CONSCIOUS AND NONCONSCIOUS MIND ACTIVITY

What Is a Thing?

"A rose is a rose is a rose"—how many times should the word be said before it takes on its specific meaning? At what moment does it turn into an object of thought and become what it is? How does a word—or a picture, for that matter—hold a meaning? The answer that is proposed here is straightforward, though perhaps unexpected.

8 | *Making Sense*

To reach the answer, two words that complement one another are helpful:

Denotation: The specific object or idea to which one refers
Connotation: The various associations that arise in the mind when thinking of an object

Choose any word, for example, *silence, tiger, ripen, blue*, and it can either function as denotation or it can give rise to connotations. Which of these two options arises depends on how we think about it. As a denotation, a word takes on a certain identity. It is that which we know as *silence*, as *tiger*, and so on. As a connotation, qualities we associate with the object suggest divers related experiences: *silence* might suggest solitude, separation, intensity, connection, presence, and *tiger* might suggest excitement, a flame, agility, fearlessness, terror, and so forth.

The distinction between denotation and connotation can be observed on the level of function. For this one need merely ask: For what purpose is a meaning evoked? In denotation, the purpose is to give presence to an object and determine its identity. In connotation, to the extent one can speak of purpose, it is to prolong a certain quality. Connotations serve to extend a general sense, enlivening it and at times remolding it. Connotations arise almost unnoticed and dissolve within an interplay of further meanings.

In this chapter, these two modes of mind activity are contrasted so as to highlight their differences. The purpose is to render the assumed barrier between conscious and nonconscious activity transparent, for it becomes evident that we create the separation between the two. But then, who is this *we*, this *I*? In this first chapter, the dual functions of mind will be described so that, step by step in the following chapters, a clear view can emerge of the words we commonly use to describe our shared experience as living beings, words such as *self, subjectivity, objectivity, reality, mind, intent, freedom*, and *beauty*.

Denotation

What gives an object its denotative meaning? Do the various attributes of an object serve to produce its denotation? To have the thought *rose*, how many of the rose's qualities need to be called to mind—one, two, a thousand? Even though this question makes little sense (there is no quantitative entry requirement to conception), it serves to highlight the fact that it is one thing to think about an object via its aspects and something different to simply have the concept of an object. Where does the specific meaning of an object lie? A search for the essence that makes a thing what it is—that makes water water, a rose a rose, happiness happiness—is futile. No such key essence is to be found, and yet water, rose, and happiness clearly signify three specific things. How does this come about?

Once it becomes clear that the entity posited by a concept, for instance, a rose, is *not* found among its specific manifestations (petals, thorns, a garden, etc.), the quest to find the content of a concept begins.

When observing a rosebush, one could note impressions that do not unite to form a specific object. For instance, sunshine, thorns, clay, fragrance, butterflies, and wind might all be noticeable, but nothing indicates which among them is specific to *rosebush* and which ones are not. Furthermore, each of these aspects is, in turn, a concept, and the same question pertains to it and, again, to the concepts that are needed to explain it. (The solution to this regression comes later in this chapter when the complementary expansive function of mind is elucidated.) Without the gesture of reaching for a concept, attributes do not signal an object. Nothing distinguishes the rosebush until the mind determines that there is an object to be known. And then, as soon as one affirms that a thing is there to behold, petals, fragrance, color, leaves, and thorns become part of the rosebush, whereas butterfly, wind, sunlight, and ground separate from it. How exactly this happens is the subject of this chapter.

It might be argued that a rosebush is an independently functioning unit and has, independent of the intentioned act of the observer, an objective identity of its own. Whether so or not, the fact is that one needs to recognize a specific presence to which relevant attributes can be tethered and irrelevant ones distanced. In claiming there is an object, one assumes an attitude that calls together the diverse qualities that give form to that object.

As a further example, take the word and concept *water*. I attribute *thing-hood* to water and recognize it as a something that has a place among other things. When did this happen? Observing water, or thinking of it, I may notice numerous attributes: the sensation of wetness, the play of light, its movement, the sound it makes, its taste as well as a wealth of previously formed conclusions about freezing, boiling, clouds, snow, the exclusion zone, the density at 4 degrees Celsius, the chemistry of H_2O, and so forth. None of these alone says the same thing as *water*, and all of them together do not either! And, in any case, how could anyone think simultaneously of so many aspects? That which gathers these as attributes and brings them to be part of the unity I aim for, namely, *water*, is not found in any specific attribute chosen. Instead, it has its origin in a prerequisite attitude that I, the subject, adopt. This attitude is what gives rise to the formation of concepts.

How exactly does this happen and what role has the perceiver in producing what is perceived?

Reaching For and Finding Concepts

Two separate moments are involved in the formation of concepts. The first is how the subject approaches the object-to-be before the concept is formed. It is the act of *aiming at an entity*. The second moment concerns *the entry of the object into consciousness*. These moments are determined by two particular attitudes the perceiver adopts.

The First Moment: Aiming at an Entity

As an aid to understanding the requisite attitude for the formation of a perceived object, the following scene is proposed.

Imagine we are in a forest where fog settles in and the surrounding trees fade into the fog. Before the arrival of this fog, objects were identifiable, and recognition, it seemed, came on the heels of perception. However, now, in the fog, it is difficult to recognize objects, and the time lapse between seeing something and understanding what it is increases. For a moment, our minds produce no conceivable object as we peer at some unclear thing through the heavy fog. There is an expectation that some object will take form, and this expectation might be accompanied by a feeling of uneasiness and restlessness that probably has to do with the need to grasp some identifiable thing. During this experience, our conscious minds try to make sense of what is there, evoking different possibilities; for example, the outline of a tree may suggest some animal or strange being. The impulse to place a definite object behind impressions inhabits most of our conscious activity. While imagining possibilities of what might be there, we are engaged in a process of identifying objects and forming concepts.

If there were no innate drive to produce what can be recognized as some thing, a different state of being would arise. We would become one with the experience of impressions and relax into the passing sensations. Released from the intent to perceive an object, we would not hunger for meaning, and the activity of concept formation would cease.

It should be clear that concepts are not ripe berries we pick freely but result from what we bring, through the presence of guiding intention, to our experience of the world. We hold a particular attitude towards the thing-to-be that is instrumental in producing the concept that ensues. It is a certain kind of expectation and has to do with the intention to pinpoint a specific entity. When this attitude is present, all that relates to that thing-to-be becomes attributes of it. Anticipating the imminent arrival of an entity gives rise to a context, a field of meaning that arises from what one knows and observes, as described earlier for the concept *water*. Meanings gather round, so to speak, and eventually the concept emerges. Without anticipation, nothing would assemble diverse features, generate a context, and lead beyond this to the formation of a concept. The disposition of aiming at *entity-hood* is instrumental to the formation of a concept. This detail, when overlooked, leads astray many a discussion on meaning, leaving the impression that units of meaning somehow stand on their own, independent of the particular consciousness that gave rise to them.

> *The subjective attitude of the perceiver unifies and objectifies what enters perception.*

To arrive at the perception of an object there is the attitude of anticipation that links qualities to an object. It is similar to the attitude one has when asking, "What is it?" This question need not be formulated explicitly, but, while receiving what arises in consciousness, we reach out with our mind for some unit meaning that integrates the impressions received. In our attitude is the expectation, or call it belief, that there is something to be identified. This act of reaching for unit meanings leads to the formation of concepts. Its presence as an intention gives rise to all we know as the world.

The subjective attitude of the perceiver unifies and objectifies what enters perception. In setting our expectation on finding an entity, an entity emerges to answer the call.

The Second Moment: Receiving the Gift of a Concept

The movement of understanding ends with the accession of meaning when we become aware of the presence of a concept. The concept somehow entered the mind, and with it we are able to recognize the presence (in our mind or in the world) of a particular entity. But how did it come to us? Between the preparation stage of gathering what will become attributes and the arrival of the concept in the mind, something unknown and unintelligible happened that allowed the concept to take form.

How easily this unknown is overlooked, making it seem that having a field of attributes is what creates concepts. It is not. Concepts are not assembled out of information bits gathered by the conscious mind. A very different mind process is needed. To describe the formation of a whole and its entry as a concept into consciousness, the complementary connotative attitude of mind needs to be taken into account. The following discussion opens the way to an understanding of the activity of the other half, one might say, of the mind: the out-of-consciousness or extraconscious mind.

Connotation

One might question whether it is at all possible to describe processes involved in creating connotation since any description will necessarily be in denotative terms and cannot account for the complementary connotative side of the mind's activity. Even so, with license for imaginative thought, there are ways of portraying the dance of the mind, even where the specific steps may not be fully delineated. In the description that follows, it is helpful to hold one's attention on the overall process being described and not linger on the paragraph-by-paragraph portrayal of its diverse aspects.

The connotative mode of thinking leads in a direction that differs fundamentally from that of the denotative mode. For example, with the thought *water*, the way opens for limitless associations to surface in the mind. Whatever they might be—*rain, washing, current, drown, joy, the moon, purity, life*—each requires no entry permission. They are there, so to speak, in their own right, freely taking on meanings without heed of contextual or logical connections. They arise intuitively as unfettered, interchanging presences and need no rational justification. Here objects function merely as the carriers of connotations, as catalysts for what manifests, and are of no further concern. Instead of particular qualities being subservient to objects, as in the denotative mode, qualities rule the play by releasing an interchange of meanings that are liberated from the objects that gave rise to them.

A burning candle may express remembrance, celebration, joy, sadness, absence, beauty, intimacy, and so forth, with each of these, in turn, suggesting other connections. All are personal associations quite removed from what the dictionary would describe as a candle. The connotative mode moves through an ever-widening field where associations arise upon associations. One could imagine a lattice of interconnected meanings where none claims attention as a specific entity—a multifaceted display of shimmering correspondences that comes alive in the absence of a subject naming the items that arise.

Connotative meanings are ever personal and subjective, reflecting something of the person who elicits them. Out of myriad possible sensations, those that are gathered reflect the subjective condition of the person who receives what emerges from expanded consciousness—*expanded* because its content is no longer itemized and restricted to fit the requirements of conscious thought. The connotative world is where free-flowing impressions burgeon out one from another with none claiming attention as a specific entity. It is available when the denotative mind with its dictionary definitions is out of play and does not break the flow by reformulating impressions in terms of specific objects conceived at a particular moment and set in time and space. Objectivity necessarily instates such a reference frame and in so doing breaks the connotative fabric.

Beyond Logic

Connotations are not restricted by a set of permissible logical links. Certainly, we assume the presence of some connection, some ricochets of meanings, of associative connections that lead from one context to another, but to hunt out the possible links would be to bring denotative thought into play, analyzing, separating, and connecting specific units of meaning. Such units are absent. An object that gives rise to connotations has no presence of its own and generates a halo of possible meanings without itself determining which should be chosen. A leaf fluttering in the wind expresses the laughter in my heart just as easily as the presence of a breeze; the sound of a vibrating string calls to mind the softness of the harp or the passing of time or a moment's sorrow. In this way, any object connotes whatever comes to mind. Out of nowhere come connotations that may be significant but are not bound by necessity.

What, then, is the attitude of the perceiver that permits such freedom and gives rise to the effervescence of the connotative mode? It has to do with the release from the denotative mode's need to formulate objects. The perceiver has to relax—yes, simply to let go—so that qualities can gather of their own accord, influenced surely by all the perceiver is and knows, but without the denotative influence that turns qualities into objects. The connotative mode arises within an attitude of *be and let be*, without the need—the intent—to erect a world to enclose one's being. Released from inducing concepts, the mind assumes the very different attitude of living in a flux of passing impressions.

We tend to identify with the logical mind and to disparage the activity of the complementary nonrational mind. For this reason, this unobserved activity of mind has not been allotted its rightful place in the activity of perception and is often viewed as trivial and inconsequential. Scientific respectability is based on the view that thinking in denotations is correct, whereas thinking in connotations is to be pardoned as the fancy of poets and artists. When faced with connotation, the rational mind ties the significance down to what it alone can perceive and, because of this, is unaware that connotation manifests a whole other way of being and knowing. Until we succeed in embracing the connotative mode and accept it for what it is—a significant other—we inevitably give dominion to the denotative mind and distance ourselves from so much that is part of us.

Thinking

With the connotative mode in view, it becomes possible to describe the process of thinking and to portray mind activity as the interaction of two modes of processing, one denotative, rational, and linear and the other connotative, unrestricted, and multiple.

The denotative, or rational, mode of thinking cognizes in terms of units. This is the mind that reaches to establish and confirm the presence of reality, the presence of a world external to the mind. Only with the denotative attitude do concepts arise as anchors for objects. Only then does an objective quality permeate phenomena. Only then do things, whether ideas or physical objects, appear as independent of the observing subject—independent in that they are understood as having an identity of their own.

In contrast to this, in the connotative mode, no attempt is made to withdraw from multiplicity and indefiniteness nor to determine either/or categories of is and is not. Too, there is no tendency to adjoin associations so as to form objects. The entry of the denotative mode ruptures the connotative world of free-flowing impressions and supplants it with recognizable entities. In this way, the rational mind works to eliminate unsubstantiated impressions, reformulating them in terms of entities that become independent objects of thought.

This leads to an interesting comparison. The cognitive object produced by the mind is not dissimilar to objects acclaimed as belonging to the physical world. In physics one speaks of the mass of an object. This, too, is a concept that has no presence as such. It is assumed to refer to the amount of matter in an object, but this cannot be measured directly. To ascertain the presence of matter, one must measure how the object is influenced by something else or influences something else. In general, the effect of the object's mass is measured in terms of its center of mass, as if all the matter it contains were concentrated at a center point, but, of course, that center of mass is fictive. There is no concentration of some essence in the center, and it is merely an assumption that proves operative in calculating physical interactions. In the same manner, the unit of meaning occupying the center of a locus of attributes does not contain an essential something that is the object. The object conceived is not *there* as an observable something. It has been assumed. The assumption that there is an object prefigures the object and allows the attributes to coalesce and produce the concept of that object.

An answer is now apparent to the question at the opening of the chapter: in order for the word *rose* to mean what it does, the perceiver must adopt two separate attitudes. One is the act of reaching through the flux of impressions for some underlying unity around which these impressions consolidate, that is, adopting the expectation that a concept is forthcoming. The other attitude is to wait patiently, to pause—typically for an unnoticed split second—and allow the new meaning, which coalesces well beyond the reach of the conscious mind, to enter the mind as consciousness of some thing.

All of this happens inadvertently. As noted earlier, to distinguish between the two complementary movements, one need only check whether the act of entering the mind serves to acknowledge the presence and the identity of something or whether, passing almost unnoticed through the mind, that quality of being dissolves into an interplay of further meanings. The first is denotative, the second, connotative, but of course by checking which of the two it is, the connotative play will have been interrupted. The result of these two attitudes or forms of intent is a concept that enters consciousness fully formed and infused with meaning. The conscious mind awakens to the presence of a formed object that, itself, it did not produce.

This is quite an event. To restate it with other words may make it more obvious. All in a moment, a huge range of information—definite and indefinite, certain and improbable, remembered and imagined—comes together, forming a rich texture of meaning that offers the perceiver an understanding of what is perceived. It is as if all knowledge can play into the moment of perception and establish the meaning of what is perceived. The intuition of meaning is a miraculous moment in which the conscious denotative rational mind finds itself in possession of a gift that was drawn in from far beyond its reach. There is no construction yard where pieces are assembled in procedural steps; this is not a way to create units of meaning. It is true that it can take a little time, maybe even a few seconds, for a concept to form in the mind, and this can delay the moment of perception. But when it arrives, there is the cognition of a single thing. It is a flash of intuition that has no measurable extension in time or space, though it may well be preceded by a sense that something imperceptible is taking form. At the *aha!* moment, meaning crystallizes into an object that is grasped, recognized, remembered, that is to say, perceived as a new arrival. Whether a thought or a physical object, it is the concept of some *thing* and alights in consciousness as the intuition of meaning. The meaning revealed is limitless (although the dictionary may suggest otherwise), and yet it comes to consciousness in a timeless moment.

This astounding aspect of cognition is largely taken for granted in the belief, preposterous though it is, that an object of cognition is simply a piece of information. In some contexts the complexity of the mind's achievement is noted and becomes a subject for research, as, for instance, the often-cited case of facial recognition. However, our impressive ability to recognize faces is not one rare outstanding feat; it is what happens every time we perceive an object, every time we understand a concept. It is certainly an astounding feat of nature, but it is not unusual.

Those who hold a viewpoint that equates the mind with the brain attempt to contain this uncanny event in what can be understood. Yet, that approach has a unidirectional bias in that the activity of the brain is supposed to sustain the mind. We need, however, to ask, has the contrary proposition—that thoughts, although immaterial, activate neuronal activity—been excluded?

An Initial Sketch of the Dual Process of Mind

At this point, a preliminary view of the process of concept formation can tentatively be proposed.

At first, there is denotative intent that concentrates on the object-to-be. This is what seeds the process and brings aspects and qualities to gather around some core meaning even before that unit of meaning takes form. The expectation to find such a unit of meaning is like the emission of a call that brings such an object to manifest.

The next step in the process pertains to a release from denotative intent. This is accomplished by releasing the mind from the rational thought process and is the *letting go* mentioned earlier. One might imagine that beyond the reaches of linear thought, qualities and aspects provoked by the denotative call for an entity somehow come together and blend to form a meaningful unit. Without trying, as yet, to put the details in place, it is clear that this crystallization of aspects into a concept takes place outside of what is accessible to consciousness.

The third step is the entry into consciousness, the moment when suddenly some thing surfaces in the mind and becomes known. The conscious, denotative mind finds itself in possession of an object that it represents as a word or a picture or a sound or a feeling or whatever. A concept has formed.

This rendition simplifies the process into single acts, while, in the mind, there must surely be any number of such processes in progress together. Many units of understanding are forming at the same time, but with their entry into consciousness they become sequenced as our one-at-a-time thoughts. With this overall view of the mind engaged in the process of concept formation, a question already noted flares up afresh: What binds individual moments of thought to a coherent sequence? This innocent question echoes deep into who we are and only reaches its denouement in the final chapters of this book.

Mind Activity beyond Consciousness

A full view of the mind necessarily must include the out-of-consciousness activity of mind. But then, how evident is this dimension of the mind? At this point, it would be useful to give further demonstration of its presence and of the way consciousness is sustained through coherent processes of which we have no direct knowledge.

Sight offers a helpful analogy of how one can be conscious of only one thing while the mind and body are engaged in more extended activity. When we see something, our attention is on the object we see and not on the fact that we are seeing. For example: when you see someone, you notice that person and not the fact that you are engaging the sense of sight. The act of seeing slips by unnoticed while our conscious mind acknowledges the object seen. With thinking, there is a similar process: what we think of catches our attention while the fact of thinking does not occupy us. The act of cognizing is transparent to its object. The object that comes to mind is the thought we acknowledge, whereas the act of bringing it to mind is ignored.

This is generally what happens, but not always. At times our attention is drawn to the process of the mind, as in the following example. If we have a question for which an answer is not forthcoming and we think that reflecting on the matter may bring an answer, we become aware of the fact that the mind is actively searching for a solution. Trying to remember something or faced with a conundrum, any number of items might flit through consciousness without our giving them much heed. What we sense is the expanded mind spontaneously at work, free of our conscious control, actively scanning for a solution.

But this example raises a further question. Why, at all, should answers arise? What sets the mind on the path of an answer? What brings pertinent bits of disparate knowledge to assemble, integrate, and flash out as a possible solution? These few questions suggest further questions, and the unexplained capacity of the mind to do what it does becomes ever more intriguing. Faced with a question or a problem or an action to perform, knowledge of immeasurable complexity is delivered both to the mind and, in cases where a skill is required, directly to the physical body. Did you personally actually play any part in its punctual arrival? You may have formulated the need and willed the arrival of a solution but nothing more. It all seems to happen on its own. When the conscious mind tries actively to assist and direct the process, it is likely to upset the flow and interfere with the achievement—for this there is the caricature of a perplexed centipede desperately trying to figure out which foot to move next! Conscious involvement becomes an impediment. In this context, it can be noted that the word *will* has also the meaning of accepting what is and going with the flow, as in *to be willing*. This *letting go* and ceasing to make an effort is a necessary part of accomplishing physical and mental tasks.

From this point of view, it seems inconceivable that letting go is overlooked at schools, and children are even marked on the expenditure of effort while non-effort, so essential for growth and learning, is maligned. Willingness is not even considered, never mind cultivated, and with this, the very sense of learning is lost.

Further examples of this unacknowledged, effortless activity of mind are given in what follows. The moment someone wishes to say something, words come to mind ready-made as sentences, prompted only by the person's intention to say some particular thing. Out of all the knowledge of language available to the speaker, how did the appropriate words in the correct structures come forth? A curt answer is to say that language is innate and programmed into the mind (whatever that is taken to be), but surely this is equivalent to saying, "I have no idea and yet consider it to be explained." Language is just one example of the mind finding answers through processes that are beyond comprehension. To take a very different example, when a tree is blocking the roadway ahead, various possibilities of how to get past it come to mind. But what brings pertinent solutions that serve the needs of the situation to enter the mind of their own accord? It is clear that coordinated activity was needed to produce them. We speak of *logic, memory, imagination, creativity,* and *intelligence*, though they do not tell what is actually going on. Perhaps words like these also serve to hush what is too amazing to be faced rationally, and they allow us to accept the fact that somehow, somewhere, and somewhen, in a realm beyond our conscious control, very exacting and controlled preparations are enacted.

A common example, experienced repeatedly by some, of this independent action of the nonconscious mind is the case of going to sleep with a question and waking to find oneself thinking of the answer. There is no dearth of dramatic examples of occasions when the mind, without involving consciousness, performs processes that imply precision and discernment.[1] To take a famous case, Poincaré, the acclaimed French mathematician, gave precise descriptions of his personal experiences of this dimension of mind. Having worked for two weeks on a major mathematical problem called the Fuchsian functions, Poincaré left the unsolved problem aside and went on an outing. "Having reached Coutances," he relates, "we entered an omnibus to go some place or other. At the moment when I put my foot on the step, the idea came to me, without anything in my former thoughts seeming to have paved the way for it."[2] The idea that came was the mathematical solution for the problem he had been working on earlier. Poincaré points out how, having let go of the question, it worked itself out in some unobserved part of the mind. A second aspect is the fact that he knew instantly that it was correct. Later he went home and verified this mathematically, but already with the intuition of the answer came the certitude that it was correct. We formulate a question and do not really determine the moment or the content of the response. From many such examples, it becomes clear that, unobserved, the mind is at work creating solutions. Leaving the mind on its own undirected by consciousness seems to assists the process of coming to a solution.

Every moment of realization is a mind creation quite beyond our rational capabilities.

In these examples of unexpected realizations, the problem and its solution are separated by a time interval, and this makes the realization conspicuous and surprising. But surely a constant stream of such mo-

---

1. Jacques Hadamard, *An Essay on the Psychology of Invention in the Mathematical Field* (Princeton, NJ: Princeton University Press, 1949). In this little book, Jacques Hadamard, a mathematician, gives numerous such examples that he collected by sending a questionnaire to leading physicists and mathematicians of his time.
2. Henri Poincaré, *The Foundations of Science*, trans. George Bruce Halsted (New York: Science Press, 1913). Also quoted in Hadamard, *Essay on the Psychology of Invention*, 13.

ments of illumination burst upon the conscious mind to answer immediate needs. Spontaneously and whenever we require it, we find the word, the phrase, the meaning, the gesture, the image, the name, the melody, the quality, the proportions, the movement, the context, the rule, the example, the relationship, the invented link, the remembered link, the hidden link, the new formulation, the projected outcome, the innovative idea, the novel expression that is needed. Every moment of realization is a mind creation quite beyond our rational capabilities. The power of the mind to serve individual needs is tremendous and is enacted without assistance from conscious *me*, excepting the desire for a response and some degree of preparedness to receive the result.

Each time something dawns in our mind, it is a surprise and is, on some timescale whether micro or macro, unpredictable. Between every word we speak, every thought we think, every moment of consciousness, our mind has in some manner disappeared into the unknown to retrieve the substance needed to sustain our reason and intentions. It is not possible to give an account of the mind without including this wider function.

Describing the Activity of Mind

It is possible, here, to insert an alternative way of describing what has already been discussed of the two fundamental states of mind reflected in the words *denotation* and *connotation*. The contrast between these two modes of mind activity can been described as reciprocal forms of movement.

The mind activity that results in denotation must surely be a centering process, a focusing on the object perceived. Such thinking converges on specific conclusions or units of meaning. With this centering movement, diverse bits of information coalesce to form a unit of meaning. By becoming attributes of a particular thing, they generate the object that arises in our mind. The activity that engages connotations, on the other hand, involves a mind that is free of any such centering process. It must function in the opposite manner, expanding beyond anything specific and into a flux of associative meanings. This, admittedly, is not saying very much, but it does open a way of portraying the differences between these two processes. It is useful to assign specific words to these two movements.

Further options, beyond the words *centering* versus *expanding*, are the *contraction phase* and the *expansion phase* of thought. In more graphic terms, these could be imagined as a *centripetal movement*, whose outcome is a specific piece of information, and a *centrifugal movement*, bringing escape from denotative reality and release into a multiplicity of possible meanings. The *centripetal phase* alludes to the contraction that gives rise to self, consciousness, objects of thought, and, by extrapolation, reality and the universe. The *centrifugal phase* comprises the expansion that dissolves the boundaries of perceived objects and reaches what has not been conceptualized—the unchartered territories of proto-information, unformed and never manifest as objects of consciousness.

Centripetal and *centrifugal* are chosen as initial handles to grasp hold of that which needs further clarification. These words usually appear in relation to physical processes; however, in the present context, they do not imply movement in physical space but something taking place in the mind that enables the arising and dissolution of meaning in the form of concepts. The first term describes the coming together of impressions to form a unit of meaning, and the second, the dissolution of such meaning, while what generates such movements, for the time being, remains hidden. Not knowing how this is achieved should not deny the possibility of speaking about it. A parallel to this is gravity, for it describes a centripetal movement, yet no cause is evident. Kepler thought the reason behind the observed movement was in sacred geometry and possibly in magnetism; Newton was not at all at ease with the aspect of influence at a distance contained in his own proposition. A contemporary of Newton, de Duillier, and, a short time later, Le Sage looked at the same facts only to elucidate them with arguments that turned Newton's reasoning on its head by explaining the same phenomena, not with an attractive force but with a force that repels. In more recent times, relativity concluded that somehow nonmaterial empty space affects the behavior of matter. The debate continues today without a consensual answer in view. These examples show that referring to a centripetal process without offering a palpable explanation of why such a process arises has scientific precedent! But this is merely an anecdote, not an excuse. By describing carefully our experience of processes that deliver meaning, we can arrive at an understanding of what is involved.

Reality and the Early Renaissance

Through denotative intent we perceive a world that appears objective. The fact that it rests on a subjective act is commonly overlooked. Without the subjective stance of a perceiver reaching for an object of perception, neither things nor concepts nor an objective world would be forthcoming. A clear example of this is found in perspective drawing.

When the field of view portrayed in a picture has been unified into a single space with a vanishing point that is the complement of the position of the eye of the viewer, objectivity reigns. Every item in the picture has its own space relative to all else that is portrayed. The apparent independence of objects set in objective space, however, is an illusion. To create apparent objectivity, the tether to subjectivity has been lengthened to a maximum so that only at infinity, which has become a dimensionless point in the image, is the picture locked into the individual personal subjective moment. Take away the painting's vanishing perspective point and the scene, too, must vanish, with nothing remaining. Objective reality is anchored to the vanishing point—a jolly paradox! Incidentally, this is a simple example of Gödel's theorem, which states that a complete definition of what is the world (an internally consistent system) is necessarily dependent on a factor, or factors, not part of that world.

The transformation to perspective drawing in which everything contained in a picture is unified into a single viewpoint and thus forms a snapshot view of reality happened at a particular moment in Western cultural history. Works from the years preceding the Renaissance show a progression towards a unified perspective, but the full transformation came when multiple views were integrated into a singular viewpoint in which each object has its own space relative to all else. This happened very suddenly. The progression leading to this moment became an abrupt and total shift when, at once, everything present was included in one all-inclusive framework taken as absolute. The changeover came in 1427, or very close to that date, when it appeared in the art of Masaccio in Italy and in the paintings of van Eyck in the Netherlands and, at the same time, was generally adopted as the standard view of the world. The change was not simply the introduction of a technique for painting but a whole other way of seeing the world. What generated it was the assumption of absolute objectivity, or, in the context of what has been said here, losing touch with the subjective origin of the objective world. This transformation was an all-encompassing event in the consciousness of that historical moment. For example, the same transformation, at exactly the same time, took place in musical composition, as can be noted in the works of composers of that time, such as John Dunstable. The phenomenon of objectivity in music that is parallel to perspective in art has to do with harmonic relationships anchored to a particular key structure. The changeover came with the prominence given to the dominant or fifth note in the diatonic scale. Through this, the temporal melodic progression in music was tethered to a vertical static harmonic structure that forms the ground that determines the relative position of all the notes of that piece, at least until a further key change installs a new tonic-dominant relation.

It is revealing to discover how artists and musicians of that time understood this transformation. Vasari, the artist and art historian, born in 1511, was sharply critical of painting before the change to unified perspective. To him, that earlier art was blatantly less accomplished. The only praise he accorded to pre-Renaissance painters was to those who made significant steps in the direction of realism and of what he understood as acceptable. Paintings from before the change appeared illogical and poorly executed to the mind-set that prevailed after the transformation. With the changeover, all of a sudden people were unable to fathom how a view of reality could be set out in anything but objective spatial coordinates. This attitude is not unique to painting and is found, too, in the writings of Johannes Tinctoris, an acclaimed composer and musicologist (to use today's term) who died in the year Vasari was born. In one of his twelve treatises on the theory of music, he expressed essentially the same opinion about music prior to "the new way of making lively concord," that is, the changeover described here. In 1477, he wrote, "Although it seems beyond belief, there is not a single piece of music not composed in the last 40 years that is regarded by the learned as worth hearing."[3] To us, such categorical statements seem hard to believe, but we must remember that our ears have been liberated from the rigor of the formal harmonic structure that made pre-Renaissance music sound primitive and strange. Debussy and Bartók had important roles initially in piercing this harmonic bind and enabling us today to listen with appreciation to music of different periods and of very different cultures.

The shift in viewpoint that crystallized at the beginning of the Renaissance reflected a fundamental change in the sense of self. The possibility of gathering diverse knowledge and skills promoted the resourceful individual we now refer to as "the Renaissance Man," but this transition includes a less obvious fact. The gain in individual freedom came at the price of a transmutation in what self signified. What passed away was the experience of being an involved subject enacting a role in society and participating, voluntarily or not, in some greater plan that was the sense of the universe and, in its place, what emerged was the untethered actor acting in the world without a predetermined role. Events carried no meaning in and of themselves because the world was more and more identified as being physical reality and was understood to function independently of the subject and with its own laws. The guardian of objective reality was rational conscious thought, and this, not intuition, held jurisdiction over what was acceptable. Relationship was defined through measurement, through

---

3. Johannes Tinctoris, *Liber de arte contrapuncti. Liber primus. Prologus* "Neque, quod satis admirari nequeo, quippiam compositum nisi citra annos quadraginta extat, quod auditu dignum ab eruditis existimetur." English version from Paul Griffiths, *A Concise History of Western Music* (New York: Cambridge University Press, 2006), 44.

quantification of the observed, and this brought the spawning of meaningless functional connections, of accidental interactions, of physics and modern science. It promoted a material autonomous world that was indifferent—oblivious even—to any conception of inherent value.

While in the arts the Renaissance viewpoint came to expression all of a sudden and the basic transformation took place almost simultaneously in different countries, in science it took time to come to expression and was formulated gradually over the whole period of the Renaissance. Could this mean that the rational mind takes more time to formulate and, perhaps, to accept what is intuitively present and ready to come to expression in the arts? Does it suggest that rational thinking can hinder intuitive truths from reaching a person's understanding?

A very similar time lag occurred five centuries later, following the breakdown of the objective worldview in the shift away from classical science that took place at the beginning of the twentieth century. The change, which included a fracturing of what before seemed to form an independent, coherent whole, came to expression directly in the arts, whereas, on the level of reasoning, it certainly seems to be taking much longer. Still today implications of the new physics are only beginning to take a general hold on attitudes in science, philosophy, linguistics, and other areas of reflection. This study, offering a reappraisal of how concepts are formed and a view of the presence of purpose in all we observe, is also a latecomer, lagging well behind the early twentieth-century changes that initially made place for it.

The Transience of the Perceiving Subject

In the process of reaching understanding, the subject is sometimes present and sometimes absent. The perceiving subject and the object perceived arise in synchronicity; they appear together and disappear together. Self as a cognizing subject makes its entry at the moment when a concept forms in the mind. The subject perceiving and the object perceived form a couplet that disappears the moment cognition is achieved. To say this once more, when the object is recognized there is a witnessing subject, but with this achievement of cognition, both subject and object are released and no longer occupy consciousness. In this way, consciousness is potentially available and able to acknowledge a subsequent moment of conception, and until that happens, there is no conscious perceiver. Between moments of consciousness, the mind is released from the centripetal movement of producing objects of perception and is carried into the centrifugal activity that leads beyond consciousness where, imperceptibly, it connects with the source of meaning that nourishes every moment of consciousness.

In order to describe the imperceptible mind, the word *virtual* as it is employed in physics is appropriate. *Virtual* refers to something whose presence eludes all that is explicit. Mind, then, is the immeasurable implicit that becomes actual—explicit—at the very moment of cognition, when object and subject are linked in consciousness. One could imagine an undulating movement that is the rise and fall of explicit moments of perception forming and dissolving out of the ongoing activity of the virtual mind.

The loss of a perceiving subject together with the loss of the object perceived is the entry into nonconsciousness; the presence of the subject together with the perceived object is the entry into consciousness:

— The first movement is the expansion phase, during which the activity of mind moves beyond single meanings and thus beyond consciousness. Impressions proliferate without being anchored to a specific object, and linear conscious thought, unable to follow many effects simultaneously, gets left behind. This is the virtual state of the mind with no witnessing subject and with no object to reflect its activity. Entering this state comes with *loss of consciousness*.
— The second movement is the contraction phase, during which the mind's activity impinges from without on the consciousness horizon, entering from what was nonconscious into the limitation that allows for perception of single objects. It is the experience of perception, of being a perceiving subject, and this state comes with *loss of nonconsciousness*.

A precision is needed here to avoid misunderstanding. The experience of being a perceiving subject does not require the thought of being a perceiving subject, or what may be called self-consciousness.

Considered from this angle, the conscious self is not the independent, controlling entity we might imagine it to be. It is subservient to the mind, for it owes its very presence to the mind. Self the observer arises within the activity of mind as it conceives of some object. Without mind achieving consciousness, there is no observer. But if self has such a fleeting presence, what does that say about the living person I understand myself to be? The chapters that follow bring out the implications of this question, leading, finally, to a more precise view of what the concept of self entails.

Feelings into Thoughts

Actually, this out-of-consciousness world is not completely hidden. A channel of communication exists between it and our conscious selves. What is sensed from the world of multiple meanings penetrates consciousness as indefinite sensations and feelings. These register our connection to what lies beyond the horizon of the known. Through feelings, the inaccessible can be intimated.

To state this in more concrete terms, here is an example: *Entering a crowded hall, you are delighted when all of a sudden you notice the familiar face of a friend.* The conscious mind, at that instant, may focus on some aspect of that person, for example, his name or his smile or the thought of where you last met or his response to seeing you, but the spontaneous feeling you have on finding him is far richer than this and includes innumerable aspects that reflect his temperament and personality, certain shared past experiences,

Because of the ability of feelings to combine multiple aspects, they enter where consciousness is barred.

the possible significance of the present encounter, and so forth. Feelings are able to access a wealth of impressions that remain beyond the horizon of conscious thought, and these are not encountered as separate items but experienced together. Because of the ability of feelings to combine multiple aspects, they enter where consciousness is barred. Our physical senses offer an easy-to-understand instance of this. Take the taste of something delicious, a fruit or whatever. It is composed of many fragrances and flavors that have combined to produce something that might be unnamable but that gives a particular experience of taste, as, for instance, the flavor of a durian or of fresh spring water.

This exemplifies the ability of feelings and sensation to achieve what the conscious mind alone cannot do: to step beyond linear sequencing and perceive multiple aspects instantly as a single experience. And, too, feelings and sensation do what the expanded mind alone cannot do: they bring multiple aspects to combine as a single moment of awareness. Feeling oversteps the separation between conscious and nonconscious activity and offers another way—other than the expanded mind feeding concepts to the conscious mind—of accessing the content of nonconscious dimensions of the mind.

Sensations and feelings have a part in everything we perceive. They enable us to access infinitely more than the momentary content of our conscious thought and reach into the fullness of the activity of the expanded mind. The significance of this will be pursued in chapter 2, with the exploration of sensory perception.

Experiencing Multiplicity and Duration

Impressions received from sensations, feelings, and intuitions are free of the duality of rational thought, but only initially. Drawn to these experiences is consciousness, and with its entry begins a very different process whereby the manifold interacting sensations become fused into a single item that consciousness can grasp.

Here are two examples of experiencing the plurality of an unidentified sensation that, for the first moment, is held purely as a quality of being. Hopefully, one of these examples suggests similar experiences that the reader has had. Imagine experiencing the sensation of physical discomfort, and then, only an instant later, you realize that it is the stinging sensation of a mosquito bite. Or while walking in the street imagine all of a sudden feeling a pleasant sensation, and, only some moments later, you realize you passed a bakery and it was your response to the smell of freshly baked bread. The indefinite inkling that was carried as a general feeling is, in a later moment, taken up by the conscious mind, where it becomes the focus of attention and enters the centripetal mind process that formulates it in denotative terms as a particular thing. The feeling may continue, but the mind has transformed it into a concept. It has been tamed into a presentable form that can be communicated, and as such, its earlier expression as some inconceivable, vibrant, multifarious quality, hovering where only the nonconscious mind ventures, is expunged. The fullness of the experience slips out of reach, and what you grasp are recognizable things: the stinging pain of a mosquito bite, the fragrance of freshly baked bread. In this transformation, the immediacy of the impression of an unidentified sensation is released; what had momentarily been wild and indefinite disappears, and in its stead we find something recognizable that has been trimmed to fit the norms of subject–object relationship. In achieving this, an air of magic is dispelled as sanity and normality are reestablished through the comforting assumption that self is inside us while all we perceive that is not imagination makes up the outside.

This is told as a fanciful tale but is, in fact, a description of how feelings and sensation function, essentially, as organs of perception.

A further aspect that comes with feeling is a possible sense of duration. A feeling can take the form of a concept and as such is no different from any thought content. The concept of a feeling occupies our conscious mind for a moment only and becomes an item in the succession of all that forms conscious thought. But given the fact that the thought of a feeling—joy or sadness, for example—is typically accompanied by a sense of experiencing that feeling, we tend to cross over between the thought and the related feelings with ease. We experience the ongoing exchange between the idea of that feeling and the sensation that accompanies it. In this way, compared with thinking, feelings tend to bring a more pronounced sense of time as duration.

A fact, not always recognized, is that conscious thought is only capable of knowing time as a concept and not as the experience of time. The sense of duration comes with the loss of consciousness. The ability of feeling to communicate both with the expanded nonconscious mind and with the conscious mind offers a noticeable sense of the passage of time.

Conscious Moments and the Noncontinuity of Thought

In order to produce a concept, a gesture, or any expression, myriad correlations have to be realized on some unobserved level of mind. The thing we perceive might be a word or a scene, but the understanding it brings is the integration of a multitude of impressions realized uniquely for this manifestation. To set out a sentence is not a matter of shuffling concepts around as one would arrange furniture in a room because, to continue the simile, neither room nor furnishings are present as independent objects. Whether newly formed or recalled from previous experience, everything that enters consciousness constitutes a meeting between self and an object of thought—an encounter that is a specific moment in a great unfathomable process.

This suggests that consciousness is a sequence of such encounters. It could be understood as being formed by successive flashes of meaning, of realizations, that intermesh to form the continuity of thought. A succession of such moments appears continuous only because, during the gaps between the arrival of each momentary content, the conscious mind absconds. During each intermission, it becomes the expanded out-of-consciousness mind that, in terms of the conscious mind, is oblivion. To put it another way, the conscious moments we string together and believe to be continuous are like dots that can be linked together to form a drawing. In the gaps between the dots, consciousness is absent, and the mind recedes into the nonconscious, allowing the next meaningful bit—dot—to coalesce. The meaningful bits surface out of the general background of nonconsciousness that was repeatedly described as multiconsciousness. A more appropriate image might be the one proposed by David Bohm, although in a different context.[4] He tells how drops of ink stirred one after another into a viscous solution form what becomes a homogenized mix, and yet, by reversing the direction of stirring, they reappear one by one as separate drops. The ink drops, in the present context, are concepts. From a state of imperceptible dispersion in expanded *out-of-consciousness*, they come together and form objects of thought that produce moments of consciousness. Rational thought collects these concepts and strings them together with no awareness, on our part, of the myriad spaces of oblivion that permeate and sustain every thought.

Every concept that functions in our conscious mind relies on the outsourcing of the expanded mind. The concept has been fetched from beyond the horizon of consciousness. What we consider to be rational thought coalesces moment by moment as newly gelled units received from hidden reaches of the mind. What is noted here is the fact that *subject cognizing object* is but one particular moment in a more extended process of which we are, in general, ignorant. We observe the superficial movement that arises in the sequence of items that form our conscious thoughts and elicit the meanings we recognize, yet it is the all-embracing processes of the nonconscious mind that sustain this flux. While thinking and perceiving, we drift in and out of conscious awareness, oscillating between the centrifugal expansion phase of the mind and its centripetal contraction phase. Richly endowed from hidden sources, meanings coalesce and surface to become the sequenced moments that form the movement of conscious thought.

---

4. David Bohm, *Wholeness and the Implicate Order* (New York: Routledge, 1980), 149.

The next chapter describes how sensory perception is achieved and offers a different view of the same dual movement. The processes described there are parallel with the ones presented here and lead to conclusions that coincide with those of this chapter. The topic of sensory perception brings, too, the added bonus of a new range of examples that serve to clarify and expand on what has been told so far.

Before moving forward to chapter 2, the second part of this chapter brings further illustrations and an expansion of key ideas already presented.

Conclusions

A. Two complementary processes are active in what we call mind. One is known as being conscious or being awake (to one's thoughts and surroundings), and the second, although nonconscious, is nonetheless an activity of mind. Neither of these two modes on its own could produce what we recognize as the world and ourselves.

B. The first mode is denotative and functions in a linear manner. Its end is always some singularity of meaning, a concept. It begins by assuming reality and proceeds to substantiate it by positing a center of meaning that integrates diverse aspects into a single object.

C. The second mode is connotative and functions through correspondences. It is the unconscious interplay between multiple impressions. Objects with no common contextual relationship cooperate in giving rise to similar qualities. In this mode, meaning is always multifarious and is not restrained by rational thought.

D. These two modes are distinct experiences. One is bent on finding unit meanings and thus reaching stability; the other is free of this attraction to things and requires no steadying anchor point and opens to a changing kaleidoscope of multiple associations constantly forming and dissolving. Both modes arise through a personal attitude that an individual assumes, and in tandem they produce all we know.

E. Pointing out these complementary modes is a way of describing the activity of mind and the intellect's ability to make sense. It brings out the fact that the rational mind receives objects in the form of concepts that result from the activity of the connotative mind.

F. The conscious mind is oblivious of the transition into consciousness. The activity of the out-of-conscious mind yields what arises in the conscious mind, and just as memories arise without our being conscious of how they came, so every meaning that arises in the mind is the result of some out-of-consciousness activity. Divers aspects fuse to become the attributes of each concept we recognize, and this happens out of consciousness in the activity of the expanded mind.
G. A further mode by which we can access meaning is through feeling. Feelings are not restricted to the linear processing of the rational mind and reach through what are barriers to the conscious mind. However, to reflect on a feeling is to engage the rational mind that forms conclusions and conceptualizes the feelings into specific items.
H. Reception of objects by the rational mind is a moment of perception in which both self the observer and the object observed are engendered. Together they form a moment of consciousness. In between such moments, unacknowledged gaps in consciousness go unnoticed precisely because they are not conscious. This allows for our experience of consciousness as continuous. The full experience of continuity is created through an untold number of such processes in progress at the same time. This will be described in chapter 2.
I. The belief that physical objects are separate and independent is a construction of linear rational thinking, which means, of one part of the dual activity of mind. To the complementary expanded mind there is no distinction between real and imagined nor between object and subject.
J. When all activity of thought is reduced solely to the rational function of the mind and the complementary connotative dimension of mind is deleted, the result yields a view where objectivity is an independent fact and all that is perceived as the world is independent of the observer. With this erroneous understanding, the act of perception is assumed to be a physical event and not a creative act that generates a specific reality. Believing objects to be independent leans to a view where all can be deemed meaningless. To realize this error and reintroduce the subjective dimension of perception is to restore meaning as an integral dimension of everything we know.

K. The two complementary modes of mind activity function together to produce understanding, yet they cannot actually interact, one mode being out-of-consciousness while the other is in-consciousness. How they function in tandem begins to come clear when another constituent distinct from mind is identified, namely, intent. Getting to know what it is and how it functions is the overriding theme of this work, and for this reason intent will be a constant companion in the chapters that follow.

PART II: THE SUBJECTIVE MOMENT OF PERCEPTION

This part looks at implications of the new understanding of perception that is taking form. It includes three parts:

— The phenomenon of integration that produces a concept
— The temporal present and the word now
— Truth and being true

These three parts are preceded and followed by interludes containing reflections tangential to the theme. The first of these considers perception as a creative act; the concluding interlude considers the effect on twentieth-century thought of neglecting the role of the subject in perception.

Perception Is a Creative Act

Everything we acknowledge actually comes to us as a revelation. It may be that we are blasé and have lost our sense of surprise and tend to take all for granted. The wonder of the baby turning an object in her little hands and the joy of the small child seeing a bird hop nearby may be lost by the adult who replaces such moments of wonder and joy with a sense of déjà vu, with "I see it's a thrush." At the root of this adult attitude is an unstated premise: things are there whether acknowledged or not; all happens without specific reference to me, the observer. In actual fact, observations come because the subject is ready to receive them. This is how perception works. It does not begin with an object standing before the senses; rather, the object marks the completion of the perceptive process. From within us comes an act of invocation that allows for the encounter with what is perceived.

There are different ways of illustrating this point. One instance is that of a person with autism for whom stimuli given by a physical object seem to make no impression; even though the person's sense organs are functioning, the object is not recorded by consciousness. For that person, things that we would acknowledge as present are just not there, suggesting that an added ingredient beyond receiving the stimuli is required. Whatever produces the state of autism, this example serves to illustrate that for presence to register and something to appear in our consciousness, there must be the expectation of intelligibility. Expectation is like a call we send out to welcome a forthcoming offering—an offering that will reach us not simply from our immediate surroundings but from the vast hinterland of the expanded mind, thus making what is perceived something of a cosmic gift. To receive meaning, something needs to be emitted. With poetic license, it can be thought of as the incantation that allows a particular object to take form and register with the receiver.

Every meaning is an answer, the fulfillment of a quest. Without the quest for intelligibility there would be nothing to behold. As in the example of autism, indifference is oblivion. Without the impetus to make meaning there could be no meaning, and to ignore this fact is to reduce all that is known to physicality and the act of perception to an irrelevant, dispensable accessory of what one considers the objective world. This is a view that sees the world as self-contained and independent of the present moment of the observer. It assumes that living organisms respond to stimuli in the same manner as material objects for which every event is considered to be a reaction, that is, the response to a previous cause, and where the universe was wound up to a certain state of entropy, a certain energetic level—however this happened—and its unraveling is a tale of passive responses. This view omits the personal act, the expectation of intelligibility that propels every perceptive achievement; it omits the fascination that animates perceptive acts both of the small child and of each one of us. It is concerned only with outcomes, with afterwards, and it presents a world where nothing leads forward and no place is given to the incantation that makes all possible. Thinking along these lines enlivens our imaginative capacity, and, if to leave the context of what has been said, we might ask even wilder questions such as what if intent formulates an omnipresent incantation that produces reality? Why not imagine that birds through their birdsong call the world out from oblivion, and each being does it too, but in its own way—the circling flies in the center of the room and the butterflies spiraling upward—all spinning the thread that brings their world and this world into being.

Letting imagination run brings mystery closer and can reveal the massive presence of what is unknown in all we experience. Assuredly, in this study, imagination is not the path forward but rather makes an entry from time to time so as to sustain a light touch and a subtle mind while carefully worked-out considerations are put forward. It helps us be ready to accept what is unusual and, in the case of intent, to see how accounting for its effect in acts of perception brings a refreshing view of life where perceiving is no longer a response but a creative act.

The Moment of Integration

It's teatime!

The kettle is boiling. You take a spoonful of tea leaves and put them in the teapot. You are in your home, it is your teapot, and the fact that all is familiar and you have done this many times before play into the experience. Imagine now if you were in someone else's kitchen using an unfamiliar teapot; the experience would be quite different—handling the new shape, judging the quantity, your attention drawn to new aspects. Even moving about in the new kitchen would have a less evident quality. And why is there the difference? Because a lot of information you call upon in the home situation is not available in the new, unfamiliar situation. While performing the task at home, the familiar aspects never enter your conscious mind, and yet they make a difference. To emphasize this, just imagine how different it would be if you never before made tea and were just following instructions. You would be less inadvertent and, perhaps, less at ease in your movements, especially if you never before tried to spoon tea leaves out of a container. How to hold a spoon, too, is an ability that is not simply something one does or does not do. It is a personal skill in the same way that being able to balance while riding a bicycle is a skill. In a sense, cognition is a skill, too: the ability to call a wealth of information in at a moment and integrate it into an understanding. Whether the unspecified information is destined to become a concept or a physical act, we draw ceaselessly on ever so much more than the rational mind can know or deal with—even in just preparing a cup of tea.

Noticing the spoon, tea, and teapot, knowing them for what they signify, is quite an achievement, and employing them to prepare tea an equivalent achievement. The first is a realization expressed in the form of a perception; the second is a realization expressed in the performance of a skill. Actions of both mind and body are expressions of intelligence, even if we have a culturally inherited tendency to give intelligence of performance a lesser status. This comes of giving dominance to the rational mind that attributes intelligence to itself (the intellect) rather than to physical skills.

What is being described in this teatime example is the transfer of content from the expansive, connotative, unlimited mind to a limited, time-and-space-ruled world. This passage is the heart of living experience and animates every moment of our existence. It is not contained within the physical universe. To an objective universe, there could be no difference between the expanded mind and the conceptual mind, and there could be no transformation between such states. Classical science came with the belief that it studied all there was and that anything else was unreal. Within this attitude, there is no place for a process of life that is built on a creative act that introduces into the universe something that simply was not there beforehand.

To inject a pertinent historical aside: in cosmology, in the middle of the last century, a shock factor accompanied the pronouncement of the Steady State theory that envisaged continuous creation throughout the universe. It offered an alternative to the hypothesis of a Big Bang. The doubt and discomfort it created were surely due, in part, to a nonrational factor: that of accepting a creative presence in the universe. The Steady State theory, envisioning continuous creation, necessitated the presence, here and now in our lifetime, of something that is not part of the universe, of some source of continuously created material. This idea was new and uncomfortable to many.

A similar surprise accompanies the realization that we draw upon sources not part of the physical world whenever we recognize an object, when we perform an action, and, simply, when we prepare some tea. To draw upon such sources requires an act of creation. It might be helpful to imagine the coming together to form something new as a passage through the eye of a needle. A freshly spun thread, drawn from wooly sources beyond all that consciousness knows, passes through the eye of the needle, and, with this, marks a moment of consciousness. This passage determines the present instant and gives presence to the subjective *I* that realizes the objective world. With this moment of realization, the passage through consciousness ends and that specific item returns to the unknown.

Who can say this integration occurred? Only the person witnessing it, for only a personal self can make it happen. Although we commonly consider the world together with our physical body to be objective, a view such as this leaves no place for any question concerning the drive to coherence that produces a realization and the emergence of meaning. To question these, both subjectivity and intent need to be admitted as functioning parts within the process. The opening chapters draw attention to the presence of subjectivity and intent, and then, in the subsequent chapters, more detailed descriptions lead to some answers and further enigmas.

The Temporal Present

This first chapter shows that the temporal present can be clearly defined, and this despite a growing literature suggesting the contrary. Contemporary discussions on the subject are often concerned with the distinctions between conflicting positions and are less inclined to set out what is known and not known of time. In considering the experience of time, a return to everyday language makes it easier to hear afresh what accumulated experience embedded in language says. The approach followed here is to note what is not understood and to leave it untouched while pointing out what does make sense and can be helpful in describing the experience of time.

Now is employed to refer to the present moment and signals the moment when consciousness alights upon an object. Here are some everyday situations that exemplify this. "*Now* it's time to leave" and "*Now* I remember" and "Will you begin *now*?" "No, I'm feeling too tired right *now*." In each case, saying *now* is accompanied by a particular thought. In saying, "Now it is time to leave," the thought might be of something to be done or of noticing the late hour; in saying, "Now I remember," the thought is probably the thing remembered. In saying, "Not now," the thought may be about how the person feels just then. The "just then" is *now* for that person because it is the moment in which that person registers, as a thought, the feeling of tiredness. *Now* is always anchored to a person's experience of coming to a particular realization.

Now refers to a particular event, namely, the experience of perception. In this work, as stated at the outset, the word *perception* is used to refer to what one grasps both via the physical sense organs and without them. It is the realization of meaning, the aha tremor that happens when, under the influence of denotative intent, an influx of impressions becomes integrated, producing something recognizable. To say *now* is to acknowledge the moment of noticing something, and therefore, what determines the present moment is this specific event: consciousness waking to the realization of an object. The present has no other determinant. By this and by this alone, we know when it is now, and that is now.

The Paradoxical Present

In this description of the present moment, there is something of a paradox. Two separate experiences of time are superposed, one momentous and the other minute. On one hand, there is a prodigious, multilevel happening where the expansive mind reaches deep into past, present, and future, without when and where distinctions, and gathers impressions that coalesce and will eventually become a concept that manifests as a particular meaning. On the other hand, this gargantuan task seems to pass in an instant. Time goes to zero, transformation stops, the process of forming meaning is brought to a standstill, and, in that stillness, consciousness awakens to a specific object. A description of what happens depends on one's point of view, whether from within the coming together of impressions or after the event when what is realized—something seen, heard, thought, or felt—has been received into conceptual, restricted consciousness as a concept. Of these two contrasting experiences, the first is multidimensional, constantly changing and far too rich to be able to enter consciousness; the second is the reenactment of experience as thought.

Often, when questioning time, only the second is considered. Only the object whose emergence concludes the act of perception is noted, and the formative process that gives rise to objects is ignored. This one-sided view leaves the idea of a present that has no duration, and as a result, it becomes impossible to understand how it could include all that it does, namely, the process of bringing together an unlimited wealth of information and of knowing it all in a moment.

To suppose that thinking is entirely composed of concepts that form in our conscious mind would be ridiculous. Every comprehension we have is so much richer than the unit of meaning we momentarily cognize. To reduce thought, understanding, conversation, literature, and life to cognitive units of meaning is only plausible when one ignores most of what is going on in living experience. Such a view may encourage the further misconception where nonconscious activity is understood to be the neurological activity that does not register on one's consciousness. The danger with this is that it divides thought into what is manifest in consciousness (denotations) and what manifests physically in the brain and body (neurology). Out of these, one cannot form an understanding of mind because the mind's reach into the nonconscious realm is overlooked. The expansive part of the mind's activity is lost from view, and the fact that something is missing is not even considered. This section, this chapter, and this book come to establish the fact that something is missing.

The Fluid Movement of Thought

The birth of a thought is also its passing. Its entrance into consciousness is also its exit. Anchored to nothing, it disappears in an instant, leaving place for a new thought. We can recall the earlier thought, of course, but recalling it is a separate creative moment that engenders that thought anew and not the prolongation of the same moment of consciousness. In entering consciousness, the formed object persists no more. It becomes merely another item in a parade of momentary cognitions that drop away, thus generating the temporal process that seems responsible for leaving it behind.

> *The birth of a thought is also its passing.*

There is yet another way to describe how thought and consciousness proceed through a sequence of momentary realizations. It has to do with the fact that to perceive is not the passive recording of what is already formed but is a formative act. Vision is not simply a camera shutter opening to record what is present but is the engagement of a whole process of image formation. Each image that takes form in consciousness engages a vast array of interactions within the visual system, and for this reason sight is not simply an imprint but is made up of acts of seeing, of image formation. This, necessarily, is noncontinuous. Were an image to persist in our consciousness, it would block the entry of a subsequent image, and we would be unable to follow changes taking place in what we observe. The same is true for objects produced when employing other senses. The duration of the presence of an object in consciousness determines the speed with which we can follow events. That is to say, perceptual acuity has a resolution factor determined by the duration time of each *frame* that occupies the conscious mind. The longer a conscious moment lasts, the lower is our ability to distinguish and follow what is present, which is to say, the less precise is our resolution of what is present. In optics, there is the smallest unit that we can resolve with the naked eye, telescope, or microscope, and so too for consciousness, there is a temporal resolution limit to what can be observed. The resolution is a measure of the rate of *falling away from consciousness* of concepts that enter the mind. Prolongation in consciousness of the concept of an object that is seen, heard, felt, or thought leads to loss of specificity in what enters the present moment.

With this understanding of acts of perception as sequenced moments, it is possible to speak of quanta of consciousness. Each quantum of consciousness correlates with a perceived object, with the birth of meaning to a perceiver. This describes the process of concepts being registered and ejected by consciousness. The time spoken of is the duration of the presence of a concept in consciousness. A very different tale is the time it takes for the concept to form—the time it takes for the expanded mind to gather the content that gives rise to the concept that enters consciousness. In chapter 2, this other aspect will be considered.

Given that thought is a series of punctual realizations, how is it that, when seeing or hearing or feeling something, we have the impression of a continuous, uninterrupted perception that does not drop away but lasts some time? In looking at a tree or any object, the experience we have is of continuous, uninterrupted vision, and this impression of continuity comes of ignoring the nonconscious periods between moments of perception. Ignoring is precisely what nonconscious means. This amnesia and partial amnesia bind moments of consciousness into a seamless flow. Actually, when we prolong the view of the tree, we re-create the moment of vision by reengaging repeatedly with what we are looking at. Seeing the tree is not continuous. Between moments of reconnecting with the sight of the tree are less focused moments, and the presence of the tree is absent and then returns. Also, at times, our attention momentarily switches to other features of the object only to return to the tree as a whole. These interrupted and varied perceptions give the impression of continuous seeing because of a fundamental assumption we make: we attribute permanence to the object. We assume the tree is *there* continuously, and this attribution, a belief structure, sustains the continuity between individual moments of seeing.

When the present is reduced to what consciousness perceives, it is without extension and marks the empty spot from which time extends to the future and to the past. When the present is understood as a nonconscious interplay aspiring towards the realization of specific meanings, it is anything but empty and includes the experience of progressing towards an outcome. To speak of the present, both views need to be taken into account: the outer one, which knows only waking to a momentary act of conception, and the inner one, which is the experience of duration.

When One Says "Now"

The word *now* is the expression we use to denote the jolt we feel when something registers in consciousness. It marks the moment when the unobserved activity of drawing from what is unknown delivers its product to consciousness. Unlimited numbers of such moments are in progress in the expanded mind, and although they interpenetrate, each one, under the influence of denotative intent, proceeds independently towards a meaning that will finally enter consciousness. Each will take a temporal position in the sequenced activity of thinking and, in so doing, will mark the ending of time—not of some universal time or another conception of time but of that particular experience of duration. With this, a personal time bubble bursts, punctured by the dimensionless point of the concept it engendered. This event stands at the juncture where the unrecorded flux of impressions available to the expanded mind crosses over the consciousness threshold to become the experience of perception. It becomes an event perceived by a subject that now possesses a particular piece of knowledge (concept) or practical know-how (skill). *Now* is the marker we use to signal the demise of an experience and the gain of the potential to know or to do. It registers the experience of realizing something.

The process of thought moves between *unconscious everything* that reaches across time and space and *conscious nothing*, where the present has become dimensionless. Saying *now* refers to both of these, to everything and nothing, to the present and to what has just ended. The word *now*, in bringing together these incompatibles, holds its own special meaning. It denotes the experience of coming into oneself and, as such, is the experience of being. To say *now* is to be witness to a passing moment in the flux that is known only to a personal subject.

These thoughts end this excursion into the present moment. The final section of chapter 2 includes further remarks on the temporal present.

The Nature of Truth

When perception is understood as the integration of multiple aspects gathered in the expanded mind, it brings an unexpected bonus: it is then possible to understand how a subjective act, without reference to any exterior presence such as objective reality, produces what is no longer subjective. One such case has to do with establishing truth. This section is a brief excursion into philosophy and proposes a revision of attitudes that find values—and truth, in particular—to be arbitrary.

In discussing truth, a familiar question is whether there is a way to determine truth without referring to external physical events. Rational thought alone has little else to propose, and in fact, our habit of entrusting the task of *truth sensor* to our conscious mind has undermined our intuitive sensitivity to truth. An example of *sensing* truth was noted earlier, where Poincaré tells of his conviction that his intuition was right. Today, to a large extent, we have learned to doubt that our intuitive sense of truth reaches beyond personal bias and subjective judgment.

Truth refers to what is ontological, to the fact that something has a self, that it possesses an *itself*. It refers to the fact that a thing is what it is. For instance, to claim beauty is beauty is to claim that beauty is true. If this sounds like a tautology, be patient yet for another moment.

From where does this self, the self of beauty, enter what we call beauty? One might ask, true beauty, true love, true anything, what is it when justified neither through reference to an external physical presence nor to an arbitrarily determined structure of values? Who and what determine the ontological level of a thing? The answer is surprisingly simple: no single criterion and no group of criteria determine the truth of a concept. An object's ontological independence—its being what it is—does not depend on the presence or absence of some element but comes with the act of concept formation. Through the fusion of myriad aspects, an object takes possession of what it is. The transformation from scattered effects into a single whole establishes the truth of the object, both that it is and what it is. The very fact that it came together is its birthright, that is, its right to the meaning it has. Once the overall process whereby a subjective act creates a whole is recognized, the fabric of truth becomes manifest and we can speak about its nature. *True* is a reference to meaning, to anything that holds meaning, which is to any concept. It is not I, the subject, who puts truth into it; it is not something external to me existing in an objectified world either. The fact that such a meaning *could and did* come together and manifest gives it truth. By coming into being, it takes on a truth factor. This is not something added a posteriori but something that manifests independently of any conscious act on the subject's part, excepting the initial act of becoming conscious of the object. Through the act of perception, what is perceived reveals itself to be true.

Truth, meaning, value, all these need to be sensed for what they are. They do not require judgment; they require perception of their presence. To miss the distinction between evaluating and perceiving leads to a view in which values are arbitrary and depend on the whim of an individual or on some external source of arbitration. Understanding concept formation shows it is not so. Subjectivity manifests in the act of perception, and not in its content. The qualities that form the content, even though they rest upon the ability of an individual to decipher what is present, are not the result of an arbitrary choice. They are not judged but perceived.

Every perception enters consciousness through the coming-together movement of the expanded nonconscious mind, and truth is instated by the fact that, out of multiple features, unity is formed. If the formation process does not succeed, a concept will not emerge and there is neither meaning nor truth. Whatever is realized becomes the property of an individual consciousness, yet its meaning issues from itself. Success or failure to form is a fact that is witnessed and not a fact that depends on arbitration by the perceiver. All-that-is allows what forms to form, and it is from the potential of the unknown, the potential of all that might be, that an object manifests as something true to itself and enters our conceptual mind. This happens through the activity of the expanded mind and can sometimes be intimated through feelings.

To be and to be true arise together.

To be and to be true arise together. Whether this relates to what one has decided to call objective reality is something very different and has to do with correspondence to a belief structure, that is to say, to what one believes to be real. Paring down truth to fit the constructions of the rational mind is to leave unacknowledged the marvel of finding oneself in possession of something that expresses meaning, its own true meaning. Accepting this opens the possibility that *meaning, being,* and *being true* are three interpenetrating aspects of everything we come to know.

When the Role of Self Is Ignored

One typically imagines that making sense and understanding something are accomplished with the rational mind, yet this prevalent view ignores intuition and does not consider the creative role of perception. Without these processes, no one is present to receive the meaning content of what is transmitted, and in place of a personal subject, there could merely be a functioning system that responds to inputs but essentially lacks what is required to turn responses into perceptions. It is a view that disengages subjective experience from what is accepted as being real. Without connection to a personal subject, nothing expresses purpose and the result is meaninglessness.

The notion of individuals divested of any meaningful function in the world is what set the stage for attitudes that became influential during the twentieth century. Existentialism arose as an expression of a futile combat for meaning in a senseless world. It is possible now to see the root of the recurrent emptiness as an expression of rationality unaware of its own limitation, the limitation being that it cannot produce a meaningful whole. Only a process that goes beyond restricted conceptual consciousness can give rise to an understanding of what is integral and meaningful. As the legacy of the view promulgated by classical science, rational thinking, denuded of intuition and subjectivity, was unable to accommodate a sense of purpose.

In science this view was a direct result of assuming continuity of space and time. If noncontinuity were the case, the subject, as perceiver, would have a constitutive role because breaks in the fabric of reality (noncontinuity of space, of time, or distortion of their unit measure) would make each observation a unique event dependent on an observer. The requirement of continuity gave closure and objectivity to the universe, reducing the subject to the role of a surveillance camera recording facts. The powerful effect of this view on our culture remains today, and to many, it is far from evident that an observer has a creative role in determining what is observed.

The subject's role in forming concepts has been detailed in this chapter, and the implication is of a world infused with intent. A spontaneous impulse that generates direction and purpose is an inherent dimension of the experience of being alive. Further examples are cited throughout this work. To occult any reference to purposefulness and to excise it from descriptions of life and the world are acts that contradict a natural impulse, and inevitably, this impulse produces alternative ways for meaning to enter living experience. This is what happened. There came the attempt to inject values from outside, whether from moral philosophy or simply in the form of a personal whim. This, in essence, is artificial insemination of meaning by thought and is recognizable in the doctrines that gave rise to a plethora of "isms" that promised salvation and wrought havoc on society. People thought up socialism, communism, back-to-nature trends, and so many other movements invented with the idea that meaning can be, and needs to be, inserted into existence. Ideologies and institutions arose to fill the void created by the loss of the role of self since together with this came the loss of all meaning.

To take one example, humanism was proposed as a solution to overcome meaninglessness, but when the attempt was to find a source of meaning within what is external to the individual, say, within society, it could never answer the call, and for an obvious reason. Humanism has to be based on some value present in an individual human being, and where no such value is recognized, humanism shows itself to be hollow and pointless. In this case, a society, constituted of individual human beings, is then a society of ghosts—of beings lacking inner direction who have no further purpose than to await, in vain, the arrival of meaning from beyond. The idea of a material world lacking meaning and purpose infiltrated twentieth-century literature, art, philosophy, science, and other disciplines. It gave rise to a barren image of life, as reflected, for example, in the theater of the absurd, which portrays a pointless search for meaning in a world where nothing is capable of holding a purpose. Futility enters when the connection between knower and known is ignored. Without recognizing that perception is the personal achievement of a perceiver, the subjective self becomes irrelevant—a view that is surely grotesque when contrasted with personal experience that intimates quite the contrary. Our every gesture, whether a smile, a tear, a frown, laughter, disgust, love, wonder, sadness, hope, compassion, rage, or happiness, that is to say, our whole instinctive human vocabulary, expresses values that have meaning to the subject and as such are animated by intent. They express purpose and direction. To deny this and lose touch with all we are is surely a great blindness.

With the understanding that perception is a personal achievement, meaning infuses everything. All that otherwise appears as empty gestures suddenly takes on purpose. This chapter, earlier, described the presence of the quest for meaning in the form of denotative intent. As shown in later chapters, intent arises where a present state, anchored by a subject, stands in a relationship with a future outcome that is valued. Without this positioning, there are no questions and no answers; there can be no quest, no expectation, and no fulfillment. Anchoring the act of perception in a subjective here and now gives rise to the presence of relationship across the universe, an interrelation that grows out of the subjective present moment and reaches to what will be, what is, and what was. The description of the role of intent in sensory perception is developed in chapter 2 and will be expanded in later chapters to include the role of intent in all we know and in the person we consider ourselves to be.

Loss of self, as described here, is a feature of our Western culture and its place is limited. To those who uphold this culture, it seemed to apply universally, but it has in fact penetrated only a minority of the world's population. Even where Western traditions rule, its acceptance is far less extensive than we might be led to believe by the intellectual trends fashioned by academic institutions and the media. Among many who remain indifferent to the proclaimed trends are people with folk traditions. Popular traditions retain a strong sense of self and meaning, so much so that Kodály, Bartok, Shostakovich, and Vaughan Williams—among many other musicians, artists, dancers, and writers—were able to draw upon folk traditions, albeit hesitatingly, to initiate a revival of meaningfulness in the aftermath of the hegemony of objectivity.

There is solace in the realization that the calamity that resulted from the extradition of self arose essentially out of a misunderstanding and that its time is over. Very different views are emerging today, views that include the presence of personal meaning in all one knows and does. Examples of this change are interspersed throughout this book.

[2]
Sense Perception: Sight and Hearing

THE MOST COMMON procedure followed today when entering a discussion on sensory perception is to retrace conclusions that issue from recent neurological research. This is not at all the approach this chapter follows. The purpose of this study, rather than to present physiological facts, is to reflect on direct sensory experience common to everyone and to take note of subtle components of what happens when we are engaged in seeing and hearing. It may come as a shock to find that an approach so lacking in sophistication leads to original insights into the process of perception. No claim is made as to the nature of the carrier of our sensory abilities and the role of biological systems. By leaving these questions aside, quite a different field of study comes into view: the significance of qualitative distinctions between what one observes with centered perception as compared with what one receives through periphery perception. Recognizing these two systems as distinct and complementary opens a way of describing how a subject realizes an act of perception. This chapter explores visual and auditory perception.

Prefacing Remarks

To eschew a common misleading assumption, a precision needs to be made. The discussions presented in this chapter do not start with the assumption that a person is a receptor of stimuli. This would, from the outset, put the quest on a false path because what this chapter researches is this very question, namely, objectivity and the construction of what is real. To start from such a point of view would reduce perception to the presence of stimuli, on one hand, and a receiver on the other, leaving as sole variable the degree to which the subject is receptive to the stimuli. Actually, reality is not some predetermined presence waiting to be observed but grows out of the act of perception. It is premature to enter this conundrum now, before all the pieces of the puzzle have been laid out. However, it is misleading to start with the supposition that stimuli producing acts of perception are independent, objective phenomena. Such a supposition is based on a belief in a particular view of reality that is challenged in what follows.

Reality is not some predetermined presence waiting to be observed but grows out of the act of perception.

Concerning the words *fovea* and *periphery*, what follows shows that the functions of the fovea and periphery are not restricted to the visual sense but are related to sense perception in general and to the way the mind produces a conscious thought. For this reason, once the precise functions alluded to by *fovea* and *periphery* have been clarified, these words will also be used to refer to mind processes.

PART I: VISION

Periphery and Fovea Perceived Spatially

Within the field of vision, all that is perceived is not of equal status. There is a quality attributed to an object placed in center field that is very different from that attributed to an object on the periphery. Although this is a well-documented fact, its implications are not often considered. The fact that the eye has a greater concentration of receptor cells in the fovea implies there is a difference in what is seen, but it does not yet show what the function of that difference is. To do so requires taking into account the subject's experience of presence and the varying degree to which different impressions enter a person's awareness. Only then do the full implications of these contrasting types of vision become apparent.

Fovea Vision

When we look at an object, we bring it to the center of our field of vision by turning our head to face it or by moving our eyes. In centering the object, we single it out as an object of interest. The centering movement of vision is part of the dynamic of fovea vision, and it serves the process of cognizing an element of meaning. As noted in chapter 1, the unity of what is recognized is not found in the object itself but in an attitude of mind. Bringing that which is detected to the center of the visual field is animated by the intent to identify it.

There are special cases in which the tendency to bring the observed object to center field is less active. For instance, seeing can be animated by a desire to enjoy what one sees—the beauty of a seascape, for instance. Here, the goal of identifying the object recedes to allow for a different purpose. Another example is when a particular object is kept in view, not to identify it but to allow some new understanding or appreciation to arise within us. These are instances in which seeing is not primarily animated by an interrogating mind-set.

Most often, however, looking at something has the goal of identifying what is seen. Once this task has been accomplished, prolonging sight by repeatedly engaging the object of attention is unfulfilling and of no interest (at least, in cases where the object itself is not changing). After seeing an object, one tends to look for something further to identify in that object, and typically, one's attention is drawn to certain features and details of what was seen. One is not obliged to take this centering path, and there are alternative options such as choosing to go directly to something else or to remain with the overall view. However, our natural disposition to question what is being looked at moves the visual process in the direction of identifying ever finer detail in what we see. Acts of seeing comprise constantly shifting views superimposed on an overriding movement that is the tendency of centering upon what enters our sight. The object that forms in fovea view represents a moment in a zeroing-in process driven by the inherent design of entering further into what is seen, as if reaching towards the formative element within every perception.

To escape this tendency while at the same time keeping the object in view, we need to go into some *spaced-out* state of consciousness, such as an alpha state. This act, as will be noted later, is tantamount to the elimination of fovea vision and the imposition of periphery vision throughout the field of view. Surprisingly, something of this nature happens between every moment of perception.

Seeing an Object

As an analogy, consider the way a cow looks out at the world. A cow's eye structure does not permit fovea vision, and this may be part of the reason for its unremitting stare in which no specific object seems to awaken recognition. Face to face with a cow, we can have the feeling that the cow is looking through us rather than at us. The impression given is that the cow somehow sees without *looking at*. We, on the other hand, *look at* but (to exaggerate the fact) ultimately *see* nothing but component parts! When we prolong the act of seeing without releasing our attention, the object seen is replaced by its constituents as we concentrate on details.

This might seem very troublesome, with things continuously slipping away from our visual grasp; however, it does not worry us. Our belief in wholes, in things in and of themselves, functions irrespective of changes in fovea seeing. We simply assume the presence of the object being looked at; we assume its continued existence qua object even while it is being taken apart in our dissecting fovea-mind process. Unruffled by the wondrous apparition of things ready-made in our consciousness, we proceed methodically to put them through the reduction process, extracting parts from wholes. Blinkered by a one-sided fovea view reflected in the denotative attitude of the thinking process, we remain ignorant of the fact that every whole, every object we set our attention upon, arises through another way of being. Both the ability to form unit meanings and the faculty to attribute continued existence to them are required to produce what we see around us.

The Intent to See Something

The centering movement described can be viewed from a different angle. If fovea vision is considered to be seeing what lies at the center of the field of view, something is missing from the description. Unaccounted for is the élan that drives the act of centering. Fovea vision, thus, is a process driven by a particular attitude of mind. This fact should not come as a surprise. It is precisely what was found in chapter 1 with the denotative mode of thought. The inherent driving attitude has to be included in any description of the process.

This attitude lies at the root of a movement of convergence in which everything seen serves as precursor to some smaller thing, suggesting the need for ever sharper vision as the units become more miniature. In this view, nothing we see is ever *it* in itself. This is the futile search for an irreducible fundamental element—futile, yes, for already from the outset it is evident that the surmised irreducible atom of existence will never hold back the reductionist process powering the search. Every atom of existence found—call it quark or whatever—each in its turn is pierced by the dimensionless point that is the spearhead of the fovea process of seeing driven by convergent thinking. Necessarily, it is a dimensionless point because it is not a thing but a principle, the principle that rules the process.

In this fovea process, wholes turn into parts, every answer becomes another quest on a smaller scale, meaning eludes every effort to encase it, and the act of perception loses the object it identifies. Similar to the tale of the thief in whose hands precious objects turn to dust the moment he touches them, every conscious act of looking to see what is *there* loses what it reaches for while taking hold of it.

This attitude of mind has dominated Western thought, research, and invention. It is the outcome of ignoring the complementary peripheral movement of the mind and of relegating any occurrence of it to a lesser state of reality. *Less real*, here, means less acceptable, and this discriminatory attitude arose because reality—an assertion made by the rational part of the thinking process—was given universality as all that has ultimate significance.

The Disappearing Object of Perception

Reducing what is seen and heard to what is most central is the process of zeroing-in on a denotative object. What arrests the process is not some kernel of reality that our senses bump into (!) but the formation of a concept in the mind. The moment an object is recognized, the convergent process is momentarily arrested. For example, noticing a strange sound in the background, you might listen, trying to catch what it is. Let's say at a certain moment you realize that it is the wind in the trees. With this, a concept has arrived: there is a known object—the wind. At that instant, "ah, it's the wind," listening ends even though you might reengage your audition the following instant and listen once again to the wind. Such an interruption in the listening process also occurred shortly before, when you noted the presence of a background sound. Every time we acknowledge something, consciousness is occupied with recognition during which listening, looking, and sensing the object end for a split second.

There is sensing, and then there is a pause. Concept formation is that pause. By rapidly refocusing on the object of attention, we stay on task, and the interruption in the perceptive activity goes unnoticed. The pause is camouflaged by the fact that the activity of perception continues on other levels since, no doubt, many diverse concepts are forming at any one time. However, the principal reason for not noticing the time lapse during which a concept is forged is because this activity takes place out of consciousness. This whole scenario is a replay of the discontinuity mentioned in chapter 1, where the process of concept formation was traced. Loss of consciousness in the mind's activity and discontinuity in seeing and hearing are two separate ways of stating the same thing.

What a tale this makes! Centered fovea attention reaches towards the formation of a concept, yet the instant the concept arises, conscious connection with the sensory object is severed—a rather surprising account of what is going on in perception. As an object becomes ever more centered, all that is the periphery recedes further and further from attention. The actual formation of the concept could be imagined as the moment when all attention goes to the center and periphery disappears—but the loss of periphery is exactly what makes the centered object disappear! At the moment of exclusive fovea attention, half-mindedness is achieved. The denotative mind has succeeded in its pursuit of full dominance and, just as this is accomplished, the lights go out. Nothing is observed. Sensory experience relayed to consciousness ends and perception is interrupted.

This is a description of denotative, fovea-riveted attention that inadvertently, one might say, moves to attain exclusivity; its tendency is to become the exclusive proprietor of the sensory object, and this means sealing the object off from what it is not, and this means from what is around it spatially and from what temporally comes just before and after it. The apotheosis arrives as a momentary blackout at the very instant when the object is formulated as a concept. And then, one moment later, it is as if nothing at all happened—nothing was interrupted, no special arrival presented itself out of nowhere, no telltale mark is left of the uncanny event, and we, the perceivers watching and listening, continue on our merry way, taking up the next item that catches our interest.

For this process to be evident to all, individual differences in the way a person forms a concept must be accounted for. Transformations from sound to concept, from picture to concept, from word to concept, and from sensation to concept are all the same in that they all form concepts. However, we have personal sensitivities, and each individual will find that one of these connections makes sense, whereas other connections might not make any sense at all. Frequently, though not necessarily, the person interested in this work from a philosophical standpoint has a verbal bias, and will find the *word to concept* connection to be the most obvious, and will assume gaining a concept means having a word for the object. Not so, for example, with an architect or engineer, who typically has a spatial bias and for whom what is pictured can, unnamed, directly form a concept. This subject returns in the final section of chapter 5, in the interlude on the work of Antoine de La Garanderie.

Visual Periphery Transformations

Vision is achieved through two distinct and contrasting processes. Complementary to the concentrating process already described is a visual function that does not converge on a center, and it has to do with *periphery vision*.

Differences in the appearance of an object when viewed with fovea vision or when seen with periphery vision are well documented. As it moves out from the center of the visual field, an object progressively loses detail and clarity. It is gradually stripped of all specific markers such as color and form to become, at the outer periphery, nothing more than the presence of movement. What is moving out at the limit of periphery vision has become imperceptible, and we can only imagine the object by recalling what was previously present in center field or by anticipating what will be there when fovea vision is directed at the perceived movement.

To follow the same sequence from the outside inward, there is at first, at the outer periphery, only a sense of movement. If we have no previous knowledge of what the object might be, it produces a strange sensation that we relieve by turning our eyes towards the object so as to bring it into fovea vision. In so doing, the initial presence grows to include qualities that make it into a perceptible entity.

What is being described here is the transformation of a visual object as it changes position in the visual field. In center field, it is most distinct and most obviously present—we are sure it is there. An object seems to possess a greater degree of reality when seen with centered vision. As it moves farther into the periphery of our visual field, consciousness diminishes, and typically we sense a need to perk up and verify it is really there by switching to fovea vision. Far from the center, an object loses definition and becomes what could be called more absent. In fact, it can hardly be called an object anymore.

When the phenomenology of vision is considered in this manner, surprising distinctions become apparent: loss of reality, increase and decrease of presence and absence, and even a sliding scale of consciousness. One might ask, are these genuine observational facts that can be tested by anyone? A definite *yes* is the answer. The terms of the description may be strange, but the facts are plain and verifiable.

A general reticence to give due importance to these qualitative distinctions of peripheral vision is the outcome of a stuck state of mind, of a belief. It can be compared to a similar mental block that happens in our first attempts at perspective drawing. Making realistic drawings often fails when we are led by fixed concepts of how we believe things to be (i.e., a circular object should be round, the top of a door left ajar horizontal, etc.). As soon as we take care to look and note what we actually see (i.e., the apparent oval form, the angles subtended by edges of objects and their relative lengths as they appear to the eye), our drawing takes on proportion and perspective. For many of us, our childhood efforts to draw were sabotaged by the inability to look at things the way they appear when projected onto a plane surface rather than the way we believed them to be. In this context, one should add that perspective viewing, too, springs from a particular set of beliefs, and being free of the attitude that produces perspective drawing is not to be disparaged. There are different ways of seeing, and each has its own wisdom.

This anecdote from drawing is offered as an analogy to illustrate what typically happens in periphery vision. Preformed concepts supplant careful observation. We carry over conclusions attained through fovea vision and so presume to know what it is we see when the object is not in fovea vision. With this, we overlook crucial aspects of the actual experience. Significant changes in an object as it moves about the visual field go unnoticed while loss of distinction, loss of presence, and varying states of consciousness seem to go unreported.

There is a conspicuous shift between the well-delineated, fully colored object in fovea vision and the fluid, blurred, colorless presence of an object placed in the periphery of vision. This blurred or smeared state calls to mind drawing techniques used for depicting movement in a manner that allows fovea vision to catch a vague sense of it. Loss of definition is an experience and produces a sense of instability that can suggest movement. An object depicted as smeared can be understood as the blending of many separate positions, suggesting continuous change even if denotative thought cannot conceive of what this is. Movement is a sensation, not a thought, and for this reason it is not accessible to the logical mind. That is why mathematical attempts to define movement in terms of fixed positions before and after the event inevitably lead to Zeno-like paradox. In periphery vision, one senses aspects of time and space that have fused and are no longer divisible into distance over time and into a definite where and when. The passage from fovea definition to periphery ambiguity is a gradual transition from comprehension to sensation.

This suggests that across the field of vision lies the transition from unity of being at the center to a fusion of multiple states at the periphery—a description that matches what was noted earlier about the connotative process, where out-of-consciousness was described not as emptiness but as an expanded consciousness of multiple presences. In the visual field, transition to the outer periphery brings on the loss of distinct units of time and space and, inevitably, becomes the limit of all that denotative consciousness can fathom.

Limits and Boundaries

These observational facts demonstrate that the field of vision does not stop abruptly at an edge, like a photograph. When we move our attention outward in the visual field, before any external boundary becomes apparent, there is a reduction of presence in the observed object and a loss of perceptible units of measure. The border of the visual field is not an entirely objective fact determined by what comes into the field of view. Something more than the angle subtended from the eye is needed to explain the limits of the visual field. How the visual field closes on itself requires an introspective look at the inherent properties of sight and seeing, and this is not undertaken in this essay.

To understand the intermediary states between full consciousness and nonconsciousness, subjective impressions of what is perceived need to be accepted for what they are before any attempt is made to fit them into an objective view. We may expect this is obvious, but the rational scientific approach requires that individual observations be recognized as real, objective facts. Since reality forms only when impressions are turned into conclusions, science contains a fundamental bias of concept over experience. Attention to periphery phenomena, on the other hand, points to graded semiconscious states that lie between restricted consciousness in fovea vision and the loss of all conceptual consciousness at the limits of peripheral vision. It is an area of transition between observable reality and what is unobservable.

PART II: AUDITION

Periphery and Fovea Perceived Temporally

The functioning of the auditory sense can be observed in the same phenomenological manner as was done for the visual sense, and what emerges is a description of a sensory system that runs parallel to that of vision.

To begin with, the tendency of fovea vision to reduce spatial extension in the direction of the dimensionless point is shown, in what follows, to be parallel to the tendency of auditory centering to reduce temporal extension in the direction of a timeless present instant. One is an emphasis on the *here*, the other on the *now*.

Focusing on a particular sound is a manner of listening that detects ever shorter time segments of what one hears with the goal of closing in on the now, separating what one is actually hearing, the auditory object, from the semipresence of sounds that precede and follow it. However, the very instant the auditory object is seized as a concept—a birdcall or a word—the process of temporal reduction halts. Up to the formation of a concept and possibly the very next moment again, listening is driven by the undeclared intention of whittling down what is heard to what is present while, as one might already imagine, that present moment, impudent as ever, proceeds to shrink to nothing. The implicit drive to reduce everything to an ever finer definition leads towards the Euclidean point, which, being dimensionless, lies beyond the confines of space and time.

Both vision and hearing are processes guided by a centripetal intent that gives attention to what is central while clearing it of extraneous periphery. Both are the expression of a particular mind-set—a mind set upon forming a concept. This is not at all a reference to a program mapped onto some genome. Instead, attitudes of mind are alterable to the extent that they have the directing presence of self. What this signifies is clarified in the final chapters of this work, but it includes the alternatives of converging on specific units of meaning or moving out to the indefinite periphery. These are two distinct ways of being, and how we employ these alternatives determines what we see and understand as the world.

Surrealism and the Source of Meaning

A central thrust of the Surrealist movement can be understood as the expression of the inability of this centered, denotative attitude to create its own meaning. It arose at a particular moment in the history of art when verisimilitude no longer proved challenging, having, as it seemed, surrendered all its secrets. It was a time when perspective in painting had lost its raison d'être and the subject and purpose of art were changing. Surrealism was, in a way, a last-ditch effort to make something new out of given representational structures. It retained the rules of perspective and objectivity, yet, while abiding by these, made original statements by deforming what it produced, by running together what does not fit together, and by distorting meaningful objects—twisting, stretching, and pulling them apart. It was a self-annihilating process, feeding off the meaningful forms it used to make its statements. Although entertaining, revealing, evocative, and whatever else, in its method it was the proverbial sawing-off of the branch you are sitting on.

Caught in a one-sided view of the dual thinking process with no understanding of the complementary side can leave us in that self-destructive state. Fovea thinking needs to be recognized for what it is, namely, an activity that engages meanings but does not create them. To recognize meaning as the gift it is opens the path to far-reaching adjustments in the way we understand and relate to all that is our world. All we perceive suddenly becomes something multifarious, no longer set and rigid, and the world scintillates with meanings that an individual may grasp or leave unattended. Like ambiguous drawings that can be seen either one way or another, duck or rabbit, everything we perceive shows how we look and not just what we see. An observation is a unique moment for the observer; from undisclosed potentiality it singles out one possible realization. A perception is a pregnant moment, a unique event that portends more than is directly observed, for there is always the meaning of that meaning: how it came to be, just then and there, that such an observation arises. Two crows flying westward is more than an objective fact in that it tells the tale of a world to which the subject gives presence. On one hand, self is the all-powerful creator of meaning, and on the other hand, the humbled witness of all that arises and becomes knowable. These two roles are linked; they portray the awakening of self and the loss of self in the connectivity of all. To be *alone* is a fovea view of *all one*, in which objects are separate and complete in themselves and where the wider view of the complementary functions of perception has been lost. To bring back the wider view is to acknowledge the interplay between self, other, and the world. It is to recognize the interdependence of subjectivity and objectivity, and it is, too, to see humor in the way we give universality to what is but a partial comprehension of a universe that remains ever mysterious.

Auditory Periphery

In general, we attribute periphery only to visual phenomena even though it is a property of sense perception in general. Although the presence of periphery in each medium of perception raises intriguing questions, the discussion here is limited to the visual and auditory media, and the goal is to offer further illustration of the dual processes of mind.

To understand periphery in audition, it is necessary to understand the role of temporal extension, for just as a visual object is surrounded by the visual medium, space, so the auditory object is surrounded by the auditory medium: time. In concrete terms, this means that the visual periphery is beside, above, and below, while the auditory periphery is before and after the object that is observed. It is periphery because it includes more than the specific object viewed and more than the sound one hears at a given moment. Simply stated, the presence of a sensory object encompasses more than is contained in the visual or temporary extension of the perceived object.

Transitional states between presence and absence are essential to audition just as they are to sight. When we listen to a melody, we are not just hearing single notes that sound out one after another. Tones just heard and no longer being played have not disappeared abruptly from our overall consciousness. A lingering presence of what was sounded and a premonition of what is forthcoming give the sense of melody; without this, melody would have no meaning. To have melody, what is absent in varying degrees binds together with what is fully present.

Another example of the play of periphery in audition is the comprehension of a sentence. It, too, requires integrating what has been with what is coming. We understand a full sentence as a unit of meaning and not as the succession of a string of words. This can be contrasted with occasions when, as a language learner, we find ourselves in the situation of following a string of words and waiting (in the case of German) for the verb at the end in order to make meaning of the sentence. For a fluent speaker there is no waiting and meaning comes to the sentence as a whole. A parallel case of integration, but on a smaller scale, is recognizing a sound or a sequence of sounds as a single, meaningful word.

When the temporal object is short, we ignore the linking of was, is, and will be, and when the object is extended in time, we ignore it too! To our rational mind, which functions linearly, there is no way other than bit by bit, so it is assumed that understanding comes through some logical step-by-step process of sticking words together and sifting through their grammatical and lexical possibilities or by sticking notes one to another to form a melody. It is necessary to go beyond the rational mind's view to realize that other ways are possible.

Strange Yet True: Temporal Periphery

It is time to heed any misgivings on the part of the reader as to the strangeness of what is being proposed. Yes, it is true that this manner of speaking of a temporal periphery parallel to the spatial periphery is not an accepted view, even though it becomes obvious as soon as one reflects on it. There are impressions from the past and from the future that form the temporal periphery of hearing

Hearing has a "now" with its temporal periphery just as sight has a "here" with its spatial periphery.

just as, in seeing, there are out-of-center impressions in the visual field that form the spatial periphery. Hearing has a *now* with its temporal periphery just as sight has a *here* with its spatial periphery.

What Do Periphery Sounds Sound Like?

The manner in which the visual object changes according to its position in the visual field was already noted. Something parallel, no doubt, is true of the auditory object. What does it mean that something heard has ceased to sound, which means, it no longer resonates in one's ears and yet is still partially present? What is it that is present? Does that sound lose some of its qualities, as does the visual object moving to the periphery? It is more difficult to ascertain this in the temporal dimension, and this writer knows of no studies comparable to those on visual periphery. Even so, simply raising the question suggests some preliminary answers. Listen for yourself and sense what is there. The following pointers are very tentative and serve only as a suggestion of changes that may occur in auditory periphery.

An emitted sound clearly has an effect on what follows. The simple fact that one feels a certain shock when some quality of the sound (volume, pitch, etc.) suddenly changes demonstrates there is a degree of carryover of the effect of the precedent sound on what follows, and in some manner, earlier and later are copresent in the mind. Whatever auditory sensation is not sounding at the present moment would be periphery, and as with visual phenomena, it gradually loses certain qualities as it recedes from the centered *now* of what is being heard. One must keep in mind that this is not about recalling a note but rather about the effect of notes not registering in consciousness. To our conceptual minds, it is strange that a sound is not *there*, yet its effect remains present and active. Qualities such as pitch, timbre, and volume die away, though probably at differing rates. The specifics of the note heard are lost, and yet a presence remains that is not the same as the initial note. It is preposterous, but remember that the outer periphery of the visual field can ascertain motion without seeing any identifiable visible object. Try that one on the logical mind! Something of the note is present though many of its qualities have left. If one goes through a process of eliminating sound qualities no longer being heard at a given moment, what is left?

That which is retained is *the relationship* of a sound to other sounds. Proximity or distance of those qualities previously noted is still sensed. For example, even though the pitch of the earlier sound is no longer present in the mind, the range of pitches and distance between the sounds are somehow still present. Granted, this is strange to imagine, just as the loss of color and form and the general blurring of the visual out-of-center image are strange to imagine in rational terms. In order to note the relationship between periphery sounds in our mind, consider, for example, a previously established key signature that is present in the mind while later notes are heard. This imposes structure on what is heard and places an onus of expectation on what is to come. At a certain point one might ask whether this is hearing or feeling, but the distinction is of diminishing importance as one moves to the periphery of the senses. Feelings play over boundaries, bridging the conscious with the nonconscious, as already noted in the previous chapter. Here, what is noteworthy is that feelings raised by a sound one hears are carried over into adjacent moments of hearing and beyond.

To show that structural effects play into a moment of hearing, take the example of a note that diverges from the melodic, rhythmic, or harmonic structures of a piece. The mismatch is apparent the very moment the note is played, for, in response to a wrong note, a missed beat, or an out-of-tune sound, quite spontaneously we react with "oops—an error." We therefore perceive encompassing structures that embrace all we hear, structures that are copresent with what we are listening to. Experiences such as these bring support to the conclusion that, unknown to centered attention, a different mode of perception is active while conscious perception is in progress.

Spoken language offers further examples of the same observation. When we read or listen to a sentence, what periphery effect do we carry over to the yet unseen/unheard remaining words? Should we come upon a grammatical error or changes in the direction of the meaning of the sentence, right away we notice. Some part of our sensitivity registers these encompassing structures without effort and without directed attention. Meanings from beyond the present instant are interacting with what reaches our ears. It is possible to make a distinction between what is being heard (fovea perception) and what are background supporting structures (periphery perception) even if it is no more than saying the first are identifiable and the second, though evidently present, are not conscious.

When the general concept of periphery is understood, the idea of an auditory temporal periphery is no longer strange. Interrelationships taking form in peripheral semiconsciousness and in nonconsciousness have a vital and complex role in what we hear, see, and experience. The object that comes to our attention is but a small part of what is being communicated to us at that moment.

Blending *Is* with *Is Not*

Although in common usage *periphery* is generally taken to mean visual periphery, this is only one example of a concept that has a wider application. One might ask, why was the attribution of auditory periphery not as obvious as the attribution of visual periphery? It could well be that this understanding was deterred by confusion between periphery extension in time and the function of memory. Auditory periphery is the expansion of a moment of hearing into a more inclusive temporal unit in which what was heard and what will be heard mingle with what is being heard. Usually, when a question arises as to how we grasp extended temporal structures, the snap answer is *memory*, and with that word, which by and large adds nothing at all, the question is supposedly answered. Injecting the word *memory* for what was and the word *imagination* for what is to come is a trick the rational mind employs to refer to what lies beyond its limited reach. It is a reductionist evasion that interprets the expanded sense of time as nothing but memory and imagination functioning in conjunction with momentary audition. However, the uncanny ability to listen simultaneously to the future and to the past as well as to what is a constantly changing present is something the rational conscious mind can neither explain nor perform, and so the proposed solution—memory—makes no sense at all. Still, such a proposition has a rational, logical sound to it and employs appropriate accepted terms, so it gets away with it—or did!

Behind such a flawed proposition lies a motive that is not difficult to discern. With the claim that memory is responsible for the expansion of sensibilities beyond the present moment, the lingering aspects of audition do not have to be attributed to a variation in degree of presence of what is heard. Calling it *memory* instead of speaking of *a lower level of presence* keeps the peace, for then reality can still be divided neatly into the familiar clear-cut dichotomy of either it is (being heard) or it is not!

Auditory Periphery Is Not Memory

In the visual field, everything is copresent, and displacement away from the center to the periphery is understood in spatial terms, thus giving no reason to invoke memory. With auditory periphery, the off-center part is temporal (one hears the *just before* and the probable *just after* of the sound one is attending to), and for this reason it can be confused with memory, which is to say with the recall of what came before, and with imagination, which is the supposition of what may come after. Auditory periphery, however, remains distinct from memory and imagination.

To recall something as a memory is to reinstate what one was conscious of earlier. What is recalled replaces what is seen or heard at the present moment. Even though it may occupy the mind but a split second, there is a moment in which the recalled object becomes the object of consciousness. This stands in contrast to periphery phenomena, for which nothing is recalled. Instead, there is a lingering presence of what is past and a prefiguration of a future presence that does not become an object of consciousness as it would were it memory. Periphery is precisely *not* what one is thinking about! It is what one is not focused on, not looking at, not listening to. It is, so to speak, off to the side and seeps into what one is thinking without ever taking center stage. If it did, that would mean it has turned into a centered, denotative object and is no longer periphery.

Another way of stating this is with the term *subliminal*. Periphery phenomena are subliminal information incorporated into our understanding without its presence being acknowledged.

To refer to the temporal expansion in hearing as memory is misleading, and the error becomes all the more blatant when one grasps clearly the parallel between audition and vision. Spatial out-of-center vision and temporal out-of-immediate audition function in similar ways. Given that, in vision, periphery needs no help from memory, memory is not what makes periphery. This suggests instead that, in both hearing and seeing, we are sensitive to a periphery zone where the experience of what is observed includes lower degrees of presence, reduced objectivity, and less awakened levels of consciousness as well as nonconsciousness.

Realizing this dispels the tidy view of a reality divided into *is* and *is not*. Instead, it leaves a sensory system that works by blending what is objective and conscious with effects ranging from less conscious and less objective all the way to nonconscious and purely subjective. The previous chapter showed the mind to function both *in* and *out* of consciousness to produce objects of thought; here it becomes apparent that the sensory system also works this way, producing sensory objects through an interplay of both the conscious and the nonconscious.

PART III: SENSORY PERCEPTION—A BROADER UNDERSTANDING

Fovea and Periphery in the Creation of Concepts

At this point, it is possible to review what was said in the first chapter about concept formation in terms of fovea and periphery sensitivities.

Meanings arise in consciousness as concepts. They are received by our centered, fovea-like attention as single wholes, and we explore them by identifying parts and how they fit together until the inevitable but false conclusion is reached that concepts arise and coalesce in the same piecemeal manner by which they are elucidated. We ignore the fact that the conscious mind is a fovea attention and on its own has not what it takes to forge new units of meaning. One could argue against this claim and suggest that we invent lots of things with conscious thought—a telephone, for example—and we can propose the name *telephone*. Have we then created meaning, a new thing? No, because although there is a new object with a specific identity, recognizing that object as being a whole still comes to the conscious mind from beyond the assembling/dissecting fovea-directed mind of rational thought. It comes from the part of our mind that can encompass whole units and can reach through periphery to what is out of consciousness.

The only sense of unity that restricted fovea consciousness can produce on its own is that of a good fit between the pieces—of course, each piece of this assembled unity is itself an assemblage and so forth in infinite regression until the dimensionless point comes to save the show. Against this, someone might argue that when parts fit together as a functional, interrelated whole, there is an attribute of unity, for example, the syntax of a sentence, the balance between parts of a work of art, or the integration of parts in a functioning unit like a beehive, a bee, or a tractor. But an assembled unit is not an experienced unit. To realize this, it is necessary to step beyond the confines of center-focused thinking in that comprehending wholes as wholes requires a very different information system.

Periphery phenomena have been shown to be intermediary stages between in-consciousness and out-of-consciousness. In this zone of semipresence, definitions are dissolving and reforming. Recognizing periphery phenomena for what they are points the way to what lies beyond the centered, reductive view of reality.

Intermingling of the Senses in Periphery

Although in fovea perception identifying objects is all-important, this is not the preoccupation of periphery sensitivity where, as noted in the previous section, even separation between the different senses becomes fluid.

Close to centered fovea perception, acts of seeing and hearing remain distinct from one another. Away from the center, deep in periphery, what is left of seeing and hearing comes to us as a general sensation; there is a blurred presence we are not directly looking at, there are inaudible effects that influence what we hear, and these have turned into something more feeling than sight or hearing. Impressions have lost their visual or auditory identity. With loss of sensory separateness, the division between intellect and feeling is erased, and instead there is some general sense of awareness. Objects have lost their independent presence, and what remains has no clear boundaries, no specific *where* or *when* to be in. As feelings, they have become infused with subjectivity. They are experienced but cannot be objectified. Subjective and objective, conscious and nonconscious are no longer separate. This blending of qualities brings the dissolution of what we hold to be categories of reality: time, space, and materiality. In this state, what is left is the content of an experience that is here referred to as *expanded consciousness* and that could also be understood as part of general awareness.

Leaving the secure basis of the world we hold as real can be unsettling, but with the departure comes a promise: the possibility of some new understanding of our experience as living beings. Implicit, at this point in the narrative, is a call to adventure to those eager to discover what a novel viewpoint might entail.

To See Without Eyes, to Hear Without Ears

The fact that seeing is built through spatial variation across the field of vision and recedes into a periphery of something no longer specifically visual, together with the fact that hearing, in contrast but parallel with seeing, is built through a temporal variation receding into inaudible qualities, leads to an unexpected conclusion that overturns our commonly held opinion that the eye is the origin of sight, the ear the origin of hearing. Seeing can arise without eyes when the display of what is sensed is constituted spatially; hearing can arise without ears when this is done temporally. The eyes are marvelous at facilitating this task, but it is not the eye itself that creates seeing, and though the ear is a wonderful instrument for constituting sound objects, it is not the ear that creates hearing. Sight and hearing result from specific ways of organizing and integrating information.

This realization brings another thought. It might seem to us that we possess two systems of vision, one when we use our eyes to look out at the world and a different one when, without employing our physical eyes, we see our mental images. These two apparently separate manifestations of vision are, in fact, one and the same. They are created by the presence of a spatial display in the mind. Eyes may be helpful in creating such a display, but, to repeat, it is not the eye that makes for seeing. The same apparent double system is true of audition, between the sounds we hear through our ears and the tune (or sounds or conversation) we hear *in our head*. The sequential range of sounds we know as hearing is not dependent on the ear, though, granted, the ear is mighty helpful in aligning the mind to the auditory mode of integrating past, present, and future sensations into graded levels of presence. With this understanding, the fact that there are people with strong visual bias among those without eyesight and people with a dominant auditory tendency among those who do not hear with their ears is not at all strange.

Step by step, as we conjure out its many aspects, perception becomes ever more intriguing.

Perceiving the Imperceptible

These conclusions point to a remarkable fact: effects that never enter our conscious mind have the capacity to form an object we see, hear, and touch. Previously, it was noted that the emergence of a concept signals that an unconscious process integrates multiple effects that never entered consciousness. Despite the fact that the disparate aspects producing the concept do not enter the conceptual mind, their integrated effect has the ability to create an impression of which we

How strange to think we hear what is actually inaudible.

are conscious. This is a paradox that underlies all we experience. Integration of what is not perceived is the prerequisite for every act of perception, whether of imagined objects or objects observed through our sense organs.

To exemplify this, one can point to the fact that in hearing a note or in seeing a particular shade of color we are able to distinguish inaudible and invisible distinctions. We cannot decipher the individual beats that create a note, and yet there is a change from one note to another when those inaudible beats change their rate of pulsation (their frequency). How strange to think that we hear what is actually inaudible. The same is true of sight. A slight color change that we observe corresponds to imperceptible vibrational changes in the wavelength of light that are below the threshold of what we can see. Our sense of touch, too, registers objects that, on a microscopic level and below, are beyond the range of what can be sensed. Distinctions too fine to be perceived result in obvious and real differences of experience: in a note of a specific pitch, or a particular shade of color, or a physical presence of particular consistency.

An object we observe becomes what it is after the integration of what is imperceptible, and therefore, from the viewpoint of the subject, every object perceived materializes out of nothing. It appears fully independent because the imperceptible constituents that its presence implies do not register in consciousness. What we see, hear, and all we divine is always a whole, a global structure that presents the result of already integrated effects. Perception, thus, is an intuitive act and not a process of construction by which parts are assembled to form what is observed. An object we recognize is a fundamental unit of meaning by dint of the fact that we perceive it. (The implications of this for an understanding of truth were described in chapter 1.) The perceived object spontaneously manifests as the expression of what it is. To phrase this in other words, anything that enters consciousness is already instated and identifiable, and even though it implies the presence of constituents that fused in order to produce it, and even though we are superbly sensitive to the qualities of those constituents (e.g., wavelength), we remain oblivious and totally unconscious of them.

Every act of perception signals the fact that imperceptible activity succeeded in producing an integrated single object. A caveat is added here to distance a common presupposition we bring from our experience of the physical world. In the material realm, it is accepted that invisible molecules of water gather to form visible droplets and that cells too small to be perceived connect to form visible, palpable tissue. Here the common ground between the invisible and the visible is materiality. The more material, the bigger the object and thus the more obvious it becomes to our senses. If this is taken as an analogy for what happens in the mind, it leads to misunderstanding. It may seem normal to multiply something invisibly minute till it forms what becomes perceivable, but the mind world is not the material world. Qualitative impressions do not add together in the way quantities of matter and energy combine. To have something imperceptible release something perceptible does not happen by simply having more of it. A transformation of a different order, not merely augmentation, is required, and it happens with integration. Through integration, diversity becomes unified. This happens when subliminal aspects of whatever is perceived organize themselves according to a common base that reveals a new property (e.g., from imperceptible sound effects into tones). Such a base is a prerequisite for all understanding and for all we perceive. This transition does not involve growth through the multiplication of elements as it does in the material domain but, instead, is the transformation of untold many into a single unit. This is a separate subject that has many implications but is included at this juncture merely to clarify what has been said about subliminal into perceptible and is not presented as a topic itself.

The effect of subliminal organized features on our understanding and even on our physiology is not just about what is too minute to be deciphered. It is true of macro structures as well. Consider, for example, the effect that the architecture of a building can have. It can influence one's mood and well-being, and the way it affects one comes from the integrated effect of its particular features. It is not the effect of individual elements of the building nor is it the cumulative effect of such structural elements. There is an impact—be it aesthetic or other—that comes from the integrated effect of the structural elements. The integral effect is present without our taking notice of features that cause it. This raises the question, where lies the intelligence that integrates the subliminal elements into the unitary whole to create a particular impression? It will not do to answer that no such intelligence is needed and the effect of the architecture simply penetrates autonomic biological systems to produce physical responses. This would leave unexplained the fact that a global effect, whether beauty, harmony, imbalance, or whatever, has a specific effect that is only present when the structural elements are taken as a whole, when an as yet unaccounted for function integrates stimuli into meaningful wholes to which we respond. The process surely involves the expanded mind that can sense multiple effects at once, but this does not explain how the integration is produced and how features unify to become that which carries a particular quality of impression. The perception of flavors, smells, sounds, sights, feelings, moods, inspiration, and all we know seems to occur as if something enters consciousness without requiring any participation by the subject except that of playing host. These impressions, already integrated into what they are, enter our expanded consciousness as effects and our conceptual consciousness as objects. This integration happened out of consciousness and was the transformation from many to one, from the imperceptible to what reaches consciousness. It is the transformation of macroscopic effects into a novel, independent expression through an act of integration of which consciousness was oblivious.

The fact that every perception originates from an imperceptible act of integration gives credence to the common belief in a ready-made world that is autonomous and objective. Yet, the reason things manifest as if already *there* is that they arise from the imperceptible and not that they preexisted in some way.

As pointed out in the previous paragraphs, there is the integration of what is imperceptible. This happens when imperceptible factors enter into common accord, that is, they enter a shared scale of values such as intensity, spatial relationships, and frequency. With this shared code, if to call it that, they interrelate. Through the intent to perceive, we bring about the movement towards integration. At first the process is accessible only to the expanded mind and lies beyond consciousness where there are, for example, imperceptible oscillations producing a note or a color. With the emergence of the scale—code—through which all enters the same integrating base, the imperceptible can take on macro features that register upon our senses and manifest as the things we perceive.

Periphery as a Subject of Study

A fascinating dimension is added to the study of sensory periphery with the realization that it offers a whole other way of knowing. Augmenting one's periphery sensitivity can become a personal quest, and there are ways of training oneself to dispel the tendency of conscious thought to exclude periphery. This is developed in a number of disciplines such as martial arts and certain techniques for inner development. In what follows, two commonplace examples are given.

Certain techniques of drawing include ways of disconnecting from the fovea-centered image. There is, for example, the trick of not looking at the object one is to paint but only at what is not that object, that is, at the spaces that give the outline of that object. For instance, you don't look directly at the chair you are drawing and don't see it as one normally knows it to be; rather, you see only the shapes of the spaces between its parts and of the spaces formed around it. One can become quite competent at this nonfocused seeing and do it even without sipping absinthe—a common practice among impressionist artists who sometimes painted in this way.

Another way of releasing fovea attention is to become aware of incremental change. Allowing transformation to enter consciousness demands periphery alertness in that it requires awareness of an ensemble of elements. To choose an auditory example: in a canoe on a river, to recognize gradually sounds that forewarn of rapids up ahead is listening to change. An example that includes other senses is noticing an oncoming storm—maybe not the towering cumulus clouds as, very likely, this would happen with fovea attention but sensing a change in the transparency of the air, whips of haze forming over a peak, slight changes in the quality of sounds and of temperature; these together can be periphery phenomena that enter while full consciousness is given over to other things. In general, perceiving that something is changing (not that it has changed) is peripheral, resulting from a combination of effects that initially go unnoticed.

Increasing susceptibility to expanded periphery consciousness implies a shift in attitude, from pinpointing to integrating. In a sense, it is like distancing oneself from what one perceives, taking a reclining position yet remaining fully alert. Visual periphery is enhanced by softening one's gaze on the fovea object and releasing attention from it while augmenting one's sensitivity to all that is detectable in the area that is not center field. To an extent, this is an altered state of consciousness. Sensing auditory periphery, similarly, requires softening one's hold on any specific sound by reducing the intensity with which one listens to what occupies the auditory center. Releasing one's attention from it tends to dissolve the boundaries of the now and allow for hearing to extend over passages of time that include varied components. A safeguard that keeps fovea attention at bay and restrains any one sound from promoting itself onto center stage is a general attitude that listens for the combined effect of many impressions.

Subjectivity and Perception

The degree to which background sounds enter consciousness depends in part on qualities of the sounds (e.g., loudness) and on one's manner of listening, that is, of directing one's intent. In fact, through the emission of intent, the listener can readjust to a significant degree qualities of sound that are commonly assumed to be objective facts resulting from sound waves impacting one's sensory system. Tempo, sound volume, distance, and much more can be reformulated as if our senses were equipped with a digital zoom. This fact is easy to verify by asking others how they perceive sounds and noting the differences. Answers vary just like they do when sports champions tell how they aim at a ball traveling a hundred miles an hour. Some reply that mentally (actually, through intent) they can slow down the action so as to have plenty of time to watch the ball come towards the bat or racket; others tell equally uncanny but different tales. There is great variation in the ability of individuals to readjust sensory parameters assumed to be objective, and seemingly this ability can be trained—but that is a separate subject. It is in the power of the observer to modulate both centered sounds and subtle periphery effects. To substantiate that such subjective factors influence hearing, one need but note the extent to which sounds depend on cultural factors such as knowledge of musical structures, affinity with certain tonal modes, sensitivity to overtones, to accents, to typical speech patterns, to expected story lines, and to habitual lines of reasoning. All these can function as periphery effects that modulate what the listener hears.

In vision, there is the same tale to tell: periphery determinants influence what is seen. There is a well-known example that Gombrich, the art historian, uses when he shows an English landscape painted by a visiting Chinese artist in which the countryside looks just like China does in Chinese paintings![1] What one sees, to no small degree, results from the eye of the beholder. Another striking case of readjustment of parameters by the viewer, not unrelated to this first example, arises when different people sketch the same scene. The drawings often come out to be drastically different. In one picture, for instance, objects seem miniature and almost lost in an expanse of space, while in another drawing the same objects become dominant features. Although the elements and their relative positions remain, no two pictures tell the same story. These differences go well beyond any question of variation in drawing ability and reflect different ways of seeing. Although each of us believes our own view to be objective and imagines that others see the same scene we do, differences readily become apparent as soon as a graphic record of what is actually seen is made. Factors embedded in personal attitudes mold the reality we observe and determine what emerges in consciousness. Among these factors, certain can be understood to be functioning as periphery; others are too indefinite to be attributed to the periphery of a particular sense and are related to more personal factors such as one's bearing and one's mood. Everything that bears upon one's way of being is reflected in what one perceives, and surely this prompts the thought that, to some degree, the world we perceive is the mirror of who we are.

Beauty is as genuine and present as anything that is the world.

Maybe it is necessary to make excuses for the direction the discussion has taken, for it has left periphery phenomena for more general remarks on the influence of the perceiver on what is perceived. But these are not unrelated. Beyond various known qualities that fuse to form a concept is a huge range of subliminal effects reaching deep into

---

1. Ernst Gombrich, *Art and Illusion*, 6th ed. (New York: Phaidon Press, 2002), 74.

periphery sensitivity and beyond. That an observer influences the observed to a far greater extent than generally admitted is a reminder of the general theme of this work. When one considers perception to be objective effects impinging on the sense organs, one omits the key subjective dimension. Physics and biology alone without the input of an intentioned personal subject cannot create perception.

Re-viewing Reality

An obsessively objective view of the world has led to the opinion that things we observe are quantifiable and objectively determined and that one can measure the amount of substance (matter or energy) they have—ounces, molecules, joules, photons, or whatever. The implied supposition is that objects with certain inherent properties determine what we perceive and that the only variable in perception is the ability of our senses to register what is present. We might take note of something or not notice it, but what is there is there! But this is not how the world works. There is much more to observation than the content found when measuring what is present in an object. The interplay of contextual features has a vital and complex role in determining what we observe. For example, the crucial role of attitude was noted earlier when it was shown that the tendency of qualities to fuse and form objects depends on the attitude one adopts, whether denotative or connotative. There are other examples, such as the fact that colors we observe are not purely a result of the wavelengths of the light reaching our eyes, and this means that other factors enter into the determination of the color of an object. Too, there is surely a parallel case with hearing in which tones we hear are not determined exclusively by the frequencies reaching our ears at that moment. Reduced exclusively to purely objective phenomena, little if anything of the entire world is left.

Beyond this position of extreme objectification, a different view awaits. It takes into account innumerable variables that make up every experience of reality, and it makes no claim for something objective that is independent of these appearances. Context determines much of what is observed. In one particular context, an object is different from what it is in another—here it is shiny, there it is not; here it sounds right, there it is shrill; here it feels right, and there, ungainly; here it is white, there it is gray. Size, too, is variable. It is a belief in objectivity that serves to steady our amazement at the giant rising moon. Variation in the size of objects is happening all the time, though we do not often pay attention to the different ways that objects stand out in our field of view. Qualities are variable and contextually dependent. These variations cannot be dismissed as passing inconsequential subjective features of an object rigidly grounded in reality because reality itself has no substance without these impressions. Without the quality of twinkle and darkness is there any meaning to the word *star*?

(Should this example appear too unscientific, I invite the reader to choose another one. Any perceptual object can serve.) And what meaning is there to *clown* if you take away the costume and the humor? Reduction of a perceived object to some essential kernel that is *the real thing* is a very mistaken approach. Reality has no such autonomy, and to posit it is to ignore so much else, for then all that cannot be grasped in a focused way and pointed at—beauty, for instance—can be removed as unsubstantiated, capricious, subjective phenomena. But is beauty less real than molecules or the galaxy? What an idea—of course not! Beauty is as genuine and present as anything that is the world. Excessive objectification has an underlying belief system that gives exclusivity to the denotative attitude. Then, as so often happens, belief and truth are confounded, and the result is the *nothing but* view where reality has been reduced to nothing more than an agglomeration of bits that combine to produce bigger bits—a devastating viewpoint in that everything then has to trace its quota of reality to something minute. Anything larger cannot be real. Without some way to give reality to comprehensive overriding structures, how can there be any form or meaning? Limited to the denotative fovea viewpoint, reality crumbles to dust, leaving a desert made of dimensionless particles. Instead of seeing "a world in a grain of sand," one sees but grains of sand where there is a world.

What it means to grasp wholes and to recognize the reality of encompassing integral structures has not yet been fully exposed. But imagine where this view leads. What if a flower is a particular expression of all of nature, if an individual cell is the expression of the whole organism in its environment, and if our every deed is the manifestation of a relationship with all there is. The tale of periphery presence has only just begun.

Noninterference within Periphery Phenomena

In realizing the full play of periphery in perception, it becomes evident that diverse phenomena can be sensed together without one interfering with another. As an example, the periphery function bringing understanding of a word does not interfere with the periphery function bringing understanding of the sentence in which that word appears, and these, again, do not interfere with the periphery moment that carries the meaning of the segment or paragraph, nor with that bringing understanding of the whole story being told. The same is true with musical examples: hearing a note while hearing the melodic and rhythmic phrase and this while listening to the overall expression of the song or symphonic movement. These examples are of noninterference in temporal sequences. A parallel visual example would be different objects within the same view, each with its own spatial extension:

the ring/on the finger/of the storyteller/in the park/. In visual representation each object is accorded a place that is separate from the observer's *here*, and therefore noninterference is clear and does not need special mention. With auditory phenomena, in contrast, every sound object forms around the *now* of the observer, and thus noninterference is noteworthy. Many different-sized peripheral wholes can play into our awareness without any particular one taking a dominant position. Each has its own moment, and although in clock time they are concurrent and straddle the observer's now, they do not interact. Units of meaning are embedded one in another, functioning together beyond the horizon of consciousness, yet coming to full consciousness as separate moments of understanding.

The significance of this is far-reaching. It shows that perception arises through any number of simultaneously functioning layers of experience, and thus models of cognition built on the idea of a linear response to sequenced sensory input are untenable. Encompassing structures on many different scales play into the mind together, each one creating impressions unrelated to the others. Such a state of noninterference is a common experience. Recognizing this fact opens our sensitivity to features that will be presented in the remaining sections of this chapter and relate to the formation of unity.

Multilevel communication is a feat that leaves our conscious mind bewildered, yet it is an integral part of the out-of-consciousness mind. The ability to sense wholes simultaneously on separate planes of experience is the sine qua non of having intelligence of anything at all. Only to the extent that this is understood can perception be described.

Perceiving Wholes as Wholes: The Ground for Intelligence

Specific factors set boundaries to a perceptive act and lead to the formation—the congealing—of unit perceptions. Something in the inner structure of what is perceived brings the moment of perception to a close, allowing a unit of meaning to take form. This process is comparable to what was mentioned earlier about the boundary of the visual field having an internal factor. (See in this chapter the section "Limits and Boundaries.") Although the ending, or weaning, of an observed unit may have obvious external reasons, for example, being prompted by the short attention span of the observer, there are, no doubt, more integral reasons for the formation of a whole, whereby qualities of an observed object bring it to close on itself and become a unit of meaning. A repeated element, such as a visual pattern or a rhythmic motif, by dint of repetition, becomes a cognizable unit. A sentence defines its own unit of meaning through syntax and grammar, and, no doubt, larger compositions such as a full-length drama or a symphony also have internal factors that bring closure and reveal a single unit of meaning. Our culture, like others, has produced lengthy creations that form large units, and this most certainly signifies that they are pertinent. On some level we are pleased and nourished by such grand unified structures. They are intelligible to us.

We apparently have the ability to sense large structures and very large structures as single units of meaning. If you have not yet noticed this ability, it may be that you have lived under the vague assumption that large units are built up through identifying smaller pieces and interrelating them. This is the fovea approach of setting out arguments and reasoning to conclusions. Instead of adhering to such an approach, we can allow ourselves to be carried by the momentum of the whole composition—play, symphony, film, novel, tableau, epic poem, landscape, whatever—for there is an integral impression to be gleaned. Sensing the whole requires unfocused hearing and unfocused seeing. Adding bits together will not give the sense of whole (though deconstruction may be helpful in expanding our attention to include more of what is there); rather, it is through a semiconscious or even nonconscious sensitivity that has to do with the nature of periphery sensibility that the whole is sensed.

A sense of fullness and expansiveness comes with perceiving extended objects. It has to do with the increased periphery involvement in the act of perception. For an extended object, the influx of all that comes from the expanded mind is more pronounced than in a smaller object, and the impression one has dwells more in periphery semiconsciousness where feelings are more noticeable. This prolongation of the periphery experience brings an increased sense of duration during which the object, whether thought or observed, has, at least initially, an ambiguous quality. It is suspended in the act of coming together into a whole, of coming into presence, and, at times, one can be left hanging in the attitude of reaching for the whole object that never becomes distanced into a neat concept and never enters full denotative presence.

As an experiment, pick a work of art you know well—a large sculpture, a building, a novel or musical composition—and consider whether it forms a complete harmonious whole. Pause right now to do this. Then, observe how this was accomplished. To be receptive to a possible overall meaning, what are you doing? Do you begin with a frown and set out to connect units and link them into a whole, thus falling into fovea mode? Or do you get a feeling of pulling back, of letting go, in order to access the overall impression, thus using periphery sensing? It is possible to observe how an immediate appreciation of the overall work is achieved through a letting-go mode, through the relaxed, undirected attention that is periphery perceiving. This pulling back allows what lies beyond consciousness to enter consciousness. It allows us to gain the intuition of a meaningful whole.

An aside worth bringing in here is the sad fact that this dimension is so often overlooked in schools. Students under pressure and in fear have little opportunity to realize that *letting go yet staying with it*, which is a particular kind of not-doing, is an integral part of learning. So much is lost and damaged when our intelligence is confined to analytical fovea functions, which handicap the development of the sense of beauty and the ability to connect personally and passionately with what is learned.

The fact of letting go in order to perceive large complex units seems fairly obvious. It is less evident, perhaps, that the same gesture is necessary to receive even the smallest unit of meaning. Large or small, complex or simple, all objects come through periphery sensitivity into fovea attention. With the suspension of fovea attention and as conscious activity subsides, an object forms. Like in fairy tales, all of a sudden—*puff!*—it is there. Thereafter, busy fovea activity returns to analyze or to admire the new arrival to bits while the former hiatus goes unnoticed.

The ability to span an indefinite range in forming a whole is given to us through periphery perception. The larger the unit of meaning to be grasped, the more pronounced is the periphery function that is present. Whether to grasp the architectural plan of a cathedral or simply the artist's brush stroke, we call into play this sense of a whole. Here the description includes works of art as wholes, but the same movement of understanding must be true for all that is communicated, for understanding one another, and for sensing the zillion forms of being that surround us. In periphery sensitivity, we remain receptive and open to ambient impressions; in fovea attention, we set on a path of action and, with focused attention, single out one item after another. Reception and action complement each other, forming the duo that brings us into contact with all we know. Reception of a unit of meaning is an experience; it is a kind of momentary jolt, a surprise that comes as a tiny burst of joy accompanied by the sense of being alive. A jubilant sense of fulfillment accompanies every realization of a whole, whether it comes as a barely heeded spur or as a grand sensation that wells up inside and envelops our being. Each time, even though we are far too busy to notice, it opens a fresh revelation of existence.

Unit Size Is Variable

These observations on perceiving unit structures suggest that a temporal unit can encompass very large amounts of information. A single moment in time is sufficient for a vast compendium of knowledge to coalesce into what can be grasped as a unitary meaning. The syntax of that moment may be built over a period of time of any length, yet, as when words fuse to form the sense of a phrase, a single statement is all that registers upon the beholder. The linguistic form required to create a moment of perception is what underlies the grammatical structure of a sentence, allowing it to become the carrier of a unit of meaning. It is intriguing to think that in earlier times cultures may have been able to communicate in far larger temporal units than we do today. Dance sequences, chants, and conversations may have been great, extended structures that entered consciousness as powerful wholes—perhaps not unlike the conversing of the tree Ents, a race of beings in Tolkien's epic. Examples are available from divers sources, both ancient and present, of the human capacity to retain lengthy poems, tunes, epics, visual arrays and, too, of the ability to remain engaged over a long period of time while what is being communicated unfolds as a whole unit.

It would be exciting to pursue this topic and consider the abilities of various animals and what each may be able to encompass as a meaningful sound unit or gesture, for surely some communicate in units that are far greater than what we envisage. Could it be that we humans live in a culture and at a time of nervous energy and fovea concentration that make communicating in larger wholes difficult?

These thoughts spring from the fact that *now* is expandable and so is *here*. A temporal moment of consciousness may, in measured time, be long or short in the same way that a spatial unit of consciousness (a visual object) may measure any size. Unity is not quantifiable in space and time, and the collapse of measured space and time into a meaningful singularity—a thing—is an experience that can stretch over any temporal or spatial extension. These reflections add substance to the view that it is not by searching into the smallest moment of time and the smallest unit of space that we come closer to understanding the nature of an object and the source of the meaning it holds.

A Narcissistic Effect

When depicting space according to the Western tradition, the complement of the observer is the vanishing point of a simple three-dimensional view. This is just one example among many of how to structure our visual experience. A more general case would be to consider the center of the visual field, meaning the part directly in front of where the eyes are pointed, as the complement to the position of the observer. The viewing position of the observer gives rise to the field that sets the specific location of an object—to the left, the right, above, close, far, and so forth. In this, observer and observed are coupled. Sensing the visual presence of an object (seen or imagined) brings consciousness, but more than this, the object determines the presence of self. The presence of an object in the visual fovea has the effect of reflecting the presence of the perceiver. That which occupies our attention in the center of the visual field is, in fact, the mirror of self—not one's physical features, of course, but one's presence. It complements and anchors the *here* of the observer, linking presence with position that, when coupled together, function as the origin and source of spatial positioning.

Now, the same tale can be retold in terms of auditory perception. The sound upon which one focuses and to which one gives objective presence is itself the complement of the position of the observing subject—not position in space but in time. The presence of self is anchored by what is heard. Sounds become sequenced through reference to the time coordinate generated by the observer, and what is heard as an auditory object occupies the position that corresponds to the *now* of the observer. From the now, temporality opens to what was and what will be, to the previous and the subsequent.

Perception is more fluid than we have dared imagine. What we consider as now is held in an entourage of *less now* that spreads out without any boundary. It is a mistake to consider hearing as made of a sequence of passing temporal moments, and it is a mistake to attribute vision to the detection of isolated objects separated by space. It must be clear by now that this mistake stems from a limited, one-sided view of perception that manages to ignore entirely what expanded consciousness knows. When the rational conscious mind is working alone, it isolates objects on a space-time grid and extracts them from the communion that exists among all that is. In a wider view, past, future, and the multipositions of undefined space impinge on our senses to produce an act of perception.

Accepting nothing more than what enters the here and now as real promotes a view of self as an independent entity, and this is how fovea vision and centered hearing reflect and sustain the sense of self. The other half of the mind—expanded consciousness—offers an alternative to this sense of self, something very different that does away with the purported island self and brings a new identity no longer divisible into here and now, into me versus others. It presents an identity that is plural, not singular: we, and not me.

To recognize only isolated objects sequestered from the greater mind, one is left with a physical world that traces its spatial origin to a dimensionless point of Euclid's geometry and its temporal origin to a dimensionless present that is nothing more than a fissure between past and future. The fact that, physically, this makes no sense at all was concealed by the supposition that the momentary present is infinitesimally small—as if infinity were still connected to measurement and to the physical universe. In mathematics, with the calculus, this flaw in reasoning entered respectability, and what was merely a mathematical tool was interpreted as measurement of what is real. It served to perpetuate the restricted classical view of physical reality that ignores the implications of extended mind in the elaboration of reality. It was a technique to circumvent the fact that no unit exists on its own and that the fovea-pierced object is couched in a periphery that lacks objective time and objective space and extends into the nonphysical. To the rational mind, this is anathema; it cannot cope with multiple simultaneous, superimposed impressions. Hopefully, this presentation, by tracing out the transition that periphery entails, offers a way of understanding that serves to allay somewhat the rational mind's fears of the unknown and coax it to release its restrictive hold on our intelligence so a more encompassing viewpoint can emerge.

Narcissus

> Becoming absorbed in the central object that anchors the here and now and mirrors one's presence is to come under the spell of the dimensionless point. Its hold upon us comes from the very same power that can release us from it: the realization that nothing is there! If we grasp that center with the conviction that it is all there is, we become entangled in the fear of letting go and of losing what we believe most precious—our individual self; but if we laugh at the nimble trickery whereby nothing becomes everything, we allow the world to enter us, and, expanding beyond what we believed to be our individual self, our former identity dissolves in connectivity.
>
> Could it be that the myth of Narcissus speaks of attachment to the visual reflection that anchors both self and reality and of the fixation that left Narcissus disconnected from all else and irresponsive to the entreaties of others—of Echo in particular? (Incidentally, as an echo, she offers the auditory temporal counterpart of visual spatial reflection.) To let go of the visual and auditory center that is the reflection of self is to lose all that one is at that moment; to hold on to it is to attempt to create permanence where there is none and thus to die to the movement that is life. The path out of this dilemma is to embrace periphery sensitivity and allow it to show the way towards another kind of understanding. Even though the conscious self does not exist outside conscious acts of perception, all that is does not vanish in its absence but becomes ever so much more than self on its own can imagine.

Fovea and Periphery in Balance

The dual nature of the activity of mind has been presented in three guises: as modes of thinking (denotative and connotative), as types of movement (centripetal and centrifugal), and as complementary domains in the field of perception (fovea and periphery). No one of these three descriptions is definitive; each offers limited insights about how the mind accesses meaning, and together they lead the discussion towards chapter 5, which considers the guidance system that creates such tendencies. In our culture, we give a strong bias to one half of the mind's activity while we ignore and even disparage the other half—something that is often referred to as the dominance of the masculine in Western culture. This, however, should not be attributed to the way our sense organs function. It is true, for example, that the structure of the human eye allows for fovea concentration, but this does not entrap our attitude and subjugate it to the search for ever smaller units to produce objective reality. There is fovea perception and there is periphery perception. The second balances the first. Our potential to know is balanced between these two tendencies, and therefore it must surely be misguided attitudes alone that are the reason for the lengthy historical period of distortion. It is time now to let go of this imbalance and open to a very different way of understanding. This little book, hopefully, is a nudge in the direction of reestablishing a more natural balance.

The Present and How It Happens

The temporal present was already considered at the conclusion of the first chapter. Here, some supplementary remarks that take into account what has been said in this chapter are added.

Because it is an experience of unity, the present has no measure. It is the coming together of a whole. From outside one can measure that moment and tell a person who experiences the whole: "You disappeared into the present and were oblivious of passing time for so many microseconds, minutes, or hours." The experience lived in that personal time bubble was of a yet-to-be-perceived whole in formation, and such an experience is not conceived with the conscious mind. *Time bubble* is an external, rational way of speaking of what, internally, is not conceived as time but as the experience of duration. The word *duration*, however, is a concept and with it the experience of duration has been reduced to something without extension, and this inevitably leads to paradox. Because it is the quality of an inner process, duration evaporates immediately upon being extracted from subjective experience. Consciousness uproots living experience, turning it into dimensionless concepts that are conclusions deduced from what was ongoing, and this is the reason that, for consciousness, the present is without extension. To accept that time has been sharpened down to nothing is to miss the sleight-of-hand trick by which it is done, for only to the fovea-attuned mind is there this temporal reduction to zero.

An object is never pure denotation; it depends on periphery, even if what surrounds it is but empty space or silence. It necessarily extends beyond what is perceptible to what is barely perceptible and on into what is imperceptible. An object becomes what we know it to be through the integration of a wider texture of meanings, and this process of coming together is very likely the source of the sense of duration.

How the momentary presence of some particular thing arises out of multiple features that extend into periphery and beyond requires a more technical discussion. A complement of information on this fundamental process of perception is included in chapter 3, where the process that produces color vision is presented. Here, for the curious reader, an all-too-concise version is offered in the following paragraph, but remember, please, a fuller rendition can be found later in the next chapter. One needs to keep in mind that the challenge being met is to elucidate the transfer across the barrier between what is unintelligible and what becomes perceptible, that is, across a kind of blood-brain barrier that constitutes the divide between the expanded mind and fovea-restricted consciousness. Though it seems impassable, nonetheless, as in many a tale of adventure, there is a secret to reveal concerning a hidden crossing where the transfer between the unknown and the known is enacted.

Whatever is visible is set within a field of vision that gives rise to the experience of seeing; whatever is heard is part of a similar temporal field, a field of hearing. Visibility has to do with a relation between the qualities of what is seen. For sight, this happens when the various luminosities impinging on the eye from the field of vision are integrated over some common denominator. They are related through a common scale of measurement. Audition has the same requirement: certain sound effects (volume, pitch) enter a relationship through a common scale. The moment in which this correlation (i.e., a scale) is introduced by the observer is the precise moment when the potential for sight and the potential for hearing are released and, for the observer, the world lights up and sounds out. With this understanding, it is possible to return to the initial question. The seemingly timeless moment that we know as perception is the passing shock wave of integration when all clicks together and, in a flash, relationship across the field is realized through the introduction of a common scale.

Of course, with this act of integration, an ever present enigma surfaces: Who or what holds the key to reality? Is it the observed or the observer? Getting closer to understanding the implications of this question, rather than answering it, is the principal interest of this work.

Conclusions

Vision and audition engage the dual processes of mind activity detailed in the description of concept formation. They are specific cases of the general fact that perception has its source in the nonconscious expanded mind. Objects seen and heard take form through the mind's access to what remains imperceptible.

Between the perceived object and all that is imperceptible are transitional states of consciousness known as periphery. They form an intermediary zone of graduated partial consciousness lying between full consciousness of centered perception (referred to here as fovea perception) and the expanded mind that is out of reach of consciousness. Specifically, the visual periphery pertains to spatial displacement away from the center of the field of vision, whereas the auditory periphery pertains to the temporal range that extends before and after what is heard at any one moment. The visual periphery, being spatial, relates to here and less here; the auditory periphery, being temporal, relates to now and less now. Both reflect diminishing degrees of presence, as the object recedes into periphery.

It is possible to trace the transformations that take place across the periphery. The more distant an object is from center fovea attention, the more it loses its particular qualities, its specificity. In the outer periphery, it becomes spatially and temporally less distinct and less clearly present. This implies a reduced objectivity where things are less real, leaving the observer with a reduced level of consciousness. *Less real* is a genuine experience, a state of being, and is not faltering perception. In this manner, periphery states bridge the gap between presence and absence, between objectivity and loss of an object, between distinct in the here and now and diffused or unidentifiable, between formed and formless, and between real and potential.

The capacity to perceive what lies away from fovea diminishes progressively, and it is likely that the reduced visibility or audibility results from the restrictions of conscious thought, which is unable to reduce the information to a linear sequence of items. The gradual loss of perception in periphery would then be the outcome not of an absence of influx of information but of a profusion of simultaneous changing effects that are not compatible with conceptual consciousness. There is no doubt that, via processes of which consciousness is oblivious, an uncountable wealth of information is assembled in order to establish any unit of meaning—an object—that arises in consciousness.

The merging of qualities that takes place towards the limits of periphery perception is apparent also in the blending of visual and auditory into feelings that are no longer distinguishable as being visual or auditory. The passage from fovea definition to periphery ambiguity is the transition from comprehension to sensation. This fact supports the suggestion that the influx of all that comes to consciousness from the expanded mind is multiple and interpenetrating. Feelings, as described in the previous chapter, are an inroad to these multiple states that otherwise are beyond the sensory range available to consciousness.

As the multiple strands of impressions from the expanded mind come together to form a perceived object, there is an experience of involvement and connection with what is being formed. This process is experienced as duration without any sense of measure on the part of the perceiving subject. However, measured from the outside, the time it takes for incoming impressions to form what is seen or heard or sensed may be of any length. The fact that different cultures create very large structures, both in physical size and in time duration, points to the fact that, on some level of the nonconscious mind, there is an awareness of the extended whole that can be grasped as a single unit.

An object coming to our attention is a moment of consciousness superposed on other perceptions-to-be that are yet in the process of forming beyond the threshold of consciousness. This suggests that while a specific perception arises and becomes that which is perceived, many levels of perception yet in formation are in progress without there being any apparent interference with one another.

[3]

Sight and Color Vision

TO REACH AN UNDERSTANDING of how a visual image is formed, one needs to consider the passage from the invisible to the visible—an epistemology of sight that includes an uncommon blend of physics, biology, and philosophy. These correlate with the three components of sight: light, the eye together with the nervous system, and consciousness.

The description of the process of perception given here is the reverse of how it is generally thought to be. Instead of assuming the presence of a structured external world that is the cause of our sensory impressions, the starting point is the way we make sense of incoherent sensory impressions by creating temporal sequence, second-dimension projection, and the third dimension—paradigms that structure our experience into the form that becomes the world we know.

The conclusion that will be reached is that sight and color vision can be understood as particular states of understanding. Each state arises out of the same fundamental motive: preservation of the unity of the conscious subject in the face of noncomprehension and the threat of fragmentation. The most obvious example of a conflict that proves to be an impasse and yet is subsequently resolved into a new awareness is the case of three-dimensional vision. This will be described before color vision, but first, a more general view of the role of contradiction in perception is presented.

The Function of Contradiction in Perception

It is evident that the subject making an observation is always single consciousness. Perceiving is always accomplished by some*one*. This is a fundamental requirement of perception. The subject who is conscious of something is always a single person, even though what is perceived can be multiple. When conscious of an object, I am an observing subject, one and not many. For this reason, if a situation arises that threatens this unity of the subject, it becomes imperative to resolve the possible split and ensure a single unified experience; otherwise, that moment of consciousness cannot be sustained and no act of perception will result. For this reason, the resolution of contradictory renditions of what is perceived have a major function in perception.

Perceiving is always accomplished by some-one. This is a fundamental requirement of perception.

Before entering the subject of color phenomena, a quick sketch is made of three distinct contradictions that arise in acts of perception and whose resolution is achieved through the creation of the three fundamental paradigms just mentioned, namely, one-dimensionality as sequence in time, two-dimensionality as a projected surface, and three-dimensionality as the sense of space. After the role of contradiction in producing these three experiences is noted, color vision is presented as functioning in a manner parallel to three-dimensional depth vision.

One-Dimensionality

Although multiple qualities can intermingle to form a particular experience, it is not possible to be the subject of two incompatible states of being. For instance, one cannot experience both nighttime and daytime together. No matter how complex an experience may be, we are ever one experiencing subject. The experiences of separate states of being, if taken together, would fracture the unity of the experiencing subject. To resolve the conflict of being (of having) more than one experience, the temporal dimension arises. With the creation of sequence in time, different experiences separate out into experiences taking place one after another and, as such, become my subjective experience at different times.

The Second Dimension

A second state of contradiction can be understood as being borderline between a general sensation and visual experience. It has to do with the formation of the second dimension and, together with it, the ability to recognize what we see as something other than *me*. Here is an example that may be helpful when trying to understand the irresolvable contradiction of sight without the second dimension as well as how resolution comes with perception of two dimensionality.

Imagine being surrounded by uniform illumination. It can happen when, from close up, you look into a hemisphere of uniform light or when you are in a thick mist. Looking into uniform illumination over a prolonged period is experienced more as a general sensation than as a visual experience, and you become identified with that experience. However, as soon as the uniformity of the visual field is broken and distinctions arise (such as objects appearing in the field of view), the fusion of the visual impression with your state of being is fractured, and, as the perceiving subject, you are confronted with the impossibility of simultaneously experiencing different visually generated effects, such as sensing the experience of a darker state and a lighter state. To resolve the contesting experiences into a single experience, that is, into what can be experienced by a single subject, the second dimension is formed. With its appearance, the contradictory experiences are ejected from the subject and juxtaposed on an imaginary surface. There, they are perceived as multiple simultaneous presences and as such do not fracture the unity of the first-person experience. The former state of experiencing sight within yourself as a state of being is replaced by the experience of *looking at* and sensing *otherness*.

What actually happens in this act is that the time dimension, described in the previous section as the temporal sequencing of experiences, is reduced to zero. With the advent of the second dimension and the production of continuous planar extension, all that forms the visual field is simultaneously present.

In the next section, on three-dimensional vision, a more detailed account of the subjective process that engenders dimensionality is presented.

Three-Dimensionality and the Visual Experience of Space

The experience of three-dimensional space is rendered visually through binocular vision. Two views formed from slightly different points in space contain contradictions. Elements in the field seen through one eye have positions that are different relative to all that is seen through the other eye. Consciousness cannot cope with more than one view at a time, and faced with such conflicting views, no coherent object of perception can be formed.

Commonly, this parallax displacement is explained by reference to a computational model that shows how, mathematically, it is possible to deduce, from the two separate views, the depth-of-field distances to objects. In actual fact, this clarifies nothing about the visual experience and even misleads, for crucial factors that are not part of the algorithm (e.g., the experience of contradiction and the insistence to overcome it) are simply passed over.

To emphasize the fact that contradiction is an impasse, take the case of strabismus, a condition in which the position or movements of a person's eyes are uncoordinated and result in the eyes looking in different directions. When this happens, the view through the two eyes does not match, and instinctively, vision through one eye goes blank, resulting in amblyopia. Even though the weaker eye is fully functional, the information it collects is deleted so that the view formed through the stronger eye can be taken as fact. By dismissing the contesting view and avoiding the contradiction, the organism functions to sustain consciousness of what makes sense.

Returning to binocular vision, a comparable situation of contradiction arises when the two versions of what is seen cannot be superposed. A nearby tree seen against background mountains, for example, would appear more to the left in the view through the right eye as compared with the left-eye view. Together the views create confusion and either the pursuit of a unified view has to be abandoned or some new way of seeing has to be found. The presence of contradiction gives rise to the need for a novel solution that goes beyond the manner of seeing employed for one eye alone, but this will only happen to the extent that an observer is driven by *the intent to make sense*. Sight is not a simple matter of responding to sensory input; more than that is required. Facing the conundrum that arises when conflicting views are present, one must have the tenacity to reach beyond the contradiction to a solution. The conflicting views are sustained by the quest for understanding, and, through it, one pushes against the limits of what is intelligible. Without the intent to achieve meaning, there would be no resolution and the experience of three-dimensionality could not happen.

During the experience of vision, it is possible to observe the actual process of conflict resolution. For this, one should bring one's attention to presences in the field of vision that normally go unnoticed. When looking at a scene, we can note in the field of vision ghost images of objects that are not in focus and that have no precisely determined position. For example, looking out the window at a distant scene and holding my focus there, I notice two versions of the fly walking on the windowpane. The duplication results from the separate views produced by each eye. These secondary presences sustain the three-dimensional experience even though we do not pay attention to them or, rather, because we do not attend to them. They have what has been referred to in the previous chapter as a lower level of presence. In facing contradictory views with the intention to perceive, one generates readjustment by which degrees of presence are reformulated. Some of what is seen becomes present in a lesser, blurry way, and the full palette of different intensities of presence results in the experience of depth.

The complexity of the task becomes apparent with the realization that it is not a matter of finding the correspondence between specific points on the two separate images. The view of each eye is an overall self-defined structure of relationships, and only after it has become visible can it be reconsidered and thought of as the juxtaposition of elements that can be picked out sequentially. Initially, an image forms when all that is present becomes mutually defined, and this must be the case for the view formed separately by each eye. Two independent structures of organization confront each other. This can be compared to having two different map projections of a globe, say, one cylindrical and the other conical. The task of unifying them is prodigious. To integrate one coherent system with another requires a fundamental restructuring of the interrelationships that give rise to each view. This is the reason that the commonly employed geometric algorithm is reductive and misleading.

Actually, using geometry to interpret relationships in space is only possible because we are already familiar with what we call space. Measurement does not create the concept of space. This point is more obvious in the case of color vision. A description of how color effects can be calculated on the basis of retinal sensitivities makes sense only if one already has the experience of colors. The experience we have of depth and of any phenomenon is independent and precedes whatever explication offered. What is described here concerns the experience and not the idea of three-dimensional space. To resolve the discrepancies between different views does not require a sequential operation but the simultaneous reevaluation of a vast number of discordant values. Clearly, this function is not performed by the rational conscious mind and is achieved through the nonlinear activity of the expanded mind.

Having noted how an impasse can generate depth vision, it is possible to proceed to color vision and understand that it is generated through the resolution of a comparable impasse.

Color Vision

Physics teaches that sight has to do with the response of the visual system to the presence of light of different frequencies. The correspondence between light frequencies and the color one observes is not a simple matter, and even though computational models predict which colors will appear in a given context, describing the process by which this happens is not without problems. The biology of sight has to do with the structure of the eye and the related neurology. The aspect that will be considered here is the action of the retinal cone cells. Three different types of cone cells are interspersed in the fovea of the retina. These three sets differ from one another in their ability to absorb various frequencies of light, that is, they have different sensitivity curves. This immediately suggests a comparison with the incompatible views that occur in three-dimensional vision: if luminosity readings made through different sets of cells differ, they must produce different renditions of the same scene, and these separate views will contradict one another, creating a perceptual impasse for the observer. The next paragraph gives a more detailed description of what is involved.

The mismatch between different levels of illumination is less obvious than the spatial mismatch of binocular vision in which one eye, on its own, already produces incompatible views. Each set of retinal cone cells produces a scene in which the brightness of what is observed differs from that produced by another set. Here is a simple way to think about it. Imagine looking at a checkerboard pattern made of squares of different colors. One set of sensor cells would detect certain intensities of light coming from the different squares, and because luminosity and not color is detected, this would be seen as a checkerboard pattern of various shades of gray. The view formed by a second set of sensor cells with a different range of sensitivities will not match the view transmitted by the first set. In this second image, employing other cone cells, some squares will appear brighter in comparison with the first image and others darker. Contradictory views of what is present are formed.

Actually, the matter is more complex. Not only do individual squares appear to have different luminosities but the whole range of mutually determined light and dark that generates each of the two fields of view would be different. To understand this, consider a surface we judge to be white. Although appearing white in one context, it can appear gray in another, depending on the brightness of other surfaces around it. One component determining the brightness of what we see is the intensity of the light source that is present, yet, apart from this, apparent brightness is determined by the luminosities of surrounding surfaces. In any visual experience, the luminosities of what is seen across the whole field of view become integrated, and this generates the relative brightness of everything that is seen. This binding of all into a single relationship is, in fact, the act that produces vision— but of that later. Pertinent at this point is the fact that when a scene registers on a set of cells attuned to certain frequencies of light, the scale of relative luminosities will be independent of the scale of luminosities established by a second set of cells attuned to other frequencies. The view produced by each set will be at odds with the other views. This is the same incongruence mentioned previously, in reference to integrating the information from different map projections. To offer a second analogy, imagine the task of working with a collection of numbers that have different bases, some with base 10 and others base 16, and performing mathematical operations (addition, multiplication, etc.) with them. The task requires converting numerical values. In the case of different sets of cone cells, there will be intricate variation in the images seen through each set, and the call to resolve the conflicting information is no small demand. It requires not simply the resolution of the conflicting luminosity values of individual squares but the readjustment of the units that form the basis for determining those luminosity values.

Returning to the central issue, it is clear that sets of different cones produce conflicting views that prevent the formation of a coherent single image of what is seen. With this, the integrality of the perceiving subject is threatened because the experience of seeing has been fractured into separate, unrelated experiences. It seems that no surface or object can be perceived unless, taking the easy way out, one retains just one of the views and deletes the others. But is another solution possible? What if the intent to form a coherent intelligible view is intense, and one stays with what is impossible, confronting the contradictory views, what then might be the result? What can bridge the gap between the incompatible views? It would require viewing an object as both brighter and darker at the same moment. How can a whole structure of relationships of luminosity be brought to accommodate a complete but different structure? For this, bright and dark must become what neither one is alone and form a new qualitative dimension of vision. This is achieved when vision takes on the new range of properties we know as color. Colors enable visual experience to function in situations where otherwise it would fail. How this is achieved is suggested in what follows.

One needs to realize that a color, blue, for instance, is not a visual quality that one recognizes through the blue-sensing ability of our visual system but is generated in answer to a particular visual conundrum, that of seeing something appear both dark and bright at the same time. What kind of illumination is there that will appear diminished when registering on cone cells more sensitive to lower frequencies (red light) and will appear augmented when registering on cone cells attuned to higher (yellow light) frequencies? This double appearance is what we know as the color blue, for a blue surface appears darker in red light than it does in yellow light. And so it is for the other colors. Because of the different sets of cone cells of the retina, many luminosity levels register together, and the special function of color is to sustain the contradiction and make sense out of it.

At first it may seem surprising that this transformation is going on and we remain oblivious to it, but actually, numerous examples of not being conscious of processes that lead to consciousness are included in this work. To understand the principle involved, it is helpful to reconsider how sound resolves temporal differences into a single perceptible quality. Being unconscious of the contrasting sequence of sound/silence beats that register in our ears when we hear a note is similar to being unconscious of the contrast between the structures of brightness produced by the different sets of cones. The physical event passes unnoticed, but what we perceive is the sound of a note and the appearance of a color. Our ability to plumb depths beyond consciousness is marvelous, and drawing from the unknown, we give expression to the imperceptible by creating qualities that register in consciousness—potentially beautiful qualities like notes and colors.

Spatial Conflict Resolved as Depth; Temporal Conflict Resolved as Color

Just as depth vision is a fuzzy response to conflicting spatial views and makes use of in-focus and out-of-focus elements and of different degrees of presence, so color vision is a fuzzy response that introduces a new range of qualities, that of color, with which to bridge the gap between separate manifestations of brightness. Just as depth vision offers a far more varied set of possible spatial relationships within all that fills the visual field, so color vision offers a rich panoply of relationships that go far beyond what exists in tones of gray. With this new possibility, a given tone of gray can be differentiated further through color. For example, the luminosity (or brightness) of surfaces that are green, blue, and red can be equivalent, and yet, through the effect of color, they are distinguishable.

A further distinction can be made between the fuzzy response in depth vision and the fuzzy response in color vision. A way of understanding the process by which colors are produced suggests itself from what has been said to this point. It seems that, in contrast to depth vision in which resolution is achieved through superposition of conflicting images, color vision is achieved through a subliminal oscillation between the incompatible displays of brightness. Instead of the contradictory views being concurrent, there is an imperceptible resonant, back-and-forth flicker between the different views, and this resonant effect produces color. This thought has various supporting evidence. It is known that color can result from a rapid oscillation between black and white. Today we find toy disks and tops marked with certain patterns of black and white that reveal colors when spun. When first setting out these ideas on color in 1986, this author ran experiments that produced color effects by projecting rapidly alternating, dissimilar checkerboard images of grays on a screen. The black-and-white slides were prepared from colored images photographed through various color filters onto black-and-white film.

It is important to add that the flicker effect does not need to be produced physically and can arise in the mind alone, as must happen when we hear a tune playing in our mind. Without sensory stimulation through the physical ear, the mind can generate the quality of a note that is equivalent to a note produced by physical vibrations activating the ear. Another example of this ability of the mind to produce a vibratory effect is a drawing in which a face has not just one pair of eyes, as is normal, but three pairs of eyes, one above the other. When looking at the drawing, the pairs of eyes appear to pop back and forth, and the image is not still. It is as if the mind is searching for a way out of the contradiction between what appears on the drawing and what is known and expected.

These examples suggest that the phenomenon of color vision can be described as temporal displacement creating the unitary effect that we know as color. It may well be that the different views generated through different sets of cone cells yield no final resolution, in neither a spatial nor a temporal dimension, and the conflict of opposing luminosities remains alive and vibrant. It is exactly this, the constant interplay of incongruent luminosity scales, that we register as color.

The Quality of Depth and the Quality of Color

A complete description of how color arises through the confrontation of systems of light and dark needs to include an account of all color phenomena, something that goes beyond present considerations. However, if it is correct to assume that color is a temporal bridge between contradictory views, depth vision and color vision can be seen as parallel phenomena. Both arise from the intention to resolve discrepancies that have their source in incompatible two-dimensional images of a particular scene. To resolve discrepancy in the form of what is displayed (i.e., in the position of objects), a point of view is created, and through it, the perceiver acquires a position in space and thus enters into a relationship with what is observed. Perceiver and perceived become related through a shared continuum, that of space, and the experience that this integration yields is found in the sense of depth. The feeling of being in a relationship with and sensing oneself as part of what one observes can be quite pronounced in some situations. Here is one example. If one spends a little time quietly viewing a pastoral scene though just one eye, taking note not only of how it looks but of what one feels seeing it, and then, staying with that feeling, one opens both eyes, there comes a distinct change in sensation that typically has something of the quality of becoming part of what one is looking at. This is an aspect of the experience of depth.

Returning to the subject of color, it is fascinating to find, here too, the same feature, namely, that of the integration of the subject with what is seen. Resolving discrepancies in color vision creates a relationship between the perceiver and what is perceived but instead of a connection through a spatial or a temporal dimension, the bond comes through feeling and links to our emotions. For instance, a blue that has a placid quality creates a different feeling than does a red that has an excited quality, and different tones of any color produce effects that reach deep into our psyche and emotional life. Shades of gray have no such extended repertoire. Through color, we enter a feeling relationship with what we see. This leads directly to a discussion of the psychology of color, but that is not the path taken in this discussion. The subject of color vision has been included here as an example of the process of perception.

Through color, we enter a feeling relationship with what we see.

If color vision is generated by a flicker effect or oscillation between incompatible scales of luminosity, we might sense it as a vibration or a rarefied tremor that reaches us principally through the eyes and is felt in the body. Different tremors have different names: yellow, green, blue, and so forth. If to move to a wider view of what has been told, there is, on one hand, the concept of space with the concomitant experience of depth, and on the other hand, there is the concept of color and the experience of color sensations. In both depth vision and color vision, the experience we have of being a single subject is challenged, and in both cases, the resolution achieved brings a greater degree of integration, not just between the observer and the observed, but also between concepts and feelings, that is, between what is understood and what is felt.

Ascent through Different Dimensions

To recapitulate the overall process:

When, at a primary stage, multiple experiences threaten the unity of the experiencing subject, resolution is achieved by separating the experiences from one another along a time line. At another stage, the unity of the subject's experience can be threatened when differentiation enters by way of multiple visual impressions. The solution that emerges is the creation of the second dimension whereby multiplicity is separated out from self onto a projected surface. At a further stage, the integral subject once again faces dissolution when conflicting views are encountered in binocular vision. This contention is resolved with the experience of depth vision and space. Yet again, at another stage in the visual process, the integrality of the perceiver is threatened when contradictory luminosity relationships vie to gain consciousness, and this requires a whole new form of resolution that comes with the paradigm of color vision.

It Is Subjective, but I Didn't Do It!

Like every concept that forms in the mind, color requires intention. Physics and biology on their own cannot explain the production of color because, for color to emerge, there must be confrontation and this requires the intent to produce a visually intelligible result. Without intent, contradictions will not meet in contradiction and solutions will have no function to fulfill. Like everything that becomes known, color arises from the subjective act of meeting an existential challenge with the determination (intent) that resolves it into a new understanding. Making sense is ever a personal act, and yet, the sense one makes is as objective as anything else that exists. All that issues from my ability to make sense escapes subjectivity and takes on reality, for it draws on possibilities of which I am not the author. Simply put: I did not create the color I see. I only reached out to make sense of the impressions reaching me, and what came out was the color blue. Blue is the response to a specific set of conditions confronting a subject who is determined to make sense out of them. Given this interpretation of how color is formed, there is reason to believe that beings with a common biological structure and with a similar cultural heritage faced with the same visual conundrum will see the same colors. We are not isolated in our view of color, and this is so even though the production of color is a creative act accomplished by each person.

Does this answer the puzzle of whether colors are subjective or objective? The fact *that* color arises is subjective, but *what* arises is not subjective. For example, it is well known *that* the rainbow I see is mine alone and the person beside me cannot see the same rainbow I am looking at, and yet, the fact that *what* I see is the familiar rainbow-colored arc does not depend on me. This, one could say, is objectively determined by the conditions present at that moment. A rainbow can be understood as a marriage—the celebration of the union of what is subjective with what is objective. In the same way, every time we see color, we cast our eyes on this celebration, on the coupling of subjective *me* with what seems objective and independent of me.

The Surprising Fact of What Constitutes Sight

A curious fact is reflected in this description of the visual process. For an object to enter our visual world, its presence in our field of view and the presence of a source of illumination are insufficient. In fact, no such direct route to consciousness exists. Access to sight is supplied by something different. As has been shown earlier, in cases of concept formation and of sensory perception, everything observed enters consciousness through an act of integration that takes place when a common scale is found. (See the section in chapter 2, "Perceiving the Imperceptible.") Nothing is perceptible without the code that enables the interrelationship of qualities. To make this obvious with a further example, consider what is needed to see a pattern of black and white stripes. For a black stripe to appear, the white stripes on either side are required to set its boundary, but these white stripes are defined by the black stripes bordering them, and so it continues out to the edge of the pattern and on out to the fading horizon of the visual field that closes upon itself (see in chapter 2, "Limits and Boundaries"). Suddenly everything *clicks together* in a mutually determined set of relationships. The event could be described as a shock wave of integration that passes through everything that enters that moment of sight, and this wave of interdefinition brings on vision. In terms of what was said earlier, it happens in the presence of the code that allows all phenomena to enter the same scale of values. In fact, it would not be incorrect to say the moment of seeing *is* this wave of interrelationship reaching through everything.

This fact reinforces what was said earlier about the visual experience being momentary. It is necessarily an instant—the instant in which everything gels in a unified relationship. It is not worked out sequentially through thinking but arrives all at once in an undeclared intuition as a wave of integration that brings mutual definition to every form and every quality that becomes visible. At that moment, what is seen comes to light and the perceiver takes possession of what is perceived. In essence, though at first it may be hard to believe, what we actually perceive are the ratios that integrate all that becomes visible. When we create a common scale that integrates all that carries a particular quality, that feature becomes visible. As already described, in the case of luminosity, a common scale is established on which the brightness of what is seen is mutually determined. Similarly, there is a common relationship between angles subtended by the observed objects and between their relative positions in space. In creating a scale of values on which qualities can interrelate, we render them visible. Entering a common accord, they become objects of perception. From ratios, we give presence to all that we know as the world.

This is a reminder of an earlier conclusion (in chapter 2, "To See Without Eyes; to Hear Without Ears"), that although sight engages the eye, and the eye is a marvelous sensory organ that consolidates what is needed for sight to occur, the experience of sight is not a phenomenon that is produced by the eye. Sight is the intuition of meaning that comes to us through an act of integration of sets of relationships that are interpreted spatially.

Fun with Interference Patterns

If to enter further into the integration that forms the visual field, there is a question of background and foreground. Here's a puzzle to illustrate this. Pray tell, are zebras white animals with black stripes or black animals with white stripes? The answer depends on what you connect with as being primary, that is, on how you look at the zebra (zoological considerations aside).

The same is true of drawings that flip between two different contents, as in the common example that presents the option of seeing either a vase or the silhouette of two faces. Anchoring our vision to one view releases other features of the drawing from holding independent meaning, and this enables them to serve as background support for the initial content. Of significance, here, is the fact that the viewer has to commit to a viewpoint and only then can the integration wave propagate throughout.

In the case of the zebra, fixing one's view on a black stripe would allow the white neighboring stripes to become background for it, and from this the overall pattern can manifest. Anchoring what is seen to a specific *here* determines the rest of what is seen just as anchoring a specific *now* allows the temporal dimension to unfurl into past and future. This subjective act determines the point of origin, and it is required for all that manifests as objective.

However, the anchoring subjective act is often vague and, for this reason, not obvious. For example, it is possible that, in looking at zebras, we may have a vague view of stripes without actually anchoring the pattern to white or to black. In this case, it may well be that, unconsciously, we move back and forth between the possibilities rather than remain without a point of view. This thought suggests a wild idea. It was shown that, in certain situations, flickering between black and white produces color, so imagine what fun it would be if we could alternate between what is the chosen background and the foreground with the appropriate regular oscillatory movement and thus see wonderfully colored zebras! Each would be somewhat different because, as is told about fingerprints, no two zebra coats are identical.

But these musings have led off the planned route, so this is where they will stay while the concluding remarks return to the general theme.

Conclusions

What has been described as the wave of integration happens in each area of visual perception: two-dimensional viewing, depth vision, and color vision. In each area, an undisclosed integration base or code enables diverse phenomena to enter into mutual definition. In this, three events are concomitant: (1) the code is established; (2) it is applied to everything in the field of view; (3) the visual scene becomes apparent.

Here is an example of what is meant by the code and the integration. Imagine you are looking at a perspective drawing of a scene, and you choose to add an object to the drawing. Let's say you put a unicorn in somewhere in the drawing. That object instantly relates to everything else in that drawing: it has a position in the scene that relates spatially to all else that is present, and its apparent size, whether large, small, or fitting, is relative to everything else in the drawing. How does this happen? The integration is due to the undisclosed code that brings all together in a certain structured way, and it is the specific perspective viewpoint embedded in that drawing or, more precisely, in your way of perceiving, guided by the relationships present in the drawing. Embedded codes are instrumental in all that becomes visible. A surface area appears as it does to us only when it has been integrated into a two-dimensional mutually defined pattern that extends across the field of view, and while this happens, the ratio linking the brightness of all that fills the field of view is established. Should color be involved, there would be yet another code at work, namely, the transformation of simultaneous contradictory brightness readings into the resonant relationships of color.

All of these are codes that establish the independent presence of what is seen. The perceiver is the influence *that* makes this possible, and yet *what* actually becomes visible is a surprise and a gift from the universe. Sight and color vision, like all perception, are generated through a meeting of what is subjective and performed by the subject and what is not part of the subjective act and appears as objective.

Reintegrating self (*me* and *I*) into all we know as the world is a central theme in this work. In this and the previous chapter it was presented in terms of sight and hearing and it will return in various guises in the course of this study.

[4]
The Word *Mind* and What It Signifies

THE SUBJECT OF THIS CHAPTER is the word *mind* as employed in English. It is a curious fact that in other languages the concept can be surprisingly different, and each culture seems to have its idiosyncratic manner of referring to the ability we refer to as mind.

What do we refer to with the word *mind*? Definitions are not a precondition for understanding; all the same, a definition can prove helpful even if it serves only to distance misunderstanding. Of course, it can do more than this. Reflecting on the word *mind* brings out implicit meanings we rarely mention.

Dictionary definitions generally list the various ways in which a word can be used, thus fracturing it into possible meanings. Another approach, one that is less accepted, is to search for some coherence in the meanings drawn from different contexts in which the word is employed. Where coherency is found, there is the chance of gaining a more fundamental sense of what is implicit in the word. This approach can be justified by arguing that language is the expression of our interaction with all we know as the world; it is the interface between oneself and the beyond. Words and grammar reflect and express this interaction and give it form, and for this reason, language has a depth of its own and is capable of leading to levels of understanding not immediately apparent, levels that go beyond what the rational mind knows. Exceptions to this also can be found. Typically, these relate to elements of language that did not grow out of natural usage but were created synthetically in a piecemeal rational manner. In French, because of the clout of the Académie française, such exceptions are more obvious.

This chapter researches the significance of the word *mind* as commonly employed, and then calls attention to some implications of the conclusions reached.

PART I: *MIND* AS A NOUN

When *mind* is employed as a noun, to what does it refer? Is it an independent object, the attribute of a subject or an action—a thing, a quality, or an activity such as thought? Is it one thing, or is it a collection of many things? How do we recognize it? These questions are not meant to be philosophical. Rather than questioning, "What is the nature of the mind?" they ask, "In each case where this word is employed, what is meant?" This implies a naïve approach to semantics that leaves open the possibility that words structure a particular set of experiences.

Examples of the word *mind* employed as a noun are offered so that the significance they carry can be noted. Then, in the following sections, examples of how the verb *to mind* is employed are considered, and it becomes apparent that the same overall meaning plays into both forms of this word.

A Suggestion to the Reader

You are invited to take each example cited and, in the manner of a wine taster, catch the flavor and balance and swish the words around in your mind to sense the meanings they evoke. Such personal involvement enlivens the subject and opens a way to appreciate the specific nuances of lexical meanings.

Initial Examples

In which expressions does the word *mind* appear as a noun? In principle, it is necessary to consider all such expressions. So as not to become tedious, the aim here is to include just enough examples for the full meaning to emerge while being careful not to ignore usages that can function as counter examples.

To speak of a *sharp mind* or a *sharp-minded* student suggests the student's ability to absorb information that becomes potentially present and is available when called upon. Mind is this capacity and therefore not an observable thing but a possibility; it is the potential that enables an individual to elicit information that is called for. If we complain *my mind went blank*, it signifies that some knowledge that I believe I have was irretrievable at that moment.

To say to someone *use your mind* refers to the ability to think and reflect with understanding. To say the contrary, *you're not using your mind*, signifies that the person is acting without engaging thought or reflection. In these examples, mind is the potential for thought and understanding. To have a *good mind* or a *wonderful mind* is about the power to know, to think, to recall, and to understand. Mind is not just the source of knowing but also of understanding, which includes making connections. *To be mindless* is to be out of touch, perhaps even uncaring. It implies lack of awareness and suggests ignorance or disregard of connections.

To contrast the expression *it is on my mind* with *I'm thinking of it* brings out an important difference. Only at the moment of recall does one consciously think of a specific content; otherwise, *on my mind* means somewhere out of consciousness yet ready to manifest at a propitious moment. Mind is ever imperceptible. When the potential of mind manifests, it is no longer mind but something specific expressed as a thought or through action. The expression *something is on my mind* implies that it is available to consciousness even though I am not thinking of it at the moment in which the remark is made. The possessive pronoun *my* mind (or *your* mind) has to do with the fact that there is a bridge of accessibility between mind and the person who is connected to that mind.

We refer to the mind as if it were some specific thing, yet it does not exist on its own as an independent object and is always related to the individual for whom it functions. Mind is accessible to a personal subject who employs it, and without this, is there mind at all? Mind necessitates an owner, someone who can activate it and reap its produce.

The potential state called mind is nonmanifest and empty of specific content. Its potential comes to expression through what a person does, in thought and in action. This description containing two factors, the implicit presence of mind and what it produces, leaves out a third essential property, for no mention has been made of what brings mind's potential to manifest. The power to elicit an expression from mind has not been accounted for. The influence that penetrates mind potential and directs it towards an outcome is surely a necessary part of any description of the activity of mind. How should we account for the influence that stimulates mind and guides its potential, or some part of it, to manifest in a particular way?

Distinct from the potential that is mind and its manifestation as knowledge and as ability is this third factor: the influence that brings mind potential to materialize in specific thoughts and actions that are performed by the person to whom that mind is accessible. The directionality that permeates mind is what we call intent or intention and will be described in detail in the chapters that follow. Expressions like *I have a good mind to tell on him*, which signifies *I have the intention to...*, allude to this influence over mind. Similarly, to say *she has a mind of her own* implies both that she knows what she wants and that she has the power to hold to her intentions. *To have half a mind to do something* refers to an intention not yet acted on. *To make up your mind* is about choice, about having an intent that sets your mind on a certain course. The expression *mind control* suggests control over what mind activity does, which amounts to control over the controlling factors of mind, over the influences that determine what a person thinks and does.

The conclusion from these examples is that the noun *mind* suggests a potential realm that seems to be the source of our understanding. Mind lies beyond conceptual consciousness. Each person has access to it—to his own mind—but knows it only indirectly as the ability to source the knowledge and meaning available to him. To transform mind potential into something intelligible requires an influence that penetrates mind. This added factor is distinct from mind and is what we know as *intent* and *intention*.

Does the reader's experience concur with this view?

Mind and Knowing

In considering the word *mind*, the words *know*, *knowing*, and *knowledge* were repeatedly used. What does *know* mean? Intuitively, it seems evident, but to describe the activity of knowing is not that obvious.

When a thing is known, it seems to be just as absent as when it is unknown. For instance, I know thousands of words of a language, but they are not present in my thought or imagination. I am no more conscious of them than I am of other words I do not know at all. Where, then, is the difference? That which separates knowing from not knowing is accessibility. The thousands of words I know are immediately accessible to me when needed. Knowing is the potential to deploy knowledge. It is the potential to call information out from a stand-by, ready-for-use state.

The word *mind* refers to a potential state and so does the word *know*, which is used here to help clarify the word *mind*. Both *mind* and *know* refer to potential rather than actual states. It will become apparent, in the following sections, that this is also true of the verbal forms of the word *mind*.

It is not simply that mind is hidden and its nature has not yet been detected with available laboratory equipment. It is not there. It is forever in the potential state and becomes something that is *not* mind when actualized. Through the medium of intention, we call upon the mind, but between the intent and the resulting response no mind activity is perceptible. No one knows what happens until, as if from nowhere, comes a reply. Imperceptible mind fulfills very specific functions. From over the horizon of consciousness, it serves our ability to know and understand and act. We may think we did it all ourselves, claiming: "These are *my* thoughts, *my* insights, the product of *my* mind." But to what extent is this so? Was I there throughout the process?

This little question is, in fact, the subject of this whole study. A *yes* or *no* answer is not important; rather, the object is to understand how what we refer to as *I* both is and is not present at any particular moment.

PART II: *MIND* AS A VERB

What meaning does the verb *to mind* carry in the divers contexts where it is used? Before answering this, an aside may prove helpful. In the divide-and-conquer mentality reigning today that cleaves meanings into component parts, looking for a coherent, singular meaning for the word *mind* may well be deemed naïve. But, as an initial step, when no obvious reason to the contrary is apparent, why not trust human intuition and see what can be learned from what is given? Listening carefully to language often leads to unsuspected depths of meaning.

The verb form *to mind* can be divided into two contrasting sets. In the first are usages that have in common the idea of taking care: *to mind the farm* or *mind yourself*. The second set carries the meaning of objecting to something one dislikes, as in *I mind the noise*. The first expresses concern with the well-being of something or someone and implies some possible danger; the second expresses distaste for something. The first contains a reference to what can be injured or what can injure, and the act of minding is the attitude an aware person adopts. It shows a protective attitude. The second usage of mind refers to one's own negative feelings towards a certain event and shows annoyance. The same word serves contrasting purposes.

The two sets will be considered separately.

Set 1: *To Mind*, Signifying Caring

In the expressions *to mind children* or *mind your step* or *mind the falling rocks*, one is being asked to look out for something with a particular end in view: that of protecting someone, something, or oneself from danger. It refers to being aware, attentive, and alert for eventual trouble. However, the definition does not stop there, for it signals not simply the intention to be on the lookout for whatever may ensue but the intention to act in response to it. *To mind* includes the readiness to act, to ward off or avoid a disturbance.

In *mind the traffic*, what is being asked for is a state of mind that produces a prompt response at a moment of need. Minding is ongoing but not manifest. Minding is present only as intent; it is present as a potential, though of course it may affect how I drive in the traffic. *Minding* refers to a state of being alert to an eventuality with the readiness to react when needed.

Here are further examples. *Mind the ceiling* would most likely be said to warn someone to mind her head. But it is also possible that, moving a tall ladder, you need to take care not to damage the ceiling. In this example, mind can refer to you implicitly or to the ceiling explicitly. Very often what is to be minded is implicit, and the gesture of minding is used without specifying what is to be minded, for instance: *mind the traffic, mind that you take your keys*, and *mind you don't for-*

get to give him the message. Who gets the benefit of the minding in these situations? The assumption is that the beneficiary is there, though who or what it is is not mentioned explicitly.

In the examples of *mind* that express taking care, there is also a subtle hint of an implicit threat. The intimation is that to damage the ceiling, to be inattentive in traffic, and to forget the keys would not be good things. Implicit is the intimation *you'd better or else, watch out or else!* This implication is absent, for example, in *be careful in the traffic* and *remember to take your keys.*

Simply to observe is never the meaning of *to mind*. There are also certain regional uses of the word, such a Scottish usage where *mind* means to notice, pay attention, or remember. *Mind my words* holds something similar. The idea is to be mindfully directing one's attention rather than to observe. Another example of this is *mind the tree*. It does not mean to look at or admire the tree but to watch out for it, for instance, so as to avoid running into it. And when you mind the garden, it is not to *look at* but to *look after*, and is about the responsibility you have towards the garden as its protector.

Here is another example: *minding the dog* is taking care of it. Bringing it out for a run, feeding it, and so forth are generally implied by the infinitive *to mind*. Although the act of minding will bring about such activities, minding refers to the engagement that leads to such acts. One could very well feed the dog without minding it. The intent (i.e., looking after it) is the minding.

Why is the word *mind* chosen to express taking care? To take care necessitates being alert, attentive, observant, and *to mind* is an implicit reference to this cognitive faculty. Words that call for alert attention typically imply the presence of a threat or of danger as, for example, the expressions *watch out!* and *look out!* which, like the imperative form—*mind!*—imply taking care so as not to be injured. At the source of an act of warding off a threat, there is caring for something and, too, there is the intention to act if required. The verb *to mind* expresses this attitude of protecting by being ready to parry whatever threatens the well-being of what is protected. It is not the act itself but the potential to act, and it is present only in intent.

This does not imply that mind and intent are the same—not at all. Rather, it suggests that a mind directed towards a certain objective requires the presence of intent. Giving direction to the awareness of mind is intent, and for this reason the transitive form of the verb *mind*, that is, minding *something*, refers to the guiding influence of intent.

With What Do You Mind?

Here's a puzzle. If in order to see, we employ our eyes, to hear we employ our ears, to sing we employ our vocal cords and breath, to move we employ our body, what do we employ to mind? It seems the answer must be something we do with our whole being.

To mind refers to an ongoing intentioned awareness. It is not an act or a thought but an attitude that is a state of being. The person sustaining the intent *to mind something* need not consciously be thinking about minding and the fact of minding might even be absent from consciousness until, all of a sudden, some threat intrudes, and almost like the discharge of a potential, the potential of minding, there comes an action. With it, all of a sudden a totally new situation arises in which there is consciousness of an object (the threat) and the act that constitutes the subject's response to that object.

Minding Interrupted by an Intrusion

It is significant that it is not the person doing the minding who initiates the transformation of the state of minding into an act. Something happens that sends an alarm to the person engaged in minding and triggers a response. Even though the specific response may have been premeditated and the intrusion expected, the instance of the intrusion is an unspecified moment determined from outside and, for the person minding, it is a random event. In *mind the low ceiling* the person comes upon the object to be minded, whereas in *mind the drunk drivers* it is some threatening other that comes to the person, but in both cases there is the intrusion on the state of minding. The subject might know roughly when the object will intervene; still, when the word *mind* is employed, it is at an unspecified moment. The event comes from without, impinging on the state of minding.

Initially, the intrusion registers as a sensation and what intervenes is recorded through the body's senses. The state of minding is interrupted by means of a call from the senses very much akin to the one when we wish to wake a sleeping person.

When sleeping, although on the level of the expanded mind there can be awareness of the surroundings, we are not consciously sensing our environs. To awaken someone and reconnect that person with the surroundings, one needs to enter her mind state through the portal of the body senses. We touch her or call her or open the curtains to let in sunlight. Somehow, the act of stimulating the sense organs pulls at the conscious mind, calling for its complicity in creating perception. And the mind responds—sluggishly at times, mixing up its own activity or dream state with what is calling it from without—and enters full wakefulness, that is to say, the person comes into consciousness where the subject–object dialogue through the senses is reestablished.

Similarly, but in the waking state, what is held in the mind as intent is called upon via the body senses. A general state of minding has been interrupted—punctured—by a singular intrusion through the senses. There is a change from potential to actual, from mind to world. General awareness charged by a particular intent releases the act that is the outcome of that intent.

Minding—Before and After an Intrusion

The preceding description could be formulated in terms of two states: before the event and after the event.

Before the event has to do with nonmanifest intent. In this state, minding is about awareness attuned to the particular needs of a situation together with the readiness to act if a threat arises. It is an ongoing state of being. In conscious activity, one engages the subject–object dialogue of seer–seen, of hearer–heard, whereas in mindful awareness one is engaged in activity without extricating the intending subject. One might say, in this uninterrupted state of intention the mind flows in synchronicity with sensation and thought, and it is this synchronicity that is broken by the event that interrupts the mind, calling the self out to take a stand.

After the event is no longer about the state of general awareness. A response to the threat is called for, and the activity of minding is something in the background. It is implicit in the situation, which is where it was all the time. Something has engaged intent by breaking into the state of minding and taking hold of the conscious mind. *Before the event*, minding is a general attitude. *After the event*, it has given birth to a specific act where subject (the person) and object (the intrusion) have replaced minding (potential) with an event (actual). A wakening call through the senses has broken the fusion of self and mind, calling out the individual who is guarantor of the mind's intent. Self separates from mind and takes action in the world.

To Be Mindful

Another application of the word *mind* is in the expression *being mindful*. What does it mean? Generally, it is not used on its own but in reference to a specific concern: "to be mindful of something," and there is in this an allusion to intent. On its own, the expression *mindfulness* refers to being attentive or aware. When mindful, I am one with my senses, fully absorbed in the sensations they bring, and I am at one with all that comes to mind, not thinking it but being the thought. How, one might ask, is this to be done?

Awareness holds intent. The intent can be specific as in *minding the garden*, or it can reach out to welcome all that may become knowable as in *mindfulness*. If intent is a dimension of awareness, where is it held? To attribute it to the subject brings a contradiction. How could it be held by the subject when, as has been described, the subject as self is not present in this nondual state? Yet, on the other hand, how could there be intent without a subject that holds the intent in place? This question is reserved for the later chapters.

How uncanny language is. Certain understandings we do not readily entertain concerning the nature of world, self, life, and mind are contained in the words we regularly use. Much of the time, however, it seems we disregard what language offers.

Summary of Set 1

To mind refers to an ongoing intentioned awareness. It is a unified state and does not separate into what leads and what responds. For this reason any change of state is necessarily initiated from beyond the state of minding by an intrusion that splits the nondual state of minding into subject and object. This new state is the release from the potential state of minding to a specific act.

Set 2: *To Mind*, Signifying Being Disturbed

What does the word *mind* signify in the question *would you mind if I open the window?* The affirmative response is *yes, I mind*, and it signifies that it disturbs me. A similar question but without employing the word *mind* is *would it bother you if I open the window?* Why should the word *mind* signify bother?

There is reason to pause here and ask, could we be dealing with different lexical meanings and this second meaning evolved in a context where the earlier usage was absent? Without any sociohistorical basis for such an assumption, it would be prudent to assume that this second usage grew out of a full intuitive grasp of this word's function in language. It has already disclosed subtle levels of meaning, and this is reason enough to maintain the search for coherence among these different usages.

One question has to do with the fact that dislike is implied. *I mind* implies that I don't want it. Why is this expression invariably called for in the case of a negative experience, a disturbance rather than a pleasure? With an enjoyable breeze coming from the window, it would not be possible to say *I mind it*, implying *I enjoy (having my attention drawn to) the breeze*. Or again, one cannot say *I mind it* for something one appreciates, as for example: *ah, yes, I mind the music. Isn't it wonderful!* Why not? This is query number one.

The second question points to what is a standard snare for the foreign student of English. *I don't mind* is a statement with a negation that is the affirmation *it's okay*. It is difficult for the student to realize that the expression carries the sense *it does not bother me*—and for good reason! The expression with the word *bother* has the person bothered in the role of object and the disturbance as the subject. This is what one would expect. But the expression with the word *mind* is the reverse. In *I don't mind the cold*, one finds I in the position of subject and the disturbing effect is the object. Who is doing it to whom? What is going on in this curious use of language? This is query number two.

Before setting out to respond to these queries, it is necessary to look more carefully at the situations where the verb *to mind* expresses being disturbed by something.

Self Awakens to a Disturbance

To mind is used to register discomfort. To respond to a noise with *I mind it* means one does not feel well with it. To say *he minds when you call him by his nickname* says that he is disconcerted by this appellation—or so the speaker claims. There is no appraisal given and no opinion expressed about the object itself, about the noise or the nickname. There is an allusion to the fact that what is referred to is disturbing, nothing more. To the question *Do you mind the music?* You could answer: *Yes, I do, though I love that piece.* This shows that no criticism of the object itself is implicit in the expression, only of its effect.

Saying *I mind* signals the speaker's aversion, similar to a nonverbal *ugh*. Although in the next moment an opinion might be expressed, the initial reaction that gives rise to the word *mind* comes before any judgment is made. This needs further clarification.

On a cold day, stepping out from a warm house into an icy wind, you have, let's say, a *brrr...* reaction. It is not *I like it* or *I don't like it* or *I feel the cold*; it is simply a vocalized shiver. There is as yet no positioning of self the observer and appraiser, although, to be sure, the process that leads there has been initiated and a moment later or even during the course of the *brrr*, self awakens and takes its stand. The expression *I mind* is said as one comes out of that feeling response.

A more imaginative portrayal would be that to say *I mind* is consciousness waking to injury. Something has stung the subject, like in the tale of King Solomon taking his garden nap. Waking in pain, he thunders at the little bee, source of his hurt. His attention is captured by one little bee that interrupted his reverie on a warm afternoon. His earlier state of mind plays no further part in the tale. An irritant incursion, communicated through the body's senses, forces entry into the mind. What an affront! Awakening to face this incursion is self, the thinker and actor, who responds with *I mind*.

I mind does not necessarily imply that the mind was asleep before this. For instance, before saying *I mind the open window* you might have been carrying on a conversation, writing a letter, or whatever. How then can you awaken when you were already fully awake? This is a fabricated problem. There is no difficulty as soon as someone steps out of linear thinking, for the answer has to do with multiprocessing. This serves as a good example to illustrate that there is no such thing as a single, unified identity to our *I*. The following section clarifies this point.

Many Separate *I*'s

Employing the pronoun *I* signifies sensing oneself to be the witnessing or acting subject of some event. Each experience of *I-consciousness* is a moment in which the *I* awoke to a specific content. There is no general objective *I* or *me* experiencing all the experiences that I have. In our conscious reflection, we assume that these distinct experiences of *I* are all me. One reason for this is that they all correlate with the same body—my body. Although one can generalize the advent of subjective experience and consider it as a particular phenomenon (referred to as *self*), each experience that thought has of self is a separate awakening of the *I* confronting an object of cognition. These moments of cognition are continuously popping into consciousness, building a generalized sense of self and of the world.

For example: I am sitting on a train and I am holding a book and I am looking out the window and I am sleepy. Considering all of these *I*'s, we can conclude they are all happening to me concurrently—all happening to the same *me*. We substantiate this conclusion by noting they have all become part of my personal history. I can recall all those experiences personally. They are first-person experiences, and thus an I that remembers other I's is the self-same I—it's me! The argument holds, and this is how we build our generalized ego consciousness. It is the fact that I am able to reaccess these experiences and recall the first-person perspective I had in each that links them as parts of who I am.

In each such experience, one can find no separate quality to recognize and point to, saying *that's me*. The experience of I is, so to speak, colorless. There is no particularity by which one experience of I can be identified as fitting together with another such experience. There may be a typical gesture or a manner of which one would say, *Oh, that's him to the hilt—that's his way of expressing himself.* But it is important to note that the experience of *I* as subject is not to be found in that characteristic gesture. Similar qualities do not make different *I*'s join together as one just as similar looks do not make two people have the same *I*. The phenomenon of first-person perspective is naked of any qualities.

Thus, on the train, *I* wakes up to sitting there, and again *I* wakes up to holding the book, and again to looking out the window, and so forth. Each experience is the awakening of the *I* and has nothing to do with what the other *I* was doing. The emergence of *I-consciousness* does not mean that the previous state was some kind of oblivion; it was just a different act of consciousness, a separate event. Each act of cognition gives rise to an independent experience of self and other. Each act is the awakening of self and other, out of non-existence.

Each experience of self is separate and is empty of qualities.

Thus, one can understand that saying *I mind* is to bristle at an unwanted arrival; it is the expression of the awakening of an *I* that was not there before. Whatever else the person was doing at the time has no bearing on the moment when a new *I* emerges claiming *I mind*. This *I* is totally new. It will, in due course, be classified together with what I consider as generalized *me*, but at the moment of its appearance, it is a fresh experience of *I* emerging in relation to an object—a new experience of being in the world.

To summarize: Each experience of self is separate and is empty of qualities. The fact that one can reaccess them as first-person experiences conveys the sense that they are joined and are all part of the same *I*.

Query 1: Why Does *To Mind* Signify Aversion?

An understanding of the aspects of caring and being bothered brings an answer to *query number one*, that is: Why is the expression *to mind* reserved for adverse situations?

First, it is useful to look at the verb *to care*, which also can take on the sense of opposition. Both *care* and *mind* indicate a state of being rather than an act. The expressions *caring for a child* and *minding a child* are close in meaning, and the similarity goes further. If one asks about an unpleasant noise, the response *I don't care* means I am not bothered by it. This is parallel with *I don't mind*, whereas *I do care*, in this case, would mean *it bothers me*; for *mind* the case is the same. The parallel shift in meaning in these two verbs from caring for to disliking is further support of the claim that the apparent double meaning present in the word *mind* is something integral and not some chance unrelated usage. To care is to be concerned. Not to care is not to be concerned. *I don't care* would then mean I am not concerned by the noise and so am not bothered by it. Following the logic one step further, *I care* would mean I am concerned and don't want to be. In other words, the noise engages me when I don't want it to become an object of my concern. The verb *to mind* functions in a similar manner.

The example of *to care* was cited to show the parallel with *to mind*. Having to care when one does not choose to do so is comparable with having to mind (attending to something) when one does not choose to occupy one's mind with what is taking place just then. It suggests that it barges in and engages the mind without the speaker's consent rather like a tune one can't get out of one's head. Awareness, no longer free flowing, is taken over by the disturbance. The person, waking to the subject–object duality, finds the mind preoccupied by the undesired presence of something unsolicited. That subject (the new *I*), waking to this fact, responds with *I mind it*, signifying: against my will, my attention has been engaged. And when the expression is used in the negative form, *I don't mind*, it is about regaining freedom or, rather, about retaining it. If the person—the *I*—who awakens to the event chooses to release it, making its intrusion unimportant, the response would be *I don't mind*, meaning my mind remains unengaged by that event. From the point of view of my mind, whatever the intrusion was, it has come and gone and I remain totally Zen about it. The reply *I don't mind* exudes a sense of détente—a potential invasion has been averted and my mind is free to continue on its merry way. This meaning is apparent, too, in the expression *never mind*, which says *don't concern yourself with that thing*, as if to say, *be free and don't let it become the object of your thinking.*

Quite unexpectedly, this first query leads to the issue of will and the speaker's freedom of choice. As must be obvious by now, there can be no way through this study without careful attention to individual freedom. As for query number one, the answer is apparent. Feeling the need to be free and unencumbered by a forced intrusion on the mind's activity is the reason for the expression's particular usage, that of expressing aversion.

Query 2: Why the Reversal of Subject and Object?

Personal choice, instrumental in responding to the first query, also has a place in the second query: the apparent reversal of subject and object.

The speaker saying *this mess bothers me* is reacting. The mess, for whatever reason, is upsetting. *Bothers* suggests a causal link, the mess acting on the person. In the same situation, a subject stating *I mind* is rejecting the intrusion. *I mind it* signifies that I attach my mind to it; however, this implication is but one half of what is being said. The implicit second half of this expression is *I attach my mind to it when it is not my choice to do so*. Mind is always potential. It is the ability to form connections. When this happy state of mind is curbed by the incursion of a particular event that captures it and compels it to relinquish its free state, the response is *I mind*, and in the background of this expression is reference to desired and undesired states.

Implicit in the expression is the comparison with being otherwise, with being free of the disturbance. The subject who minds is a person in metaposition and not the passive receiver of an undesired effect. The subject is taking a personal position relative to a troubling intervention. Saying *I mind* is not about the content of the intrusion but about its inappropriateness to which the speaker takes offense. It is not by its nature that it bothers; rather, when the intrusion is there, one puts one's mind on it and this brings one into the thinking mode that is detached from the ongoing experience of mind. What a mouthful! Why not say in just two words: *I mind!* This expression does not express a negation and implies separation from the ongoing interconnected activity of the fullness of mind.

Here is an example to illustrate that *to mind* is not a causal sequence. When one is with a group of people who choose a certain path of action, one might say, *I mind taking that action*. It is the free subject who chooses to disconnect from what is happening. A contrasting situation would be when one has a strong instinctive aversion. In this case, the person would probably use the form *it bothers me* (unless, with wry humor, the intention is to make an understatement). Compare *I dislike the awful smell of garlic. It really bothers me* with *I really mind the smell of it*. An impulsive reaction calls for the causal link of *it bothers me*.

The apparent reversal of the roles of subject and object when *mind* is used is because the subject makes the choice to stay engaged with mind activity and to release immediately whatever it is that thrust itself into its attention. Even though the expressions *I mind* and *it bothers me* are frequently used interchangeably and both answer the same need (to express aversion to something), they are not identical. There is a subtle difference between them that does not surface and often has no instrumental function in situations in which they are employed. That subtle difference, however, makes all the difference. It is the little step into freedom that makes all we know as mind different from all that is understood to be inanimate, material, objective, and real.

Reflections on What Was Found So Far

The two sets of meaning of the word *mind* (caring or objecting) are indicative of the two distinct processes of thought that have been described in each chapter of this work. The word *mind* straddles the nondual and the dual states. If what the subject does is on the level of intention, thinker and thought are fused in awareness and the sense of caring is present; if the subject is called to react to something explicit, objects enter thought and there is a sense of disturbance. The former is nondual awareness; the latter is the breaking of the nondual state and the emergence of a subject–object relationship. The former has no temporal or spatial units, no exact *when* or *where*, but has duration and is ongoing. The latter is punctual and signifies the termination of the state of minding, and whatever results is the aftermath of this change of state.

The first set is the expression of expanded consciousness and the loss of self; the second set is the arrival of restricted consciousness and the awakening to dualistic perception.

Behind each of these, one can uncover two attitudes fundamental to our experience of life: that of being engaged with all contrasted with that of finding oneself alone, a single person standing in opposition to all that is not self. In the first position, self has disappeared into general awareness; in the second position, self finds itself but loses its connection to all that is. Is this a dreadful comedy of errors by which personal aspiration is mocked and, Sisyphus-like, one is forced to live a contradiction where no attainment and no resolution are possible? It is nothing of the sort! It is what results when one half of the twofold process of the mind is ignored. Reality, having been defined by concepts alone, has become intellectual property, something you can grasp and have but cannot be.

The contradiction illustrates that life cannot be expressed through concepts and being is not found in the conscious mind. In saying *I mind*, one implies this is not what one favors and that there is something else from which I am removed when caught by conceptual thought. What is lost is the interlinking potential of the full mind responding on multiple levels to the influence of intent. This fullness of being is attainable through the expanded mind that brings release from separation—from separate concepts and separate self—and opens to an understanding of reality not based on material presence. How this happens and the role of self in this process is the central theme of the remaining chapters of this work.

PART III: PLEASURE AND DISPLEASURE IN MIND ACTIVITY

Describing Qualities

This section of the chapter brings into perspective the relationship between the two contrasted meanings of the verb *to mind*. No longer about usage or grammar, it is concerned with qualities of experience, and to describe qualities, forcibly, imagery is used. The die-hard rationalist or materialist will need to give a little leeway. Imagery allows readers to identify the quality of experience being referred to and then to check it against their own experience in such situations. What is rational can be communicated in rational terms; what belongs to experience and feeling has to be known through other means.

Two Contrasting Experiences of Mind

The fact that *to mind* is linked to an experience of displeasure and the fact that *not to mind* is linked to freedom from such displeasure and to being relieved of its threat bring a curious conclusion. These facts seem to suggest that thought occupies the mind, disturbs it, entraps it, and is experienced as an imposition. As was noted, *never mind* is liberation from being caught, from the obligation of thinking about what forces itself into the mind. Thinking, it would seem, is linked with displeasure. How strange! The implication then would be that, in the opposite case, when something is experienced as pleasurable, it does not invade conceptual consciousness. Enjoyment, then, is linked to the freedom of the mind to explore without being obliged to think about things consciously.

Could it be that conscious thought is a battle of wits, and in this conflict the mind wrangles with an imposed object that threatens to take it over? This would suggest that there is another way to be and that, in a pleasurable state, the mind functions otherwise. What would it imply if thought has this qualitative dimension related to the experience of displeasure and pleasure?

The scenario would be something like this. In the pleasurable state, whatever one is conscious of flows through the mind without causing commotion, and thus, this state of being conscious without rational consciousness is effortless, noninvasive, frictionless. In the pleasurable state, awareness alights on the mind ever so gently, whereas, in the contrasting state of displeasure, the mind is usurped by thought. Can it be that thought weighs upon the mind and uses consciousness for some purpose of its own?

This suggests there are two experiences of mind activity, one related to the expanded mind and the other to the conceptual mind. They are the expansive and the restricted states of mind already presented, and can also be described in the following manner. In one, the experience does not intrude upon the drift of consciousness, upon ongoing awareness. It passes through consciousness, or perhaps consciousness passes through it (take your choice), without the movement of awareness being arrested. The mind is moving across whatever it experiences, catching flavors and impressions without having to objectify them. In contrast to this stands another very different experience of consciousness and in it whatever is experienced clings to the mind. It enters awareness only to pull that awareness to itself, drawing in the mind till the sweep of consciousness is lost, having been brought to halt on that single experience. Instead of an ongoing movement, there is a series of arrested movements whereby what is experienced is itemized.

In one version, consciousness could be thought of as a divergent beam of light that brings all it illuminates into awareness. In the contrasting version, the beam gets caught by what it illuminates and converges on it. A single experience catches the beam and, by focusing the light upon itself, takes priority over all that is being experienced. This is the emergence of the subject–object duality and the breaking off of ongoing expansive consciousness. The result is consternation; the mind is called to respond to the intrusion that has taken hold of it. It is a case of consciousness activated from outside awareness, whether by infringement upon the senses or through goals dictated by the conscious mind under the influence of intent, producing a troubled state.

This stands in contrast to the pleasurable state of mind, flowing freely, unobstructed by that which enters awareness. When the mind moves in concert with integral inner intent there is a sense of ease and lightness coupled with a sense of joy in riding consciousness as one might ride a wave. It is effortless and allows awareness to remain free of a commanding subject.

Coming to recognize processes that engage the mind is instrumental in arriving at an understanding of perception and the role of mind in forming the world we know. Although these reflections may seem far removed from everyday living, they are not. They touch upon the source of beliefs we hold about the world and ourselves, beliefs that determine what system of values we embody in our interaction with other beings and with the natural world. Experiencing pleasure, even unnoticed pleasure, has a profound effect on the way we behave.

To hold unwittingly to the belief (not formulated in words) that we are engaged in an inevitable battle that rages between aggressive restricted consciousness and the flow of the expanded mind and, thus, to go about our daily lives as if life were a matter of itemizing the achievements of the conscious mind, we place ourselves in a position of incessant struggle; there is little doubt that this strife influences all we do. For the person holding this viewpoint, the contrasting position is barely conceivable. To understand that deep pleasure is linked to the loss of self and to undifferentiated awareness surely breaks the confines of who we imagine ourselves to be. It projects the possibility of a wholly new set of interpersonal values that is all but hidden in the subject-versus-object belief system. But let us not attribute the lack of expansive peaceful values to the presence of selfishness or some other simplistic motive. It arises, instead, out of a misinterpretation that has entered what we imagine ourselves to be. Self is assumed to function as a conduit that funnels experience through the analytical mind, and this view ignores the fact that conscious self is but a passing presence that dissolves into a more encompassing view when we cease to employ the mind solely for the production of facts. Beyond all that we know as factual is an interpenetrating creative state that is out of bounds for *little me*, as this conscious moment will later be called.

Should it seem that what is being said here is a call for a mystical belief in some higher nature, rest assured that this is just a study of the mind, nothing more, based on observations of how the mind functions.

CONCLUSIONS

Two surprising results emerge in this chapter. The first is the fact that the duality of the thinking process described in the first two chapters is implicit in the meaning and usage of the word *mind*. The second is that these complementary mind processes are related to the experience of pleasure and displeasure. It is curious to discover that the word *mind* points to the fact that enjoyment is conducive to one way of apprehending the world and that this approach stands in stark contrast to the way one apprehends when experiencing displeasure. An implication in this is that, in approaching an understanding of who we are and of our relationship with intent, the pleasurable path, free from conflict, becomes more accessible.

Personal attitudes and ways of being result from the manner in which the mind is employed. This, in turn, depends on the particular forms of intent a person holds, both individually and in the greater context of community, culture, biology, history, and more. We partake in a network of intent that spreads much further than thought goes. In accepting that intent is not part of the mind and not part of thought and that it functions independently of them, a way opens to describe intent and to unravel the way it relates to mind and self. With this, all is in place to enter the next two chapters: what intent is and how it functions.

[5]
Intent: What It Is

Intention: A Constant Companion of All That Lives

Just think for a minute: If there were no such thing as intention, what would this imply? What would change if the pole-vaulter did not *intend* to go over the bar? In such a case, making the jump, running towards the bar, holding the pole, calling up the energy to overcome the obstacle, thinking of success—none of these would be. The champion would wander aimlessly at the start of the run! Even to walk implies the presence of intent: the intent of being upright and of moving forward using one's legs. Being without intent, surely, would mean total paralysis. The option of getting up from a seat would be excluded. Setting out to do something would not be possible, and one could not enter into any course of action. Acts of choice would be precluded. Life would have no questions and no answers. There would be no directed thought, no call for meaning to manifest in thought, and no desire to speak or act. More drastic still is the fact that without the presence of intent, the attitude that links traits into a single object (see chapter 1) would be lacking, and no concepts could form. Conscious mental activity would cease. Nothing would become intelligible. To function as an organism that feeds, protects itself, and relates to other beings and the environment would be impossible.

Life, it seems, is impregnated by this inapparent something. To what degree should intent be considered a constitutive part of what we know as the world?

Just as a whole organism expresses intent, so does every living part of an organism—the organs, the tissues, the cells functioning in coordinated activity, each with specific tasks to perform. Adaptation to the environment suggests there is direction in what happens, and so does the determination of every living thing to express what it is. Direction-filled activity is manifest throughout nature. Any move, any event that implies a sequel is laden with intent. Present everywhere, intent is as ubiquitous as the air we breathe and, very likely for this reason, has been forgotten and is left out of the equation of life.

Present everywhere, intent is as ubiquitous as the air we breathe.

But then, computers and robots seem to function well without this invisible substance we name intent. This fact gives credence to the conviction that a living organism is nothing more than an assembly of material parts with a system of multiprocessing. Against this belief comes the shock of discovering that nothing of life is possible without intent and that it permeates everything we know, do, and feel. The verb *to be* implies intent, and *being* is its manifestation. But all this needs substantiation. This chapter enters the subject point by point.

Ubiquitous Intent

It is revealing to linger a moment longer with the analogy of the ubiquity of intent and air. Only with the advent of unified perspective in the early Renaissance did artists begin to take into account the state of the visual medium, the transparency of air, and the play of atmospheric conditions on the visibility of what they observed. The absence of this sensitivity in earlier painting is surely not a limitation in artistic skill but instead has to do with a pre-Renaissance mind-set that did not understand reality in the same way. With the change of understanding that brought consideration of the continuity of physical space and of the air that fills it, these new features entered both the painter's and the viewer's conscious minds. Acceptance of the all-pervading nature of intent might well require a similar change.

Preliminary Remarks

Allowing for Intuitive Understanding

To speak of intent ought to be simple and straightforward. Who does not know what it means to have an intention? It is obvious, and yet the term *intention* has frequently been closeted into certain set meanings or left impossibly vague. In phenomenological studies, the word *intention* has a particular meaning, introduced by Brentano and shaped further by Husserl. Because this usage is a distortion of the commonly understood meaning of the word, readers coming to the subject from this angle will need to take courage and find their way back to the original meaning to hear what is told here.

The Words *Intent* and *Intention*

The words *intent* and *intention* are generally interchangeable. One might argue that *intent* seems to focus more on the drive that inhabits a state of intention, but such a distinction is irrelevant to the discussion that follows. The two words are used interchangeably in this text, be it with a certain predilection for *intent*.

Defining Intent

Intent signifies a state of being in which someone is determined to produce a certain outcome. It can signify, too, the outcome on its own, without reference to a subject. In the first case, the word is employed to refer to the state of the person holding a particular intent: for example, *I intend to do it. I have the intention to climb that mountain.* In the second case, it refers to the outcome on its own, the task that has been set: for example, *to go up that mountain.* The first points out the presence of the intent, and the second tells what it is, so they go hand in hand.

The Challenge

As done in the previous paragraph, the meaning of the word *intent* can be stated, but this does not answer questions about its nature and function. How do we register and recognize the presence of intent? Where is it stored? How does it manifest? Such questions come as posers, but that is no reason to pass over them and imagine the world can be described without intent. Though it remains unidentified in the physical world, it is a vital component in every act of understanding. As this chapter shows, intent is indispensable to our experience of being alive.

A Playful Approach

In entering a discussion of intent, there is neither starting point nor end point and no particular sequence to follow; rather, it is a matter of *making the rounds* and touching upon the different properties that need to be mentioned. Because intent is elusive and not the usual type of object we set our conscious mind upon, getting to know it and recognize what is constant in intent calls for a degree of playfulness. This chapter is replete with examples of intent. In playing leapfrog over them, we can train our minds on the subject and, with each jump, reconnect with our personal experience of intent.

An Initial Example

Let's imagine that I want to pass a flower shop on the way home. To what extent is that an intention? If *buy flowers* is written on a list of errands I need to do and one by one I perform each item on the list, the only sustained intent might be to follow the shopping list item by item. If, however, I set out with the intention to buy flowers, I carry a certain attitude that brings about the accomplishment of that intention. Where is that attitude to be found?

An Important Caveat about Individual Distinctions

Before entering further into the discussion of intent, it is important to note that intent manifests differently in different individuals.

Although there is a common understanding of what intention is, the manner in which different individuals connect with intent varies to quite a degree. It is important to note that it is not the concept *intent* that changes but the way a person works with it. Personal idiosyncrasies can make an example of intent suggest quite different things to different individuals. For some, forming intent is difficult; for others, it requires no effort. Some need to repeat it as a directive to themselves until the act is accomplished; other people need only think once of their intent for it to become installed as part of their personal program and for the intended act to follow. This may partly have to do with memory, but essentially it is about how intent is retained.

An example: let's say you wish to find a box in which to pack a present, but rather than going out right away to get one, you wait for something suitable to come along. There are those who need to remind themselves repeatedly *I need to find a box* (or they repeat a key word to themselves or a mental image) while between those moments of recall they hardly notice whether there are boxes around them. In contrast, there are those who do not need to consciously reactivate their intent. It becomes part of their being and they begin to notice lots of boxes, and, even without seeing one, in a situation where an appropriate box might be, they are already alert to the possibility of finding one. A statement about *installing* intent has meaning for those of the second group, whereas for those of the first group such a statement makes little sense.

A further example of this variation is setting the time to wake up. Some people, without even checking the time before they go to sleep, can wake at whatever hour they intend—pretty much to the minute! Leaving aside the question of how the process works and considering only the presence of intent, one can assume that those who accomplish this feat take on the intention to wake at a certain time, whereas others who cannot perform the task are unable to bond with this intent in the same way.

Of course everyone is constantly acting with intent. But as far as purposely installing intent, there are great differences among individuals in their ability to do so in different situations. A highly charged situation, such as caring for someone close, can permit a more hermetic person to open and take on intent more easily. These examples show that the capacity to sustain intent can differ; some remain aloof and enter intent with difficulty, whereas others do it deeply, naturally, and with ease.

Entering into intent is something that can be developed. A geologist who sees strata and rock formations where others don't notice them and a naturalist who notices birds and animals and sounds and scents in nature that are not apparent to others have primed their ability to sustain intent in particular contexts. This training no doubt increases these individuals' power to deploy intent in many circumstances.

In light of this, surely, encouraging such abilities is, and ought to be, the central content of school programs, and what's more, this is something children spontaneously enjoy. Sensing personal power through developing such skills is exciting.

It is helpful to keep in mind throughout the subsequent discussion that a significant personal variable influences our ability to connect with intent and the way we experience it. Readers need to recognize where they stand, noticing where examples seem obvious to them and where, from their personal stance, an example does not seem to make sense.

Preview of the Trajectory of the Two Chapters on Intent

On a summer day, standing by a lake, I decide to dive in. First comes the thought about what I will do; then, I go ahead and dive in. This suggests a straightforward causal sequence in which thought forms the intention that leads to action. Not at all! There is no such causal sequence. The impulse to make the dive is formulated on many levels of my being and is the result of many more things than the momentary thought of diving into the lake. Quite independent of thought is the fact that I am determined to act. This determination has to do with a charged state of being and that I am *hyped-up* for the task. The outcome results not from a thought but from an overall state that releases this particular impulse.

Intent may be accompanied with a particular feeling, but, then, it may not; it may be accompanied with relevant thoughts, and, too, it may not. This variability means that fundamentally it is neither a feeling nor a thought. In this case, what is it and where does it reside? This is tantamount to asking where the sense of purpose is to be found.

Intent is a commitment one entertains to realize a specific outcome. It is registered not with a signature on a document, not with a spoken sentence, not with a thought but is made with one's whole being and permeates one's state of body and mind. It is contained in everything a person is at the moment of intending and is present to a greater or lesser degree on many levels of being at once: thought, feeling, metabolism, neurology, muscle tension, facial expression, and who knows what further microsignals of the presence of intent are to be included. The inference, thus, is that intent is everywhere within the living system. But then, how do these disparate influences flow together to produce a specific intent? To recognize the enigma of coordinated activity is to understand what intent is.

Intent manifests as the nexus of factors that form a certain commitment. Multiple functions, distributed throughout body, mind, and whatever else, correlate to produce a particular result, and with this, the singularity of intent arises. One way of understanding the interrelationship—a curious way that conflicts with our common view—is to consider that the different parts are coordinated through the outcome. This is to say, the anticipation of a future affects the present. By giving reality to a future event through the presence of intent, events cooperate to realize that future, and with this, no record is left of how connections are made among all that participates in forming the intended outcome. These reflections, although premature, hint at something strange and wonderful that does not seem to fit with a linear progression between cause and effect and even seems to suggest that time can disappear. Classical physics knows nothing of such processes, and they require a whole new language.

Keeping an Open Mind

One hindrance to forming a clear view of intent stems from the terminology currently in use when speaking of the transfer of information. Cybernetic models of communication are of little help when considering intent since intent cannot be described as the transport of a signal through a circuit. A few words about this may prove helpful.

Given the fact that intent influences outcomes, how could it be that intent has no place in communication theory? How could intent, a *form*ative process, not carry in*form*ation? Evidently, it does and what needs to be understood is that the meaning of the word *information* has been altered in information theory to a point where it no longer includes the formative process. When reduced to yes/no information bits, information is formless. This view concurs with the classical scientific view of causality in which a cause has to do with the application of force to produce an effect; that is, the transmission of energy from one object to others. Put crudely, in this view causality is a matter of things knocking into each other—bumper cars with no drivers. If all there is results from unforeseen effects that have been produced as objects knocking into one another, events carry no information except *yes knock* and *no knock*, and, with the exception of whatever is embedded in universal physical laws, there is no place for something that lends form to objects.

In actual fact, intent *is* a formative process and is pregnant with information, but it is not transmitted in binary terms. For this reason it slips unnoticed through the web of information theory. Intent has to be inferred from the correlation between actions attuned to a common purpose. Intent is expressed through integration and not by individual events. This process permeates the inductive, connotative, centrifugal, peripheral (all synonyms) activity of mind presented in the first four chapters. Information is conveyed through what might be called a *coordination coefficient* inherent in a set of actions that together produce an intended outcome. To use a visual metaphor, the information content is the ballet that results from coordinated movements of cooperating individual dancers. This said, do not hurry to conclusions and imagine a choreographer outside or inside the overall movement who creates the composition that the ensemble is to dance, some transcendental entity prescribing events. Instead, allow this tale to unravel little by little without starting from foregone conclusions of our habitual thinking.

Intent is not a determined object one can place under a microscope to study. It is imperceptible at first and needs to be approached somewhat as one approaches a work of art in which the sense of composition and the subject matter are often unclear at the outset and require some initial time for pertinent aspects to come together in the observer's consciousness. In approaching intent, we acknowledge the presence of some influence without as yet understanding what is before us. By entering the subject in this way, its manifold aspects unfold and gradually come into view, thus corroborating the initial trust we gave that a presence was there.

In what follows, implications of intent will be gathered one after another with the goal of reaching a clear overall concept. Such clarity will come with the release of certain common notions about the way the world functions.

Subtleties of Intent

If to approach intent as one does a work of art, careful observation is required. This includes taking time to develop sensitivity to the numerous subtle *touches* or qualities that accompany the presence of intent. From among these, this section gives attention to the following five qualities: commitment and the involvement of self, the sense of power, the lack of intermediaries, the imperative call, and the sense of freedom.

Commitment and the Involvement of Self

To start from an example: If someone says: "I intend to eat more fruit," he has expressed more than a thought about eating and not eating fruit; he has made a statement about a future event. The speaker voices the fact that it will come to pass. Is intent then a matter of future predictions, like a prophet or seer telling the future? Not so, because over and above declaring "this will be" a statement of intent includes the speaker as agent in the realization of the intended result. Intent is not simply a prediction but an engagement.

A second example: The announcement of a theater performance at some future date can remain a piece of information that has no further effect for one person, whereas for another, who plans to attend, it sets a series of activities in motion and excludes other eventualities, such as doing something else that evening. To know about a future event or to hope, wish, want, or imagine going to that performance is not the same as having the intention to go, for they lack the engagement that distinguishes intent. Some manner of bond is formed between the person with the intent and the intended goal; the subject contributes in some way to the realization of the outcome through a specific engagement.

One can go further into the matter and ask how such engagement arises. What is required to have that deep sense of "I will bring it about"? This leads to other features of intent.

A Sense of Power

To intend to catch a ball, you have to assume that it is possible for you to do so. To intend to move a rock, you must assume you have the power to make it move. To try is not to intend, for intention is more than an attempt. It implies certainty. One engages one's ability to create a result. Of course, a person could, at one moment, call up the energetic level to make the commitment and in the next moment become lethargic and relinquish the intent.

In expressing intent, one feels one is instrumental in making something happen. Rather than a matter of "this will be," one expresses "through my powers this will be." There is a sense of being capable of affecting events. With it, one assumes a certain air of authority. In fact, should it happen that one feels one has no power over events, the expression of intent is not possible. A farmer may wish and hope for rain, but she cannot *intend* rainfall; the shaman, knowing that intent influences world events, is able to emit the intention for rain. To create intention, one must have a sense of personal power and the audacity to stake claim to such power. A degree of confidence, whether insistent or gentle, is present with every expression of intent.

The engagement of intent is completely defeated when one believes that events are determined by objective factors over which one has no influence. This realization brings one to reflect on our school system where precisely this belief is disseminated on many levels, from the causal billiard-ball view of the world to the view that personal achievement is ruled by predetermined quantities of something named intelligence—and then educators are puzzled that students lack motivation and personal interest! Without feeling that it is within one's personal power to influence events, the seeds of intent and personal engagement fall on arid soil (a metaphor that alludes to what happens when limited abstract thought designs a world impervious to intent).

What is the tennis player doing on the court, bouncing the ball before making a serve? Very likely, she is engaging intent so that the shot will be successful. Some do this through visualizing the ball going over the net, and others might speak with the ball. But how can this make a difference? Has a tennis ball eyes and ears and the goodness of heart to be attentive to her call? In actual fact, what she manages to do at that moment is to take what is yet undetermined, hypothetical, and place it in the factual context of the upcoming serve. The function of intent is to summon possibility into actuality, giving it a place among

To the question "What is intent?" comes the answer "the summons to enter reality."

the events of a world of time and space. Admittedly, engaging the nonmanifest in this way demands a measure of audacity.

To the question "What is intent?" comes the answer "the summons to enter reality." This describes the function of intent. A subject with intent assumes the power of creator and calls into presence, ex nihilo, an event that would otherwise be left floating in a hypothetical world of possibilities. Here lies the power and arrogance of subjectivity wherein, from beyond all that is known, the subject establishes a *where* and *when* that lends form to phenomena, allotting them a place in the world and a share in reality.

Inadvertence to the Presence of Intermediaries

In the expression of intent, nothing points to the actions that will produce the intended outcome. This is surprising. Even though intent may engage intermediaries to bring about a result—such as my hand and the door handle and a twist of the wrist when I manifest my intention to enter a room—even so, the expression of intent is not directed at these intermediaries. Intent calls for a certain result and nothing more, trusting that the required physical actions of my body and of the world will align themselves to the common purpose. Intent is free of any belief as to how events transpire; it addresses neither causes in the material world nor spiritual entities. It knows no servants and there is no allusion to that which is to carry the intent towards accomplishment. It seems it addresses directly the mysterious working of the world where compliance is immanent in all that joins to express that intent.

While driving, you come upon a red light, and your intention is to stop. The car comes to a halt. How? Somehow your intent brings into play intermediary processes leading to that outcome. If to ask, did you actually intend them, the answer most likely is "no." Of course, you could have told your foot "get over there onto the brake and push" (as might happen in a state of semiparalysis), but that would be a new intent, distinct from the initial intention to stop. There are times, too, when even the intention to stop did not enter your mind, yet there you are, waiting in front of the red light! Unconscious intent will be discussed later and at length. The fact illustrated here is that intent addresses no intermediaries.

Intent can be compared with a summons. The court issues a summons demanding that a person will appear on a certain day and hour in court. The summons does not address all that must happen in order for that person to be present in court at the determined moment. Indirectly, it engages intermediary actions—whether performed by the person who received the convocation or through accompanying factors such as the tram that goes to the courtroom, the tram driver, someone who sewed the buttons on the blouse worn that day (because the summons contains implicit conditions, for example, not to be naked), and so forth, indefinitely, including, for instance, the strength of the thread holding the button. None of these contributing factors is contained in the summons, and yet together they participate in producing the resulting action called for by the summons.

Is all of this relevant, for it starts to sound rather far-fetched? Surely, the worker in some far-flung place on the globe sewing buttons or the machine, if it is that, is beyond the pale of the court summons. If to include it, no one and nothing anywhere would be out of range of any specific intent, and even more preposterous, every movement and every object at any given moment would be collaborating in an infinity of different intents reaching to the end of time.

It seems our common views concerning what is and what isn't will need some stretching to accommodate intent. Rather than a process of cause and effect in which one action is juxtaposed with another to produce a result, intent engineers a far more comprehensive process while attending solely to the outcome. Through intent, which ignores means, what seems disparate becomes unified, an utterly strange phenomenon that strays from our usual patterns of understanding.

The Second-Person Stance

As just stated, intent is the power to call for a result without specifying or engaging operatives to fulfill the task. It implies an unstated *this must be*, ordering events to obey. In earlier cultures, the practice of sending a blessing or a curse through the power of intent was common. Intent, like the wave of a wand, seems to function as a call for events to configure themselves to the desired end. In such a process it would seem that even Humpty Dumpty would have the chance of getting together again! All parts relevant to the intended result partake in the calling.

Engaging intent requires an attitude that expresses personal involvement, and this attitude has a specific grammatical structure, the second person. Instead of speaking *about* some entity and referring to it with the pronouns *she*, *he*, and *it*, we call it before us and address it directly as *you*. With the proclamation of intent, the potential of world is no longer viewed as *it*, in the third person, but is addressed in the second person, as *you*. The change is subtle yet nonetheless significant, for it places one on a par with all that happens and allows for personal intent to extend out and blend with the guiding forces attributed to the world.

Where does this second-person relationship come to expression? For example, if I have the intention to build a cabin and say: *I intend to build a cabin*, nothing is expressed in the second person. The reason is plain: telling *about* a specific intent does not require a second-person stance. Informing another or oneself that intent is present is not the release of intent. To tell a god-power (or a tennis ball) what one wants is simply an example of communicating a message. Doing so can serve to focus intent and enliven one's connection with that intent, but it is no more than a focal point to which one directs the intent one has, the intent that is independent of the particular focus. Intent is the call for a certain outcome by commanding some aspect of the world "be thus." The imperative form, in grammar, only exists in the second person. Our tennis player, imparting intent before her serve, is calling for the complicity of all that will happen in the next moment—and this independently of whether she chooses to focus that intent on an object, on someone she loves, or on a deity. Casting one's intent is to perform an act from the position of second person. The act of intent emitted by a person charges the universe with a certain mission by making the intended outcome a foretold conclusion.

But this sounds grandiose and out of proportion with our everyday intentions. Do we constantly stake such claims on the universe or is this merely imaginative play? To take time to express this sort of misgiving is an occasion to step aside from the task of gathering attributes of intent and to question what it might all mean. Maybe this is exactly the way the world works, not the objective world of science, but rather the world I am intimately associated with. It is the world reflected in my consciousness, which is the world I know through being an intentioned living being—and, to go one step further, it is the world that my understanding has led me to accept as the objective world of science. Consideration of intent leads down strange paths.

The expression of intent is a call for a final result not by engaging the actions necessary to produce that result but by addressing the outcome directly in the second person. Somehow, doing so encourages the means to cooperate in producing that result.

The Sense of Freedom

Having an intention quite clearly includes feeling that one is able to influence what happens so as to generate a certain result. It includes sensing that one has the ability to modify events to come, whether events in the mind, as in an act of recall, or events in the world. One feels present among all that makes up the world and yet not confined by it in that one has power to intervene. Is this freedom merely an impression or is it an actual fact? To answer this, it is necessary to show exactly what is personal in intentional acts. When one can point to what is *mine* in the expression of intent, it is possible to understand where and how one is free. This chapter develops what is needed to reach the answer presented in the final chapter.

Humility

These preliminary remarks on intent lead into areas we do not often consider, at least not in relation to the thousands upon thousands of intentions we express throughout the day. Another angle showing what is involved comes when one takes note of the fact that, for a religious person, a clear expression of intent tends to call for the adjunct *by the grace of God*, as in "we will meet again tomorrow, by the grace of God." It is as if a gesture of humility is needed to redress the insolence of intending the future, as if to intend is to make a presumption that oversteps human bounds and infringes on a task that belongs to God.

But, in and of itself, intent implies humility. Intent, as we saw, is the expression of power and the ability to impose upon the future, and yet, at the same time, it is mysterious because we are totally at a loss as to why and how it works. We are humbled by our ignorance, by not knowing how we do what we do. Recognizing this fact, we concede to the unknown a part of our personal power and independence.

Perhaps it would not be too much out of place here to include some humor about not leaving place for the unknown: Once, some engineers came to God and said they had figured it all out and didn't need her anymore. To this God answered, "That's fine. I'll leave under one condition: that you demonstrate you can create life." They took up a handful of clay and proceeded to do just that. "Ah, no," was God's rejoinder. "Use your own clay!"

Intent: Distinct from Thought

To think and to intend are distinct from one another. This warrants clarification. One can have a thought about a future act without any intention to perform it. The thought of going for a walk this afternoon may be devoid of the intention to do so, and the contrary is also possible: to have the intention to go for a walk without formulating it as a thought. Thought does not necessarily imply intent; intent does not necessarily imply thought. Even though thinking about an outcome might be a factor that propels it to become an intention, it is not thinking that is the intention.

In this case there is the question: Whose intent is it? To whom or to what entity does intent belong? Before this realization, in cases where thought and intent are assumed interdependent, one could imagine that the person who thinks of the intent is the one who has the intent. For example, the one who thinks of going for a walk is the one who has the intent to do so. But with intent existing independently, disengaged from thought, the owner of intent is an unknown. This has far-reaching implications. If thought does not direct intent, common assumptions we hold about how we perform acts need to be reviewed. No longer can one assume that it is me—the self we attribute consciousness to—who rules the actions I perform.

Intent: Cleansed of Thinking

An extreme example of intent purified of conscious influences can be found in calligraphy and archery in the Zen tradition, for there consciousness of the goal has been eliminated, yet the intended result—for instance, splicing a first arrow that has penetrated the center of the target with a second arrow—is achieved to perfection. In relinquishing all control, the goal is attained. Such a practice seems utterly contradictory until one moves to a position that admits

Conscious thought responds to intent that is already present.

influences that bypass consciousness. Releasing conscious control means releasing linear thought from the delusion of having power and from thinking it controls events. When, together with all that is unconscious in intent, one is also conscious of the intended goal, the tendency is to assume that conscious thought directs the intent. Actually, the process is very different. Conscious thought responds to intent that is already present. The person stating "I have decided" is only taking cognizance of what is already in place.

The example of Zen archery serves to demonstrate this surprising and verifiable fact: that our actions are not instigated by consciousness, and this, even in cases where consciousness is present. But our non-believing minds, most likely, will not accept one instance as proof. The presence of disbelief has to be softened with other examples before the leap into a new perspective of how the world functions can be made.

By watching carefully a decision we make to perform an act, a strange fact emerges: between *recognizing* that decision and *acting* upon it, there is a hiatus. They are not sequentially aligned. This is easily overlooked and mostly passes unnoticed: walking down a lane, I want to turn left and it appears as if the act follows the thought to do so; I wish to type a word and my fingers hit the relevant keys. It seems straightforward, as if there were nothing to question. Surely, I direct my actions consciously. But when we slow the process down, silently watching what takes place, a strange phenomenon is observable. In cases where the conscious thought about an action we wish to make precedes the intention to act, we can discover that the act is initiated sometime after a conscious decision is formulated, and in its own time. The act of making a conscious decision is not at all what determines the instant at which the move is made.

Here is an experiment. In the morning before getting up, I wish to catch the moment when I decide to get out of bed. What is going on just then? Still lying in bed, I may have the thought that it is time to get up and yet remain where I am a moment longer, or I may be thinking about tasks and engagements for that morning, or I may have a wandering mind and not be thinking about anything to do with getting up. Then at some point, I push the sheet back and get up. If I look for the decision to get up, it simply was not there at the moment I made the move. It can even be frightening to discover one was totally absent at the moment of acting out a decision. One can find excuses to cover such examples such as *an unconscious decision* or *the play of habit*, but do these tell what is actually going on? They help one to recognize the phenomenon as being familiar and commonplace but nothing more. There is a moment when a consciously elaborated program has been ingested, becoming an overall attitude that no longer depends on the conscious mind, after which, out of the unknown and with no further prompting on the part of consciousness, an act is initiated. We may make a move just after thinking about doing so, and in this case the hiatus between thought and act may be so short that we are led to believe the act is triggered by thought. But because in the less pressing situations there is no such connection, there is reason to wonder if this is not true of all acts of choice. Conscious thoughts arise and disappear, but that which produces the act comes from elsewhere. It springs forth from what has been integrated into one's whole being. From an overall attitude that I have taken up, multiple effects come together and produce the act—my act!

Most actions never enter consciousness. Life would be unbearable if conscious commands were required for every gesture: moving your tongue to speak, moving your eyes as you read, focusing them at a certain distance, forming images and sounds in your mind while thinking, and so forth. It is obvious that one could hardly count the number of gestures required just to take a jug from the cupboard, and there is certainly no conscious intention behind each of them. Most of the movements and gestures we make are not controlled consciously, and, as noted, where there is consciousness, they are not instigated by consciousness. The conditions that promote every action are set in the unknown, far out of range of conscious thought. The Zen master reaches beyond thought, giving presence to more than the conscious mind is capable of directing. The surprise, though it is obvious, is that so does everyone! In the Zen tradition, the moment of choice is refined to include the complete release of thinking. But we too evacuate thought with every action we initiate but, for the most part, in a clumsy, jumbled manner without singling out the act we perform, streamlining it, and reaching the perfection of achievement that deliberate training to release thought can bring.

In all of this, the holder of intent proves to be ever more elusive. Recognizing where and when this subject is absent and cannot be found is an important part of this search and leads to further understanding.

Intent in Objects

What does it take to be in possession of intent? Can, for instance, an object have intent? We can say that the purpose of a pair of scissors is to cut, that the purpose of a locomotive is to pull carriages, but it would be strange to say that the intention of the scissors or the intention of the locomotive is to accomplish something. It sounds odd, childish even, as if one were speaking in anthropomorphic terms. Why? First, to have intention requires being able to imagine a future time, because intent bears upon what has not yet happened. Then, to know that a thought we have is an intention, we check our feelings to sense whether this is what we want. Allowing for this, it makes sense to attribute intent only to a subject we consider capable of such knowledge and feeling. It seems therefore that intent remains with the scissors' maker or the person using the scissors but does not become the scissors' intent. And yet the design of the object relays the intent of the maker. Something of intent is present in the object even though we do not attribute *having an intent* to scissors.

It is clear that the original designer, in producing an object, determined the form in accordance with a purpose and that the specific attributes of the object serve in implementing the preconceived intent. What aspect of the maker's intent is to be found in the object and what aspect is not there?

— *Present in an object* is information concerning the intent of its maker. The scissors' size and ring-shaped ends, for instance, suggest that this object can be held in the hand and operated with fingers. Information of its purpose is encoded in its form, texture, choice of material, and so forth. Properties of the object echo the initial intent and guide its possible use. The intent reemerges in the person using the object, whereas the encoded information and cues contained in its design tend to animate that particular intent.

— *Absent from the object* is the experience of intent that includes that of vying with an unrealized future so that one's position straddles two moments in time: the present and the unrealized future. Without a determined present and an unconsummated future, purpose is impossible. In order to intend, there must be entry into time at a present moment wherefrom arises the sense of a future that has not yet been realized. This prerogative is available to the person employing the scissors, but it would be curious to attribute it to the scissors themselves.

This leads to the conclusion that, even though aspects of intent are implicit in an object, to become full-fledged intent requires something more than the physical qualities of the object. Whatever this may be, it will have to include the state of reaching for an outcome.

Since material aspects of an object influence the way it is employed and the way it interacts with everything else, they have a role in the intentions that the object serves. This thought leads in a strange direction, for it means that an object with its specific qualities must be intertwined in any number of intentions that unfurl to produce future events. Everything we know is then a functioning part of innumerable movements of intent. This particular thought belongs to the next chapter on the function of intent, but it slipped in here almost inadvertently and serves as a signpost of what is to come.

The present goal is to have some grasp of what intent is. If, as just noted, intent is distributed through all that participates in the movement towards the intended outcome, one must then ask, whose intent is it? If intent is formed both by what I consider to be mine (my body and whatever) and by what appears to be other than me (world), can one still consider that it be *my* intention? What I think of as me is merely *part* of all that participates in intent. This means, for example, with the intention to visit a friend one would have to state, "The world and I have a mission to carry out." Does this make any sense? Do I extend into the world so that the world and I, in accomplishing an intention, become one? An answer to this is forthcoming, though not immediately.

Intent with No Ascertainable Source

It was shown earlier that intent is not dependent on conscious thought and, as just shown, the influence of intent can emerge from an object. How is one to put the pieces together and understand what it is we call intent? A possible path to follow is to search for the source of intent. In doing so, it is useful to continue with an example of an inanimate object as this illustrates clearly how intent is part of a whole system of relationships.

If to take a spoon as an example, it is plain that its form and properties set parameters that tend to determine what happens with it. Through its qualities (shape, size, hardness, etc.) it favors some events over others. What is implicit influences what becomes manifest. The spoon, in a certain sense, participates in the intention of the person who employs it. Let's say you use the spoon to help yourself to some soup. If to retrace the path of intent from the result (the action of employing the spoon to drink soup) backward, where does it lead? One might expect it to converge on your choice to have soup, but it does not. The action leads back into a multitude of different lines of influence that branch wider and wider into the overall situation, and with this, the more closely one tries to focus on any particular source, the more ambiguous it becomes. For example, having soup links to the time of day, to your appetite, to when you last ate something, to what you will be doing afterward, to where you are, to why you are there, to waking up that morning, to the temperature of the room (which permits the soup to be liquid, the metal spoon to have a specific form, and you to be alive), to the presence of the spoon, to the spoon's maker, to the culture of which you are part that uses spoons, and so on. This is all rather unsettling! Instead of starting out as a single cause at a particular place and in a particular moment, the origin of an intended event spreads out and is traceable throughout a whole system. It appears spread over time and it starts nowhere in particular.

The conclusion from this is that traces of intent are present in all objects and situations that relate to that intent, including, of course, the body and mind of the person involved in carrying it out. There is no unitary source that marks the origin of intent, and instead intent is embedded in an extended fabric of interactions. Influences on the intended outcome are indirect in a manner not unlike the way belief affects behavior. Having a specific intent plays into everything one does, influencing one's choice of action and the manner by which actions are performed: where one is careful, where inadvertent, where speedy, where deliberate, the type of control exerted and for how long the action is sustained, and so forth. All these factors are integrated through intent as it aligns separate acts towards a single outcome. This ballet of interconnection homing in upon a result is intent. It brings form and direction—quite distinct from physical cause and effect. This statement may appear clear enough, but further discussion is needed to elucidate what it implies.

In following intent to its origin, there is a constant branching of paths. Each path becomes multiple as it subdivides further to include factors ever more varied and distant in time and space that, together, constitute that intent. Everything that bears upon the final outcome has a role in forming that specific intent. In this manner, the path to the source of intent becomes ever more spread out in the world, losing specificity in time and space. This may come as a surprise, but it is a familiar beast! It was studied in earlier chapters on the role of periphery consciousness in concept formation, and it returns here in a new guise. The search for an explicit origin of intent leads away from anything explicit and out into something equivalent to the fading reality at the periphery of perception. In searching for the whereabouts of the source of intent, one finds it is not identifiable anywhere unless, dare one say, it is everywhere. This thought is disconcerting, for it implies that the search for the origin of an intent does not lead to a specific owner that generates intent and, instead, reveals the lack of any such origin and the lack of any identifiable presence that animates the process that brings the intended result.

Intent and Reality

The search for the origin of intent goes astray only for as long as one persists in the attempt to pinpoint a specific event in the world that generates that intent. The fact that no unique source emerges is not surprising when one recalls what was shown in earlier chapters, namely, that the world we know only comes about as a result of intent. When this is understood, it is quite obvious that intent cannot have its origin in the world that itself arises though the influence of intent.

The view reached so far is that the world we observe is a result of the denotative attitude that gives form and direction to the manner in which we integrate sensory impressions. Without this attitude none of what we observe would be. Through intending reality, one produces it, and, as noted, this means that what is assumed to be objective is in fact produced through a subjective act. (Is this not the ultimate insult to objectivity!) It also implies that to accept something as being real produces an effect. It brings about what we call reality. This immediately raises the question: What is the quality that makes reality real? How does being real differ from being imagined? An answer to this helps open the wider perspective needed to encompass the phenomenon of intent.

Reality's special quality is found in its staying power. All that is imagined enters the mind and disappears again, but to think "this is reality" is to claim there is something over which the mind has no dominion, something that can be without mind. It has duration, that is, being in time. For this to be possible, there is an edict—an unstated axiom of reality—that makes perception a mere epiphenomenon of reality. In shorthand version, the edict goes like this: *reality requires that any event and change observed in the world is the result of causal agents that lie within the world.* It claims that reality is determined by what is real, an obvious tautology that was left unchallenged.

Proclaimed reality obeys a system of causality that has the following four stipulations:

— The establishment of a time and space grid that is continuous and uniform
— That no two objects can occupy the same space and time coordinate
— That no single object can appear in more than one position on the grid
— That nothing can step off the grid

Although these principles of classical science have all been experimentally disproven in the quantum realm, they continue to sustain our common attitudes to the world. The classical view of time, space, and causality gives an independent place on the reality grid for everything known. In so doing, it makes what is real independent of the personal subject that determines that grid. Acceptance of this reality view implies that one retracts oneself from the reality one is creating and revokes all personal involvement in generating that world. There is an inherent contradiction in this, for it means personally creating what one claims is impersonal. This fact, however, has remained hidden because, once the tenets of causality are in place, all intervention is assumed to be physical and to proceed according to the edict of reality.

The requirements of reality, just defined, work fine when we know that we proclaim them and are not caught in believing they are imposed anonymously upon us. They can serve us well when we are able to recognize the implication of intent in reality and recognize our personal role in what arises. Without this understanding something very different happens and we lose our power to choose and to act.

Whose Intent Is It?

Recognizing reality for what it is opens new questions as to the origin of intent. Is the power of intent actually available to someone? Is it mine to wield? An answer to this requires a fuller discussion on self (see chapter 7), but a preliminary answer is offered here. Fusing diverse features into a single object is a personal act and is the expression of our personal power to create reality (chapter 1). This shows that what transpires on the level of intent plays out into the material world that includes our physical body, and this, in turn, suggests that on some level our intent sets the horizon of reality and of that which becomes our world. A comic rendition would be to imagine it as a game called *Integration*, played by some imaginary *intent beings*. These intent wizards (who, as will be revealed later, are dimensions of self) pick an outcome, some particular intention, and proclaim, "Let's integrate that," and by expressing this intent they expand the horizon of knowing to include that new perception, thus giving it presence as an event in time and space.

Intent, being nonmaterial, cannot itself manifest, but its influence manifests as the material world it forms. On one hand, without intent there is no material reality, and on the other hand, with intent there is far more to reality than matter strewn innocently through the universe.

With these last remarks, the presentation of intent reaches a breaking point and a new discussion reaching beyond a view of reality anchored in the material universe is called for. To proceed in such a direction, more clarity is required as to the presence of nonphysical processes active in the universe. In stating this, a curious fact comes to mind. It is ironic that ideological trends render references to what is nonphysical (or spiritual) abrasive to many an ear, and yet, the whole intellectual edifice we have created, including the view that renders the nonphysical suspect, is nurtured in an immaterial mind (whether or not it is found to correlate with particular neurological activity) and by feelings attributed to an equally immaterial self.

From here, the discussion has to move to the nonphysical, and this can be achieved in a relatively simple manner through a study of form.

How form arises and produces concepts was described in the first chapter. How form is perceived through our sensory system was the subject of the second chapter. At this point, what needs to be broached is the nature of form: what it is, how it is transmitted, and, in particular, how it finds its way into physical objects. This subject is taken up in chapter 6.

Before proceeding further and entering the next stage of this account of intent, an interlude is offered. It has to do with learning and tells about a pedagogical approach that includes intent as a fundamental principle.

La Gestion Mentale

In our society, school is a place where we come across repeated reference to intent. Take a look at typical report cards and you find allusions to motivation, will, concentration, attention, and, especially, to their absence. These comments are not directed to what the students do but to something that influences what they do, to an implicit factor that has the potential to direct and enliven learning. Apparently, teachers assume the presence of such a thing, though in not recognizing intent for what it is, opportunities to cultivate it are forfeited.

A current pedagogical approach places intent in a central position. It is mentioned here to bring a further example of intent. The field is called *La Gestion Mentale*, and it was developed through the work of the French philosopher Antoine de La Garanderie, recently deceased. He described five fundamental acts of learning (attention, memorizing, comprehension, reflection, creative thought), each of which is generated and guided by a specific intent or, more accurately, by what he names *projet* (in French). In the context of this chapter, it is revealing to take a closer look at *projet* as it appears in his work.

Here is an example of the presence of intent that pertains to the fifth act of learning, that of creative thought. The *projet*, or intent, that drives this activity is that of finding, in relation to what is present, a thing that is absent, that is not given. There are two distinct paths one can follow in doing this: one is to search within what is given for what is hidden; the other is to move beyond what is given into what is not there. Typically, the first path results from an attitude that questions *why it is so*, and the second path results from the quest for *outcomes* and novel *applications of what is known*. These two directions are the result of two distinct intentions. The first form of intent describes the mind of the discoverer, the second the mind of the inventor. Through dialogue with different individuals, Antoine de La Garanderie demonstrated that, in creative thinking, a person has a deep-seated bias for one of these tendencies and not for the other. For every person, one of the two tendencies becomes a structure of learning and a life pattern.

Such a division of mind activity into contrasting directions is not unusual. In a similar manner, there is a splitting of ways in the drive that generates and satisfies the act of comprehension. This subject is more complex than the dichotomy of discoverer/inventor, but it is possible to touch upon just one aspect to show what is involved.

In school learning, some students, when faced with a problem, first look to find the rule or the principle that applies to the given situation. From this, they deduce what they need to do. For others, first of all they need an example, a model to go by. To them, the rule is not helpful, and they get to it afterward only if they are required to state it. These two instances point to the two opposing ways of reaching an understanding. It is not often told, but there are two separate ways to respond to the questions, "What does this mean?" and "What is it?" One answer follows the impulse to explain. This person looks for a principle or rule or some point of origin that explains how it comes to be what it is. A very different answer follows the impulse to look ahead, not backward, and find what to do with it, how to apply it, or simply what can serve as an example of it. The first is driven by a *why* attitude; the second by an attitude that questions *what is it for?* In the first case, the person's intent is to explain; in the second, the person's intent is to look for applications that demonstrate what it is, and typically, this person feels quite lost until an example of what is being referred to or an example of how it is to be applied comes to mind. The dichotomy between *explicative intent* (the former) and *applicative intent* (the latter) is a source of frequent misunderstanding between individuals both in the classroom and in life, producing disagreements of historical proportions where two opposing points of view find no common ground. Unnoticed for the most part is the fact that the verb *to mean* has two fundamentally separate interpretations, depending whether it is employed by a person with explicative intent or by a person with applicative intent.

There is, in this, a parallel with what was stated about creative thought. People who, in acts of comprehension, move with *explicative intent* are nearly always those whose creativity comes in the form of a *discoverer*; those whose thought is directed through *applicative intent* tend to manifest their creativity as *inventors*. From these examples, it becomes clear how the structure of intent influences our mental performance as well as our actions in the world, and it can easily be shown how it determines our affinity for certain activities and for certain professions.

The distinction just outlined for acts of comprehension stems from a yet more fundamental dichotomy in the structure of intent: one's sense of time and one's sense of space. Antoine de La Garanderie shows how, in this too, people are divided into two mutually exclusive positions: those who think in temporal terms and those who think in spatial terms. Instead of there being some generalized way of grasping time and space, there is a dichotomy that influences whatever we wish to understand. To use the words of Antoine de La Garanderie, some people are *tempo-spatial* and through an intuitive sense of time build spatial understanding, and the others are *spatio-temporal* and through an intuitive sense of space build an understanding of time. The difference results from the specific form of intent one has when setting about reaching an understanding. This is not the place to expound further on these findings, but Antoine de La Garanderie has published more than twenty books on the subject.

It is hardly possible to resist mentioning one further observation that links with much that is told in this work—a fact that is fascinating in and of itself. The fundamental distinction between time-based and space-based intention has vast implications for society and for biology. We choose our partner in life according to specific parameters. Girl meets boy is not the innocent tale we are used to hearing, and Cupid's playfulness is not without its rules. Though hard to accept at first, the uncanny fact is that parents are of complementary (i.e., opposite) structures, one being tempo-spatial and the other spatio-temporal. (Maybe this is why we have Cupid because, on our own, how could we choose from possibilities we know nothing about?) This complementarity is true for very close to 100 percent of the population and has obvious implications on biological principles active in the world as well as on how freedom of choice functions. These contrasting structures in parents have repercussions on their children, on who is temporal and who spatial. Understanding this can be helpful, even instrumental, when engaging with children and offering them the possibility to move with ease into their vast potential to understand and to develop.

The fundamental duality noted here is very noticeable, even when overlaid by innumerable personal attributes and by individual itineraries that a person employs when reaching an understanding. The basic parting of ways between time-based and space-based comprehension is obvious and can be brought out through specific questions. De La Garanderie mentions some historical incidences of these contrasting views. For example, there is the calculus, invented at the same time by Leibnitz and by Newton. The former worked it out in temporal terms, the latter in spatial terms. Lack of comprehension and even antagonism between philosophers of temporal versus spatial orientation offers a new chapter in the history of philosophy—if not a whole new history.

The field of *La Gestion Mentale* describes how intent enters various activities of learning and how it correlates with the creation of images, sounds, and sensations that sustain the mind engaged in learning. When teachers are informed about the structures of intent, it enables them to overstep limited personal mind patterns and open up to those of their students and, too, to pass on this whole understanding to their students.

This short excursion touching on *La Gestion Mentale* is included because the subject is not widely known and because it is extremely pertinent to an understanding of intent, the activity of the mind, and the importance of the subject's position in all that has to do with acquiring knowledge. There is a further reason for including this interlude introducing the work of Antoine de La Garanderie. It is to bear witness to a unique teacher and philosopher who has been an inspiration to the author of this work. I am deeply indebted to him.

dr
[6]

Intent: How It Functions

THE AIM OF THE PREVIOUS CHAPTER was to bring an understanding of what the word *intent* signifies. Curiously, together with the addition of clarity, the concept itself becomes diffuse, less concisely determined. To describe the enigma more fully, the central question changes from *What is intent?* to *How does it function?* With this shift in emphasis, a new chapter opens.

Normally, we think of an intention as being directed by someone and imagine that the subject—me, for instance—sets the intended purpose and guides all to an outcome. However, the conclusions reached so far are these:

— Intending is not a conscious act even though it may become conscious.

— Intending is not directed by an entity or intellect separate from all that the intent influences.

— Intending has no single source and instead seems to grow out of divers actions.

Accepting these, one needs to ask afresh: What description is there of intent that is still in line with the common usage and meaning of the word *intent*? That which continues to hold true is the basic feature of commitment to an outcome. (Exactly who makes the commitment will be dealt with later.) This is accomplished through the correlation of diverse activities that participate in realizing the outcome.

The Anthill

In a functioning anthill, a little ant rolls a ball of earth up the side of the heap. It is just doing its job. Yet because it is sensitive to the presence of the queen and the influence she extends over her domain, the little ant is not working alone. It performs acts that are related to what other ants are doing, and the result is a functioning anthill. The overall structure becomes perceptible only with the capacity that the mind has to integrate elements of structure into a unified whole. Such a capacity is usually not attributed to the ant; the biologist might instead speak of instinct, preprogramming, genetic content, and so forth—terms, I might add, that speak of nowhere and nothing as if somewhere and something, for they place the unknown in the field of the known without any justification for doing so. But the anthill is real and cooperation is real and the presence of a living queen is real and crucial in many ways, so there is some shared dimension in the anthill that results in informed action. Where is it? We might accept, as is told, that pheromones have a role in this and have, apparently, a marvelous ability to carry information; still, pheromones do not tell how the global enters the specific, how a structured plan is held in place and takes form through cooperation. For this, something even more subtle than pheromones is at work, something that may not be physical at all.

Taking Form; Losing Randomness

To speak of intent is to refer to the insemination of order and purpose in what happens—no less and no more. Randomness, a state that may well never exist, is excluded wherever intent is present. Uncovering the presence of intent makes a world formed from random events less conceivable. To perceive intent is to be attentive to nonrandomness in events by noticing what unifies individual acts. This implies being attentive to the presence of what is whole. In order to gain a view of the process of intent, some grasp of how meaningful connections arise is required, and this can be achieved through an understanding of the process by which form enters the material world. It is assumed to be well understood, but is, in fact, misunderstood. This chapter will present the matter gradually so as to readjust what is mistaken.

> *Randomness, a state that may well never exist, is excluded wherever intent is present.*

Nonmaterial Presence

One after another, notes are plucked from a stringed instrument, and as if from nowhere, a beautiful melody emerges—but, from where? The melody is not the notes. Or take the case where, with a gentle caress you offer to someone, a smile forms. How does it happen? A simple and observable act has hidden depths that are not found in the physical gestures themselves. To find what is happening, one needs to peer beyond the obvious material causes. To do so, one must stay clear of the familiar trap of adding intermediary causes and effects until the chain of explanations becomes so long and complex that the missing connections between form and matter go unnoticed.

Is there a way of *seeing* that delves beyond material existence and takes account of more than what is apparent to the physical senses? Our sense organs seem bypassed whenever intent is functioning, but this gives no reason to leave the tale untold. By some subliminal process or perhaps supraliminal process, objects are affected by more than the physical influences we assume to be the reason for everything. Through what procedure does this nonphysical influence happen?

Transmitting Intent

Architect, mechanic, gardener, teacher, shoeshine worker—all create form and transmit form. For an artist, it might be a more visceral process and seem more intuitive than what an engineer does, but, in every case, the result has its source in a person's intention and is displayed through the orchestration of activities that set individual actions in line with a common purpose.

How this happens will be studied by considering specific examples. The guiding question can be formulated as follows: *How does the intent of an artist enter into matter and emerge in the resulting work of art?*

The Sculptor and the Statue

The intent of a sculptor is brought to expression, for example, through the action of hammer and chisel on stone. The actions are physical events, yet through them something nonmaterial is transmitted and the artist's intent is brought into a material object. Somehow, it seems, intent jumps the gap from artist to artwork. The influence of intent that gives a particular quality to each act as well as the correlation between acts lies hidden. The formed sculpture comes out of a thousand different influences that bear upon the actions taken by the artist. The sculptor's temperament affects thoughts and feelings, and these influence the manner in which the block of stone is struck. Mingled with these influences are the artist's skill, knowledge, experience, understanding, mood, and ever so much more that momentarily comes to bear upon the physical actions. And all of this is coordinated by the intimation of an outcome. The catalyst of this transformation, the intender, is somehow present throughout the process of making the sculpture and yet is nowhere manifest. The intention appears to be focused through the physical presence of the artist, but the unity of self to which we attribute the creation is not the artist's body. Looking to the body and its biology for an answer always leaves something missing, something that contributes to the presence of form.

Looking for the Unity of Self

Many areas of research are directed towards the question of how the unity of self is generated. Surely, in this, an initial and crucial step for researchers is to clarify what they are looking for. This can be achieved through careful reflection alone. In understanding where exactly this mystery lies and what form it takes, philosophy has a significant role in this research. Somehow there is the transfer of form, of information, into the world of objects, whether it happens through a little ant or through big Michelangelo, and we spontaneously attribute this ability to something other than the body, to something we refer to as self, or *me*.

We consider the form giver of our actions to be *me*—I call it *me* and so does everyone else. With this word, we refer to the underlying unity that holds intention and injects purpose into physical processes. But where is it and what is it? If to reply that it is made of body, intellect, and will, that would simply split the problem into concepts that themselves need clarification and, in any case, would make three things and not just one *me*. Of course, this is a vintage debate, and through the ages, the question has been presented in many different guises. In the present context, *self* or *me* is linked to the expression of intent with the suggestion that it might be the experience of having intent. We have an intuitive feeling of being a single self, a single me, but it seems impossible to point at what it is, unless—and this may well be the case—we are looking for the wrong kind of thing and failing to see what is obvious. An error in what one attributes to the concept of self can have dire consequences.

Me is our most common way of referring to the nonphysical. When in our worldview, no place is given to that which is nonphysical, *me* is assumed to be the mental activity (whatever that means) that conceives of the physical and as such becomes a transcendental dimension that gives rise to a dualistic view of matter versus intellect. Assumed to be part of the body yet never ascertainable, the belief in such a me has unleashed destruction in our society, our environment, and the world, for it is the basis of the belief in a divided world at war with itself, split into mind versus matter, heaven versus earth, and all the other versions of the same duality. This unwarranted state comes of putting a blind eye to what was described in the first chapter: that everything knowable is produced through a subjective act of integration that forms both objects of the mind and objects of the world. The act of concept formation performed individually by everyone gives presence to everything we know. Without it, all is formless. Following closely how form arises suggests a coherent way of describing self and the presence of the physical world.

Formative Influence

The transmission of form is often brushed aside in our explanations of how the world works, and yet something other than a physical process, made up of a causal chain of events, is required for things to be what they are. Just as the creation of a sculpture cannot be explained by physical actions, neither can the creation of anything, for everything has form in the sense of recognizable qualities that make it what it is. To grasp how form enters a physical object, it is necessary to find a description that is free of our habitual way of understanding cause and effect.

The Aristotelian distinction between material causes and formative causes differentiates between the punctual strokes of the chisel, a material cause chipping away at the block being sculpted, and the formative cause, a form-creating influence that brings about a meaningful result. Chipping at the stone sculpture takes place over time and implies the presence of an integrating influence that correlates the individual strokes so that together they produce a meaningful object. One might contend that all these influences function separately and the result is merely the sum total of uncountable individual nudges issuing from the artist's psychology, emotions, and whatever, which individually pass into the physiology of the artist, and there is no need for interconnection among them. But this would not explain how a preconceived result is achieved, how it is that a sculpture looks like what it was intended to be at the outset, together with any changes of intent that occur along the way.

Actually, using the word *cause* in the expression *formative cause* is not helpful because, today, the word *cause* often has the restricted sense of pushing things around and imposing on events, whereas form-giving is about the correlation of events, a nonphysical connectivity present in an overall field that includes the outcome. It is a process of induction (see chapter 8) rather than causation and involves the presence of self the perceiver and of mind the knower. When these two functions are reintegrated into the description of all that is, causation as an objective independent process breaks down and a new physics is required to accommodate the implications of subjectivity.

To be equipped with a familiar word that refers to the function being studied is itself a step forward in the enquiry. *Intent* names the process whereby an imperceptible influence brings about a movement of integration that leads to a meaningful result. How intent does this remains mysterious, but this is not troublesome here because the goal is not to explain but to form a coherent description of what can be known. We can now add to the understanding of intent the fact that it implies spontaneous interconnection.

Should a question remain concerning the act of integration through which a material object acquires form, this paragraph brings some added reflections. The form of the stone statue is ascertainable only when multiple aspects are integrated and perceived together. Mind is required to connect the toe of a sculpture to the top of the head and, in fact, to connect any molecule of silica with another. To clarify this, take the example of functioning objects. A bicycle is only a bicycle when one knows how it works or when one rides it, and a wristwatch is not a single object until one considers the parts functioning together. As for measuring time, this only becomes a fact when someone looks at the watch with the intent to read time. Observation driven by intent reveals the world, and observation driven by intent is also required to make the assertion that there is a world that functions independently of observation. There is no escaping the fact that intent is a prerequisite for all that shows relationship.

Science was able to dodge questions concerning relationship and interconnection by calling upon the laws of nature—a nonmaterial organizing presence. These hide subjectivity behind something impersonal. Still today, to say that something is *scientific* is to emphasize the fact that it has been purified of personal intent and subjectivity. In this manner, experience has been ruptured into two separate functions, one conceptual and the other physical. A universal obligatory protocol, in the form of laws of nature, is not called for in the case of intent. It relates to individual events, each with its own range of cooperating effects, and essentially, it overrides the dichotomies introduced by the scientific view.

A Sense That Perceives Integration

The basic premise is now clearer: the expression of intent is found in the correspondence between all factors that produce an intended outcome. As the unseen complicity between events engaged in bringing about a result, it is a bona fide element that must be included in any description of the world. Taking account of this hidden bonding inaugurates the search for what is missing in our description of the world.

First, a counter example is offered to exemplify how unacceptable viewpoints become acceptable when the coordination of intent is omitted. The traditional scientific postulate is that causality is universal and is the sole explanatory approach to be applied in elucidating all that we observe. It is related to the edict already mentioned (in chapter 5, "Intent and Reality") and this assumption of universality leaves no place for the function of intent. For example, take the case of an animal or plant gaining nourishment. Initially evident is the fact that a living being senses the need to feed and sustain itself by eating, that is, it senses hunger. The intent to eat is what brings about the sequel: procuring food, ingesting, digesting, transferring nutrients through the body, and so on. These processes are described in detail in the biology classroom. The chemical reactions and other processes involved are explained minutely until the causal sequence from ingestion to excretion is complete, but then the story is left there, while the fact that a living being has the need to find food is forgotten. Motive, being unidentified, is prescinded as if, suddenly, it is no longer required. There is a comical "now you see it, now you don't" to the story, as if the description of stages in the process removes the requirement for intent and the sense of hunger. On the other hand, as soon as intent is recognized and incorporated into biology, the Darwinian attitude that supposes a trial-and-error evolution totally blind to outcomes becomes untenable. (See also "A View of Evolution" later in this chapter.) This is not about science being wrong; instead, it points to the fact that the view—the philosophy—on which the credibility of science is based is erroneous and needs to be replaced.

Then comes the question: With what exactly are the omissions of the classical view to be replaced? What observable manifestations are there of the presence of intent?

As it happens, simply asking this question is all that is needed for the answer to present itself and for the missing pieces of the puzzle to reveal themselves. Signs of intent are present all the time, but lack of clarity over the object of the search lets these occasions pass unheeded. For another reason, too, they remain undisclosed. We employ different words when we refer to the different manifestations of intent, and for this reason, the fact that the different words refer to the same phenomenon is not obvious. With recognition of the function of intent, we discover that our sensory system includes the capacity to sense the effect of intent; in addition to our recognized senses, we are endowed with a sense that registers the occurrence of the integrating effect of intent.

All perception is sensing the presence of intent.

Here is a description of our sensory ability to register intent:

— When integration manifests as thought, *we sense meaning.*
— When integration manifests as feeling, *we sense an inkling* of some presence or *the inkling* to act.
— When integration manifests as emotion, *we experience an emotion, a particular state of being.*

When intent manifests in a manner that enlivens all of these, we sense an awareness of a higher order, for example, *we sense beauty.*

What has just been told gains precision when *feelings* and *emotion* are clearly defined. In the definitions that follow, the word *perceive* is used, as it is everywhere in this study, to refer to conscious perception of an object.

Both *feelings* and *emotions* refer to non-conceptual experiences relayed through the body. However, the way we experience them is very different. Two separate forms of awareness create the distinction between feelings and emotion.

Feelings register in *conceptual consciousness* as an event happening to a subject. A feeling requires a perceiving subject who is affected by the feeling. Like all that enters (conceptual) consciousness, feelings form part of the reality consciousness builds, a reality that includes a perceiving subject who perceives the feeling and anchors what is felt as a presence in time and space.

Emotions register in *expanded consciousness* and therefore do not include a separate perceiving subject who registers the effect as some thing being experienced. Like all that enters expanded consciousness, emotions are states of being, a set of qualities experienced without the intervention of consciousness and without a subject who attributes specific presence to it. An emotion is a self-contained experience without relationship to anything beyond itself. The experience of emotion includes neither the physical world nor a perceiver and for this reason does not become an event positioned in time and space.

An emotion can be spoken of, given a name, and attributed to someone; however, doing so is a separate act not included in the experience of the emotion. The description of the experience of an emotion introduces a subject who describes an object. This necessitates telling what the subject feels. With this, emotion is transformed into feelings.

In conclusion

Awareness is related to sensing intent. We are constantly experiencing intent. What was presented up to this point was that every perception is a result of intent; what is being told now is that all perception is sensing the presence of intent and transforming it into what becomes perceivable. Every experience brings awareness of the effects of intent, and this sustains the experience of being alive. Ineffable perhaps, but an experience all the same, it is the sense of the flux of innumerable unrealized impressions on their way to becoming the acts we perform and the thoughts we perceive.

Intent and the Cultivation of Values

Our capacity to enter deeply into an experience depends on our sensitivity to qualities and values that a given situation reflects. The extent to which we are inspired or moved by a story and able to understand it depends on sensitivities that have been nurtured. Qualities of being such as attention, generosity, elegance, sympathy, courage, and love can be given the chance to grow within us, and if not given this opportunity, they tend to wither. To take one example, kindness is more than a particular feature that is either present or absent in one's character. It is something that can be cultivated, possibly with approaches similar to the way compassion is cultivated through certain practices in the Buddhist tradition. Most indigenous cultures consider it evident that qualities need to be refined, and in their traditions, certain values are nurtured and developed through specific activities and behaviors. In the West, however, this has not been obvious. Instead of cultivating values, we find them imposed in an authoritarian manner by moral codes dictated by state or religion. Why are values not understood as something to be created and discovered by each individual?

The answer to this question necessarily touches on what one believes a person to be. If intent structure is ignored and no place is given to this dimension of being, individuals need to be told what to do. Value, inevitably, is imposed. Without recognizing that a person's nature is formed out of structures of intent, one fails to see the need to allow the development of personal attitudes. Then, our natural instinct to have values can be fed with any doctrine, as it was, for instance, with the dictum *man is evil by nature*—an idea that was able to serve the ends of those entering positions of power. But values are not delivered through commandments; they are generic riches present in an individual in the form of a precious potential that needs to open and flourish.

An old question of mine from long ago was, why is it that, before modern times, tables and chairs had sculptured legs; utensils, tools, and instruments had incrusted artwork; and buildings had turrets, arches, lintels, domes, and decorative relief? What happened to our artistic impulse, to our aesthetic sensitivities? What brought us to cease re-creating the fractal-like patterns that abound in nature? *Functionality* is the proposed answer, but this is wrong. Modern artifacts do not represent increased functionality; what they display is the nakedness of functionality divested of qualities. Another explanation given is that it is a matter of *cutting costs* (justified, then, by *"straight lines are beautiful"*), but today we are alert to the fact that claiming budgetary constraints is a surface excuse that serves to bury a deeper impulse. The deeper fact, here, is loss of a sense of value, which, in turn, is loss of one's deeper sense of self, which, in turn, is blindness to one's connection to everything that holds meaning, which, in turn, is imperviousness to intent.

Simply put, we do not recognize ourselves in the objects we produce. As a result, qualities do not enliven a sense of value, beauty is superfluous, decoration is frippery, and my table's legs are straight. I live separated from those who created the plain artifacts that fill my world and to whom I am grateful. Little or nothing of their intent-world is carried to me through their works. I sense this, sometimes, as a tinge of sadness...of emptiness.

This is an account of what we see superficially around us. Beneath this, deeper currents that carry meaning and nourish our actions are somewhere present. Yet, even so, this description is an illustration of how our attitude towards intent can mold the society we create.

Intent versus Entropy

With the words *intent* and *intention*, we reference the cohesion through which diverse factors produce a particular result. Even if we have not consciously defined intent in this way and wish only to refer to the intended result, cohesion is implied. The significance of this definition is brought into focus when we contrast two separate forms of relationship: intent and entropy.

To begin with, here are a number of contrasting features.

INTENT	ENTROPY
Ordered	**Random**
Intent brings unity of purpose and thus signals order and meaning.	Entropy is a measure of disorder and randomness.
Subjective	**Objective**
Intent involves engagement to a purpose and reflects a subjective state.	Entropy is information about an objective state.
Time	**Space**
Intent, being outcome oriented, implies time but makes no reference to space.	Entropy is a description of the spatial arrangement at a given moment and is without time. In cases in which entropy does not describe a physical state, the spatial aspect takes the form of a copresent array of data.

Prior to perception
Intent, as the coming together of parts to form a whole or an outcome, is the precursor of what will manifest as the intended object.

Subsequent to perception
Entropy is calculated from an already present objective state.

Self-contained
Intent is self-determined and indifferent to imposed boundaries. It is everything that pertains to a certain result and is always total and complete. What does not relate to that result is simply not part of that intent.

Externally bounded
Entropy relates to a closed system with boundaries that limit a region of space or, in the case of information, that limit the relevant area from which data are gathered. The perceiver registering the data views the system from outside, even when the entropy considered is that of the entire universe.

(This brings up a recurrent question: If information is lost from the universe, would this affect the entropy of the universe? Surely, to respond to this, one would first need to show that information is, in some way, part of what we call the universe and something the universe can lose.)

Generating meaning
The intent to achieve a certain result generates meaning. The meaning created is the outcome—a realization in the form of a concept or an act. All the factors that pertain to that intent cooperate in and contribute to its formation.

Imposing meaning
Entropy does not determine an entity; it does not form the object that is measured. Entropy makes sense only within predetermined boundaries. What constitutes entropy is the aggregate of individual events that form no-thing.

measure of togetherness; entropy is ever a measure of loneliness, for, even when small, it is a measure of how much a given system is random, which is to say, meaningless.

Intent offers a system of behavior that completely bypasses causality. Where there are life forms, there is a drop in entropy. This can be explained by considering the life form together with the environment and showing that when the closed system includes both together, there is no overall reduction in entropy and the principle of conservation is maintained. But is this really the question? Surely, the question is not about balancing entropy but about creating form and order? How does life do this? And to this question there is an answer: Through intent. But to the person with an entropy-trained viewpoint, there is no such thing. This is because intent is a whole other process and to include it is to set forth a very different world than the one commonly described.

A dramatic illustration of the contrast between intent and causality is apparent if one makes a diagram of each. Intent ends in a single point that is the intended outcome. It has no specific origin but branches back through ever more distant (in space and in time) items that are participating in that intent. This was described in detail earlier in this book (e.g., in chapter 5, "Intent with No Ascertainable Source"). On the other hand, causality begins from some initial effect—for example, striking a chime that leads to other events (vibrations of the metal, of the air, and beyond)—and dissipates through the universe. In forward-moving time, causality proceeds from a single event and branches out into uncountable effects; in contrast, intent springs from uncountable effects that cooperate to create something whole that is a single outcome. Described in this manner these two contrasting views of the world are inverse functions: causality and intent portray reversed images of the same thing.

Entropy is a still-frame snapshot of the process of causality that views a world coming apart into separate bits—today one might choose the term *deconstruction* for this. The complementary movement of coming together might then be called *holistic*, being the fusion of diverse elements to form a unity. A felicitous realization is that negative entropy—negentropy—whose presence is questioned, is alive and well and even carries a name with which we are all familiar. This antientropic movement is what we call *intent*, and its function is complementary to that of entropy.

Intent: How It Functions

A quality sensed or inferred
Intent is never an object of consciousness. Either it is an experience sensed by the subject or its presence is inferred from the result it produces.

An object recognized
Entropy is the state of a system, an what is measured manifests in the behavior of its constituents.

The intent view
For intent, maximum entropy is formless. It is without intent and carries no meaning. On the other hand, zero entropy is the presence of meaning.

The entropic view
For the entropic view, the introduction of intent lowers entropy and manifests as order. Wherever intent is lacking, there is disorder and an increase in entropy.

In this last point, in one simple fact, we find an epiphany for this whole discussion of intent and entropy. That which science recognizes as natural and formulates as a basic law of nature (the second law of thermodynamics) is loss of meaning. To the objectivity-seeking scientist, the opposite extreme of the natural process of entropy is a state in which all degrees of freedom are lost. This, from the viewpoint of intent, is what a personal subject intuitively registers as the presence of meaning, direction, and purpose!

Further Discussion: Intent versus Entropy

The familiar tale in physics of Maxwell's demon, who is positioned at a trapdoor letting certain molecules in and keeping others out in order to produce a lower entropy state, appears in a different light when the contrast between intent and entropy is noted. Loss of entropy, to the extent that it is gain in intent, is not achieved through the demon's kind of intervention but through integration—something the rational mind knows very little about. It is to allow for the possibility that molecules by themselves lead the way to the low-entropy state or, more correctly, to a formed state, and everything in that intent-rich environment is conducive to that end. It is achieved through the influence of purpose, not causality. If to include the tale of the demon, one needs to imagine it as having fun doing what the molecules themselves are doing, cooperating in their purpose rather than tricking them! Intent is a

Objective versus Subjective

Entropy and intent reflect two contrasting views of the world. One is the objective view of classical science in which laws of nature rule the world and every action results from preceding causes. The other is a subjective view of a world without laws that authorize what is possible. In it, events are directed towards a specific outcome, and to be alert to this world, a person is attentive to where activities lead and to the correlations that produce a particular outcome. To sense the objective world, a person is unconcerned by such correlation and, instead, is attentive to local energy-based interactions.

Entropy and intent are opposing structures of perception that never meet. When we focus on one, the other necessarily disappears. The physical cause-based world dissipates; the purpose-based intent world anticipates, and its direction is always towards the realization of meaning. The principle acting in the one is loss, that is, a downgrading of structure; the principle acting in the other is gain in that it creates form and meaning. In the causal world phenomena are determined by what precedes them; in the intent-infused world, phenomena show the creation of meaning that promotes yet further unrealized meanings.

A Synopsis: The Intent Circuit

In this chapter, numerous examples of intent were proposed, and the phenomenon has been described in a number of contrasting ways. Right now, before proceeding further, a merry challenge awaits: to formulate a concise, integrated summary of what has been understood so far.

A reminder: The usage of the words *consciousness* and *perception* is in accord with what is noted in the *vocabulary key* in the book's preface.

The Intent Circuit

A. A perception is intent reaching its intended outcome.
B. We perceive it as an object placed either in the physical world or in the mind.
C. When we refer to a particular intent, we name the intended outcome. There is no other way to refer to intent.

D. In naming the intended outcome, we have formed a concept of that intent.
E. The concept serves only to refer to the intent. It is not the intent.
F. Intent is an experience, a sensation, not an idea or a thought.
G. To refer to the experience of intent we speak of *having the intent to…whatever.*
H. We sense intent as an engagement to produce a particular result.
I. An engagement is a duty one assumes. The outcome is what is due.
J. Engaging is the act of assuming a purpose.
K. Purpose arises in a context where an outcome affects what leads to its realization.
L. Through intent, diverse activities cohere to produce a common end.
M. To cohere implies relationship.
N. Relationship is not a physical property. It is nonmaterial. (See in chapter 7, "Self as Belonging.")
O. Relationship is sensed as a feeling, but to acknowledge its presence and recognize it require consciousness.
P. What enters consciousness is the form of the relationship, the way it manifests in time or in space.
Q. What we call *intellect* is the faculty to recognize form, that is, to decipher relationship.
R. Intelligence of form is consciousness awakening to a specific meaning.
S. The perceived meaning is an object of consciousness.
T. *Objects*, *meanings*, and *forms* are what consciousness recognizes. They enter consciousness as concepts.
U. The emergence of concepts in the mind attests to the influence of intent.
V. A concept is intent that consummated its purpose.
W. Meaning is the wake of intent.
X. Intent is not meaning but the potential to form meaning.
Y. Ever subjective, ever potential, intent never becomes an object.
Z. Intent generates the faculty of perception by which objects become known.

This is a circuit. The final statement links back to the opening statement.

The Emerging Vision

This section serves to render in plain terms the view of intent emerging from this and the previous chapter. It is not a conclusion but merely a temporary stopping point to note what is becoming clear while still leaving intact all that is not understood and remains mysterious.

Whatever way we look at intent, it does not seem to have specific limits. The source of intent is spread through space and through time, reaching through the past and sustaining a vital relationship with the future. From out of the unlimited, intent gathers that which becomes the content of our conscious minds. Some examples can help point to what is involved.

Imagine looking for ibex on a distant mountain flank and, while doing so, in your mind you hold a sense of what an ibex looks like. In general this intentional act of preconceiving what you expect to find increases the likelihood of bringing into view what you are looking for. You can hold such intent without consciously expressing it and even without noticing you are holding it, as for instance in the case of someone accustomed to making such observations. In this example of seeing ibex, an intended future influences your observational ability, but might the influence be greater than this and affect the world that is observed? In other words, does the call of intent bring the ibex into view not just for the visual apparatus of the observer but in the world? This would mean that your intent manifests in the world in such a way that the likelihood of ibex entering an intent-laden reality increases. This is similar to the popular suggestion that, while driving, one does well to form the intention of finding a parking space on arriving at one's destination.

This example indicates that intent could cover a range of possible influences. At one end is a low degree of influence where the presence of intent affects the observer's manner of observing and in so doing influences what is perceived; on the other end is a more extreme case in which intent brings about an event in the world that is not physically connected with the observer. Between these are intermediary levels that represent variable degrees of probability for an event to happen. Everyday experiences of serendipity could be included on this scale— as, for example, intending to contact someone and then crossing paths with that person during the day, or to take a different example, the story told of Rolling Thunder, a Native American, calling thunder to manifest. The particular cases quoted here are not the issue and only serve as examples of coinciding events that may be considered significant or insignificant. What is alluded to, however, is the possibility that a range of variable degrees of influence upon the observed world is part of the system that is the world. It is part of how the world works.

A further example is one given earlier about waking from sleep at the exact time one intends. What if, instead of looking for causal reasons, the answer were that the intent to wake at a certain time is a call broadcast to the universe that aligns an intended future with one's present, and the response comes from no particular source in time and space but from everywhere? From that call for a future event, the influence of that intent works *backward* through all that participates in making it happen. It was already noted that the expression of intent does not prescribe the means that are employed, leaving them to arise spontaneously out of the given situation. But the *correlation* of the means is fashioned by intent, and in the present example, this suggests that the outcome of waking at a particular time can have any number of causes. It can happen, for example, that I wake on time because a gust of wind happened to bang the shutter at just that moment. On another occasion, it happens because my arm "went to sleep," and, in this manner, each occasion can have its own cause or no apparent cause. All one can say about the process is that the tendency to awaken inhabits the situation and plays itself out. To some, this way of considering events leaves them uncomfortable, but comfort is not a criterion for being right or wrong. Should you find this description of events a bit spooky, it merely calls attention to the belief structure that determines what you consider acceptable and inacceptable.

These examples carry the suggestion that events do not result from disparate causes but happen in response to a future-determined outcome. The question "Why does something happen?" is answered not by pointing to prior events but by finding the purpose. Only through recognizing what is being accomplished can one answer why something comes about. There is direction to what happens and, recognizing this: events have purpose, motive is present everywhere, *being* is a state infused with meaning, and our subjective view of things—what we understand—has an influence on what actually takes place.

In contrast with this, the classical scientific explanations that are widely accepted are built on independent cause-based reasoning applied to events. These serve to predict what will happen and to interpret what did happen. Such cause-based reasoning is invariable and with it, necessarily, a given cause must always produce the same effect.

Instead of this, intent brings a different viewpoint. It requires specific understanding of each individual situation. The correspondence between divers actions has a purpose-based reason that manifests only with an understanding of where the observed events lead. In this view of the world, the active principle is intent and any interpretation of what happens depends on the observer's sensitivity, on the ability to sense form and direction as well as the cooperation that manifests the purpose of the activity. In other words, a description is not the reproduction of what is observed but is always an expression of how a particular subject integrates what is observed so as to perceive meaning. To acknowledge is to act upon the world. By forming an understanding of what is, we become an integral part of that observation and have an active role that influences what we recognize as the world. Intent implies a way of seeing and of being that eliminates the scission between subjective knowledge and objective reality.

Where Past Becomes Present and Present Intimates Future

This view of the world stands in stark contrast to the standard view that extends reality to the past but not to the future, or to use a metaphor, to a world in which the past is considered as solid ground on which the present stands while the future is *castles in the air* and assumed imaginary until it plays itself out physically in the present. The view of the world that emerges with intent contrasts with this and is of a future that is an integral part of all that happens while the past loses its reality. This can be told as follows.

Through intent, present activity is influenced by what will be and carries import from and to the future. In this way, the future is active in the world. As for the past, the sources of intent are multiple and come from any distance in time and space. The influence of these sources manifests only to the degree they have a present effect; they participate in intent only because they affect present events. In and of itself, the past has disappeared, for there are no autonomous events, only effects. This fact is revealing in that it confirms that intent has no place for classical causality, a world fully dependent on past events, and instead the field of influence of intent is not through a sequence of events but through the formation of meaning.

This is a separate subject, namely, seeing events from the point of view of their impact on the present. It is significant that the structure of the English language includes such a point of view, and there is a grammatical form that expresses just this: the perfect tense of the verb (e.g., to have done, been, seen). Grammar explanations that use a timeline to demonstrate the perfect tense become a jumbled mess because what this form expresses does not relate to time sequencing. It is about feeling and, more specifically, about sensing the impact of some event that happened in the past. This subject is to be part of a separate publication by this author.

Here is a concrete example of this state. A piece of bogwood—a tree that died long ago and lay submerged for millennia—carries its history in its present features. These contribute to making it what our conscious mind recognizes as bogwood, and, too, these guide the effect it has on all processes in which it plays a part, whether pipe making or sculpture. What is active are present effects of past events. These generate the meaning of every object. To the extent one is at ease with the concept of meaning, this is straightforward. However, where the computer is proposed as a model for what happens in the mind, attribution of meaning is not obvious and a few words of clarification are in order.

In a world reduced exclusively to objectivity, things can only be understood as composites made up of bits of other things. We may call these things atoms, feelings, actions, teddy bears, or galaxies, but they would remain essentially meaningless if there were nothing that fused the parts into a single whole. Words are not merely signs that refer to things but are formed by all that comes together to generate the concept of that object. This was detailed in chapter 1. Objects, when recognized for what they really are—subjective creations—become fully integrated wholes that carry meanings in a meaningful world. The activity of integration that brings objects to form in our mind also produces connections between all we understand as real. Taking note of this connectivity reanimates our benumbed sensitivities that rendered reality meaningless and illusory.

The skeletal view of a world of objects lacking rhyme or reason goes hand in hand with the assumption that rational thought is the arbitrator that decides what is real. This does not necessarily mean that feelings are denied, though some did deny them in certain situations, as in the case of Descartes, who promoted animal vivisection without anesthetic, professing that nonhuman animals have no souls and thus can feel no pain. In this intent-vacant view, our sensory system is still accepted as the connection we make with reality, but it is then concluded that *what* we sense and feel is grounded in biology, neurology, and chemistry—in other words, the basis of what we experience is physical and not feeling itself. Even when feelings are accepted to be what a person feels, they are subsumed under a broader, more fundamental category of reality that is comprehensible to rational thought and understood as the interaction of material objects.

In this material view, the nonphysical roles of mind and intent have been left out, and forcibly, our intuitive sense of having a creative role in producing meaning is relegated to nothing but delusion. A change—escape, one could say—from this view is the integration, or reintegration, of intent into all we know. Every perception is an act wielding the intent that allows, in its wake, for the emergence of meaning. Meaning is what consciousness harvests from the activity of the expanded mind and is the fundamental unit of all that is. It manifests as the ever lively present. Everyone wakens to meaning—to a world that presents what is recognizable and exemplifies our ability to comprehend. For this reason alone, the world is filled with vibrant meaning that carries our understanding towards future realizations. The past is the process of integration that becomes present meaning, and the present is carried to further realizations through the action of intent, through intimation of a future. Without the role of purpose, nothing becomes knowable and there would be neither world nor object-seeking scientist.

Romanticism and the Pursuit of Meaning

This reference to the limitations of the material view of perception prompts a historical anecdote. The Romantic Movement that began towards the end of the eighteenth century came as a response to the lack of subjective meaning in the rational scientific view of the world and, more generally, in the intellectual climate of the Enlightenment. Romanticism did not challenge this rational view and instead turned to something different, looking to find meaning and a sense of reality in what is irrational. Depictions and descriptions of feelings of love, admiration, inspiration, and such were presented as the meaningful reality not found in rational science. It seems, however, the adjudicator empowered to decide what is real—whether the material world or the irrational emotional world—was still the thinking mind, but it is not with the intellect that we create meaning, and this escape from sterility did not give place to a satisfying answer. The rational mind, unable to create new wholes, is impervious to the movement that leads to meaning and to the sense of engagement that gives expression to purpose. The inherent futility of the Romantic enterprise did not preclude grand creations in the arts and careful works of reflection; however, an answer to the quest for meaning is found in a more fundamental change that includes the reintegration of subjectivity in all that is known. The recognition of intent for what it is suggests a very different answer to the quest for meaning.

The "Motor" That Runs the World

A simple way, though somewhat crude, to describe the shift from a cause-based world to a purpose-based world is to say that it is a case of having a new motor installed. No longer is the world powered by a system of propulsion in which every outcome is the result of prior events that push or tug things around. Instead of reaction, the world manifests attraction. These are two fundamentally different processes, not simply opposite directions. With intent, things do not happen because the future *causes* what is observed. Cause is generally understood as the application of an exterior force (exterior to the object or to the particles of the object) that pulls or pushes matter around. Meaning does not work like this. Everything that is identified with a particular intent animates its own participation by aligning itself with what will be. This alignment can be thought of as an interior quality, and thus, from their very nature, things participate in the attraction towards meaning not yet manifest. *The attraction towards meaning not yet manifest* can serve as a definition of the function of intent. It is the process of homing in, where mind and world concur in producing a new manifestation. Evolution is towards a future that will make sense.

Evolution is towards a future that will make sense.

This noncausal process requires careful consideration because this fundamental *other way* has been all but excluded from our descriptions, both of events in the physical world and of the processes of the mind. Chapter 8 enters this subject fully and gives an account of a misunderstanding that brought the marginalization of noncausal processes. There, as a way of approaching this other way of understanding, the process of induction is described, defined, and differentiated from causal thinking. With an understanding of how induction works, a separate way of comprehending process emerges, and it serves to deepen the understanding of the nature of intent presented so far.

A View of Evolution

The implications of this understanding of intent—should it prove tenable—would be powerful. Here is one illustration of what is involved that relates to a belief system that has deeply penetrated our understanding of the natural world and of social behavior.

With the action of intent, natural development moves towards a functional result, and what sustains the process is that future option. This nullifies a central premise of the Darwinian interpretation of what we observe in nature. For instance, there simply are no dangling intermediary stages of development in evolution. There need be no *missing link* to bridge the transition stages of a wandering, arbitrary evolution. Every living thing evolves towards what is possible, and the world is not made up of evolving bits that, through fortuitous accidents, broke away from what was. In the macro world and, too, in the quantum world, no transitional stages of anything are to be found, neither as partially evolved organs nor as nonfunctional leftovers—even though, in the past, such explanations surfaced to hide gaps in understanding, as for example the function of the appendix or of glial cells or of dental complications attributed to a supposed evolutionary shrinking of the jaw bone. In time, one after another, these interpretations prove to be flawed. Any change that takes place, whether on a subatomic level, a molecular level, a cellular level, on the level of an organ or of a whole organism, responds to the presence of an intended outcome. All features evolve in a correlated way in order to participate in a particular possibility of being. And why is this? The answer is because its movement is an expression of intent. The influence of the outcome is present from the start, and it brings all that coheres to form that outcome to come to pass. As with quantum phenomena, there is little doubt that the result gives direction to what precedes its manifestation, and, too, that only what is possible is undertaken. The result, one could say, gives the green light for the process that will produce that result to go forward.

Trial and error may be our present way of progressing towards further understanding, but it is not the natural way and in all likelihood reflects the degree to which we have become estranged from natural processes. Evolutionary processes set out in the direction of a goal that is known to be achievable; otherwise, they do not set out in that direction. This is not only true on the quantum level where photons do not make test runs to verify whether a particular final state is available but is true throughout nature: the behavior of larger molecules (spontaneously organizing themselves into amino acids), of enzymes, of organisms, and of ourselves, as when we engage in a task because, intuitively, we sense it is feasible. (Had Brunelleschi relied on calculation and the skepticism of his contemporaries, Florence would never have had its magnificent cathedral dome.) The ability of the world to self-organize is systematically ignored, and underlying principles by which this happens (aesthetics, for instance) are doubly ignored. Recognizing this fact of nature brings a fundamental change in the logical arguments that apply to what we observe as the world. It implies not just that a search for intermediary incomplete structures and for functionless developments in biology is futile but that the Darwinist attempt to justify (with an ever-expanding compendium of interpretations) the presence of a physiological feature or a social behavior found in nature proves groundless. If we accept that formative processes guide evolution and events, a very different world presents itself for observation and appreciation.

There is no place anymore for an understanding that reduces all interrelationship to local interactions on a space–time grid. The search for understanding—whether scientific or personal—opens into new directions and necessitates approaches that will include the action of intent.

Thinking and the Action of Intent

The suggestion that the movement towards meaning describes a world that responds to the presence of intent brings to mind a more obvious case in which the same uncanny result arises. How is it that our thoughts respond to our intentions? What produces logical coherence in thought?

Described in the first and second chapters was the fact that, prior to the formation of a concept, there are no spatial or temporal dimensions, no time or space, with which to structure understanding. Links between words, ideas, images, feelings, and all that is are only set in a time structure when they become our thoughts. Without this, that is, prior to thought, there is the affinity of all to produce meaning in an unlimited number of ways. One could say that from all that has the potential to become meaningful, droplets of meaning condense as concepts. Although beyond our direct control, the condensations fall into meaningful patterns—words into sentences, and these into statements that form arguments or into mental images that cohere to form thought sequences. They follow one another, producing relationships that give meaningful continuity to thought and, too, can exemplify what we know as logic. We recognize the coherence of our thoughts and of our conversation, and we assume ourselves to be the authors of this coherence and, thus, take ownership of our cleverness and ability to perform as rational beings. This happy measure of hubris comes out of not addressing the question: What leads one thought to the next? This is to ask, what sets the sequence of images, sounds, and words that enter the conscious mind? The miraculous way words come together to produce meaningful sentences was noted earlier (see in chapter 1, "Mind Activity Beyond Consciousness"), and in a similar manner, larger units come together to form meaningful thought constructions. There is always a possibility of being incoherent, of jumping from topic to topic and flying helter-skelter through associations, but this is not how we communicate with one another and with ourselves. We produce ideas that interlock to form constructive progressions of thought. Although we can filter what enters our mind and choose certain items over others, most of what comes to mind arises spontaneously. One thought follows another, and we do not really know how and why. Thoughts tend to show coherence we did not consciously produce.

This leads to the conclusion that the thoughts we have are induced by intent in ways that we do not understand. This happens out of consciousness and apparently beyond our conscious control. But it is rather strange. When one thinks and speaks and acts coherently, is one not the individual who makes it happen, the one manifesting this intelligence? Could it be that some greater, unobserved processes of intent influence what I believe is my doing? But, if so, would this influence of intent be the influence of *my* intent? Where am I in all this? These reflections lead to another topic that is discussed in the chapter that follows: What is the self that I name *me*?

Beyond Meaninglessness

Take a handful of coins and drop them on an open space, say, on the carpet. When they settle, look at the pattern they form. Consider it aesthetically as would an artist or master who looks at the forms and shadings on a painted canvas and appraises whether they create balance and harmony. As a youngster, I used to experiment with this and was amazed that the pattern from the undirected fall seemed to be more aesthetically pleasant than when I performed the task consciously by placing the coins (or whatever objects) one by one. Could the aesthetic quality I recognize in the pattern be more than my imagination in the moment of viewing it and have to do with a determining factor that overrules blind chance? Test it further by taking one more coin and placing it somewhere with the others without disturbing the quality of balance of the overall pattern. It is not easy! This game seemed trivial, yet I wondered and I wondered. If coins come together to show balance and harmony, what would be the intent involved? Would it be an expression of some aspect of all that is, or might it be me that affects the display? If an expression of all that is, then what is the carrier of intent? If my state has some influence on the result, could something so diffuse and of which I am not conscious be my individual intent? Turn the page to follow the trail, but take heed not to become entrapped in the expectation of an answer. Rather, let our purpose be to wonder together.

[7]
The Self We Know as "I"

Understanding Subjectivity

Words That Refer to Self

I, *me*, *self*, and *myself* are words that refer to one and the same presence. In the discussion that follows, these words will be employed interchangeably. In some cases, they will be considered as a state of being and spoken of as "the I."

Even though everyone has an intuitive grasp of what is being expressed when saying "I," stating exactly what this *I* signifies invariably leads to an impasse. This is a foray to meet that challenge, so hold tight!

Who Is *I*?

When spontaneously we use the word *I*, as for example "I'm on my way" or "I remember…" we feel the *I* to be close by. When saying *I*, it seems to me as if just behind my actions, my conclusions, my perceptions, I am there making them possible. I am there, seeing what my eyes show, hearing what my ears relay, tasting what I taste, thinking what I think, feeling what I feel, doing what I do. Yet, close as it may seem to be, this *I* remains imperceptible; instinctively, I know it is there, and yet no such entity can be found. Am I present or am I not? The usual tale is that I'm sandwiched between past and future in a squeezed out-of-time moment with a self that occupies no space. But how can that answer be acceptable when I sense that I am a full-fledged being living in a world that exists in time and space? There is a contradiction here and something is not right.

Sensing the proximity of self comes from being anchored to a specific here and now with which I identify. We could think of it as local *little me*, and we sense its position is nearby in the time and space location from which I experience the world. To find its content, however, is an entirely different matter and requires reaching into the vastness beyond all that is here right now.

Who is that absent presence? What is its identity? The answer comes with the realization that who I am is both more than I dare imagine as well as far less. I am *greater me* that can be traced back into all that forms my world, and, too, I am *little me* that cannot be found because it is nothing at all. This can be stated otherwise. If *greater me* is the full intentional dimension from which one draws the way of being one manifests in the world, it is necessarily limitless, reaches through all of space and time, and, as such, occupies no definite position. In contrast to this is *little me*, a handy way of referring to the source of our first-person perspective in the world. It can be thought of as the point where that vast *greater me* drops anchor in the world of time and space and secures itself to a present in time and to a specific position among all that we experience as the physical world. Taken as such, *little me* is a hole in the space and time fabric, formed neither of space nor of time, that marks a certain here and now. That is all it is. It marks a position—the position I have as a physical being living in this world. All we commonly perceive of this physical world is centered on this position, but whatever has to do with *what we are* and *why we are as we are* is a very different matter and has to do with our form as an intentioned being. Intention is not physical. It is forever a potential state, and so, in order to understand who we are, we must pass through the hole, the emptiness of *little me*, to reach beyond the physical world that carries the imprint of intent as outcomes but never as intent itself.

> *Who I am is both more than I dare imagine as well as far less.*

This implies that in first-person statements, *I* stands for what is absent from the perceived world. When someone, living here and now, says *I*, that person becomes the spokesperson for the absent *I*. Becoming a mouthpiece for *greater I* signifies being in the world, which signifies being at a particular moment and at a particular place, and—from that anchor point—speaking for that which has no fixed reference point. Speaking in the name of the absent *I* is the *little me*, who says *I want, I see, I do*, each statement reflecting aspects of the tendencies of *greater me*. From a position fixed in time and space, *little me*, as spokesperson, tells something of how *greater me* manifests when implanted in a specific context. To make this very plain, one could imagine that instead of saying "I want" and "I see" we would say "the *I* wants," "the *I* sees," revealing in this way that everything said is told by *little me* in the service of *greater me*. *Little me* is transposing into a particular situation the general attitude and bearing of *greater me*. What those qualities are will be shown in the two sections that come after this one.

What emerges already from this initial description is a far step from the kind of self we are in the habit of inventing—a self that lords over all, directing the thoughts we create and actions we take. Such a view of self as a transcendent observer/actor is a persistent knot into which our thinking has tied itself. It gives rise to caricatures such as that of a separate me, head perched high, running the business of my life through conscious acts or, possibly, the caricature of an almighty masculine persona thundering his intent through the universe with god-fearing subjects meekly acquiescing, or a third rendition nominates a substitute for that god-power in the form of laws of nature that have dominion over absolutely everything because, in this view, all existence is obliged to adhere to the laws science attributes to nature. These are three humorous, misguided versions of a severed self and they stem from the erroneous assumption that purpose-directed activity is possible only under one condition: when an intelligent being endowed with conscious thought premeditates the action that is taken. The error in this is surely quite apparent after what has been presented in the previous six chapters. Purpose-directed activity is necessarily independent of thought, for it happens with intent and in the absence of consciousness.

A new understanding is needed: one that loosens the distinction between intellect and inert matter, between subject and object; one that allows a zone where presence with duration is experienced and where the impression of intent can generate movement towards meaning.

180 | *Making Sense*

Forming the Concept of *I*

With the division into *little me* and *greater me*, the question of *I* has not been resolved, but a way of speaking about the subject of self has opened. The next step is to consider specific questions. How is the anchor point of *little me* formed? By what process did we arrive at the concept we already have of *I*, and what exactly are we referring to when we say *I* and *me*?

Chapter 1 told of how a concept's content emerges from a fusion of aspects, most of which are imperceptible and do not themselves enter consciousness. The way this happens through the influence of denotative intent was described in detail. In the present context, we can trace the same process and examine how, in the same manner, the concept of *I* is created.

Let us now follow this process of concept formation in the case where *me* or *I* is the concept being formed. With denotative intent, as always, we set out to find an entity, and in this case the entity aimed for is our personal self. What happens when we do this? In terms of the twofold movement of mind summarized earlier, one movement is set on producing a denotation and the second, the connotative, gathers meanings from the expanded mind beyond consciousness. However, in the case of oneself, only the first movement is possible. In answer to the denotative quest comes a focus on the moment of experiencing, on the here-and-now moment that is the formation of an object as a concept. But, where meanings should come forward to produce a concept, the process fails. No attributes of the concept of self come to mind. There simply are none! One might object and say there is the content of, say, one's physical traits, tall or plump, or of one's temperamental traits, being kind, careless, enthusiastic, or there is the content made up of one's achievements, but all these are external miscellanea one attaches to self. They arise later and are not the reflexive movement that is the source of the sense of self.

Half the process of concept formation is all that is accomplished. Denotative intent manages to settle on the moment of recognition of *I* but cannot bring content to what is being pointed at because attributes are lacking. This is the emptiness of *little me* that has no qualities of its own and is the up-front anchor point of intent that reaches back though all the universe. Between these two moments, punctual *little me* and expansive *greater me*, what exactly do we allude to when saying

I? Actually, reference is to both of these, but it is accomplished through a different process. The fact that no content comes to mind to give meaning to the concept of *I* implies something quite different is involved.

That which gives the sense of self is a little pull, yes, a little tug that comes from the purpose in which I am involved. Through intention, I am engaged in a certain purpose and sense a certain call to act—whether with my mind, emotionally, or physically. To state this more directly, it is not on the level of concepts and qualities that I sense my presence and that I am able to refer to myself but through the feeling of being prompted to act in a certain way. I become me through relationships and behaviors that I, an intentioned being, generate in the world. This engagement in life is what I sense as my self, and it is a manifestation of *greater me* that gives the form of my intervention or, one could say, gives form to my participation in the world.

In this way, *I* refers to all that forms my presence: the way I smile and cry and go about a task and, too, what brings me to smile, to cry, and to act. It includes all I feel and all those sensitivities that give rise to my feelings, to my understanding, to my gestures, behavior, thoughts, and all that forms my way of imagining, hoping, enjoying, and being bored. Nothing I am is irrelevant, and all that I am is there in the word *I*, not just what I am sensitive to now but what makes me sensitive to what I am sensitive to, including my purpose, values, mission, vision, and all that is my way of being. Every time we say *I* or *me*, all this is called in. Quite baffling, is it not?

Our understanding of self reaches far beyond the rational content of the concept *self* and delves into intent and into all that makes us a living being. To say *I* is to sense *I am* and the connection to all that is. This fact surfaced at various points in the previous chapters and now it becomes even clearer. Intent and being are intimately bound together. Being and intent become presence and *I* is the moment when such unity is acknowledged.

All beings have a sense of self

It is noteworthy that what determines our sense of being and our sense of being alive is intent. The same is surely true for *all* that lives. This realization creates a break with Western traditions that, since earliest times, have held a disparaging attitude to non-human forms of life (more precisely, to beings that were not male humans). The prevalent assumption was that beings that are different from us are of lesser intrinsic value. The misconception involved is blatant once we realize that the experience of self, of *I am*, registers with intent and is not at all dependent on the formation of concepts or on verbal communication. Sensing that I am a living being is not in any way the privilege of human beings; all animals and all that lives have this sense of self that comes to expression through intent. It is this purposefulness that animates all beings and not the vacuous concept of self-preservation, a *survival instinct*, that is supposed to exist as some senseless functional motor pushing every living thing towards self-perpetuation. All beings are the manifestation of intent; realization of this intent is the accomplishment that we aspire to—you, me, and every living creature. For us, as humans, just as for all beings, it is an intuitive experience and stems from our intent relationship with all that forms our world.

In conclusion

The descriptions in this section point out the reason why self has long escaped detection. Self does not register on the receptors that were used to search for it. What is required is an antenna that picks up intent. As has been plain all through this work, self has its form in intent. I know I am because I sense a connection to the intentional being that I am. This sense of *I am* registers upon mind or body only to the degree that they manifest the presence of intent. The source of *I am*, together with the source of intent, is spread through everything.

This dynamic view of oneself is held, in English, by a little word of one letter, and to question what it signifies leads our reflections as far as we are willing to go. The trail we are on is still marked for a limited distance ahead, and readers are invited to take part in this journey for some way yet before stepping aside onto paths of their own making.

Self as Belonging

The little tug of intent (mentioned in the previous section) is what brings a sense of self, and it comes from intentions that mold one's individual engagement in life. This set of commitments (intentions) is a kind of identity zone. Each act or thought one performs that enlivens this zone gives the feeling of being in touch with oneself—one's self that is sensed as a way of being, as the personality and character with which one is familiar. Self-identity, the sense of being someone, comes through participation in one's own nexus of connections. There is nothing absolute about a particular nexus, and it takes on reality through repeated activation of the same commitments—rather curious since it shows that habits have much to do with the person we consider ourselves to be and the person with whom we feel at home.

When I look up at the night sky, I sense a moment of elation. In addition to a general sense of wonder, this experience has a particular quality that has to do with my fascination with astronomy and a lifetime of involvement observing, studying, and speaking and thinking about celestial objects. This interest is an engagement or commitment I uphold that makes glancing at the sky an act of reconnecting with myself. I reconnect with the nexus of intentions that influences my pursuits. Self is sensed as the recrudescence of a certain attitude one entertains that fosters the formative process to which one is committed. It is like the artist who, with each brushstroke, reconnects with the art-being she is and with the sense of what she is doing—painting a painting and so much more. The same is true of the musician composing, the player performing, the parent parenting, the businessman reckoning, the beggar waiting, and the nun or monk meditating the emptiness of self. The sense of participation can come from a tradition one upholds or from a role or attitude one typically adopts and with which one connects through one's actions and thoughts and feelings. Identity, one could say, is a sense of belonging.

The connectivity implicit in everything one does is a manifestation of intent. The first two chapters of this work described how intent is necessary for every act of perception. Now we find that all a person comes to know reflects biological, cultural, psychological, and further structures that are part of the nexus of intentions of the perceiver. Thus every observation, which is to say, every moment of consciousness echoes the identity of a person and, whether attested to or not, awakens to some degree the sense of self. Every moment in which consciousness is aroused signals participation in the formative process that is the passage of intention into action, and this generates what we experience as a connection with self. Through intent, one constantly re-creates the world one knows, and with this comes self-identity, not due to the object perceived but because of the nexus of intent re-activated each time.

In this view, self is not a thing one can point to but the action of a formative process that creates connections that enliven one's identity as an intentioned being. We are part of all we know and all we interact with and are thus part of all that is. Surely, this is what we feel spontaneously all the time—a sense of being in touch with our surroundings, our imaginings, with nature, and with life.

In order for this description of the experience of self to become obvious, one must cast off the common belief, most likely unacknowledged, that to be part of something is to be physically connected with it. Connection is never physical. *To be part of* is to partake in form, and this means being part of something nonmaterial. As an example, you are *part* of a train journey not because you are materially transported in the carriage but because you partake in its movement and travel together in a certain direction. It is participation in the train's vector and not in its physical composition. The carriage, too, is part of the train for the same reason (traveling together with the locomotive or relating to it so as to form the concept *train*) and not because it is hitched to the locomotive. And did you know that your nose is not yours simply because it is attached to the middle of your face but because you partake in a common purpose—whether actively or by its participation in forming your face. Self is the formative process that brings connection and allows things to link together and be part of one another. We experience self as a sense of participation and nothing more. It is empty of being any separate thing and yet, as the manifestation of a nexus of intent, is so much more than any individual thing could be.

Relationship as described here is very different from the way it is usually thought of in the physical world. It is different in that no one sets a time and place to meet, for there is no when and where and instead relationship takes place in being, that is to say, it happens through mutual participation that gives form to some way of being. It is not an encounter between two objects but a communion where being is shared. And who is to tell whether, even though we do not recognize it, this kind of intercourse is present in all we know and is happening between beings everywhere in the world including plants and animals—all of them expressing relationship and intermingling in ways we are not attuned to perceive? If so, the world

The world must be permeated by an overwhelming intimacy.

must be permeated by an overwhelming intimacy that surely, were we to drop the dominance we give our rational filters, could be sensed and known and shared.

The Song and the Silence

One can find a rationale for the materialist who denies self just as for the scientist who excludes it, for they concentrate solely on the world of the self, that is to say, the world to which self gave rise but never itself entered. Thus, although reflected in everything they observe and consider, the self is not the object being studied. With this, the tale of *I* has been left unsung because *I* is not about anything—it is not about any thing. It is becoming.

Tales and songs in our culture are typically *about* things, about discoveries and behaviors, about feelings and intuitions, about love and conflict, about all that is and all that can be. A very different song is that which is not about but *is*. It manifests as the song of becoming, and so, when it ceases, there is nothing. The difference between being *about* and thus pointing at what is and actually being that which is, is enormous. The song of *I* accumulates nothing, builds nothing. It sings the sense of identification, not of self with anything (that again would be *about*) but the identification arising within all that is. It is a song of exultation at the coming together of all that is; it is the ecstasy of fusion—ecstasy at the fact that it happens and not of some particular me that fuses with something other. It is about the intercourse that takes place at the horizon of all that is real and that makes reality possible. *I* comes no closer than this. Out beyond the world we know, in a totality that subtends all our concepts, I am. And never doubt it, you are too, your *I* and my *I* with nothing to separate them.

An object always stands in opposition to the subject taking it in. But the subject, it turns out, is a vortex with a hole that leads out beyond everything real. Instead of an entity that completes the duality of subject–object, there is nothing. No *I* is present in reality to form duality. Playing with words, one could say the subject, who is the in-taker of all experience, is in fact out and is only referred to in absentia.

Isn't this fun! It's like *Hide and Seek* or, maybe, like *Snakes and Ladders* with one long slippery snake that slides you right off the game board! Who wants to play when the rules are being broken, not by a player but by the pieces that constitute the game? In chess, the queen can do it. She can leave the board and come back again without anyone being concerned with what she's been up to; in fact, she can be producing clones of herself. But try doing it with the king—try bringing him back after a checkmate exit. Who can tell, maybe he's always been waiting in the coulisses for just this. What needs to be outside in order to have a chessboard game or any game? What encircles the stones marking territories on a *Go* board? What closes any space and any concept? What makes for a world of stars, galaxies, and mysteries that closes around us—whether at measurable distance or in the immeasurable?

Beyond everything that is known is the knower, and we forget to take this into account. Actually, we forget not so much because it is left out but because it is left in. With a vague sense of what is going on, we attribute presence to the observer and imagine it to be a subjective presence somehow contained by a preexisting world, but then, when looked for, it recedes beyond the bounds of all that is known simply because it never was there in the first place.

Dimension comes to the world and encloses all within infinity through participation, through the communion among all that is. The movement of communicating is self, and it includes all selves participating in the realization of this world. Self stems from intent, and intent resides in the unknown, in what is imperceptible beyond all that is taken as reality. Intent preempts all futures but only potentially, and the bridge from potential to actual is the movement of self that ends each time an object takes on form. Every conscious moment ends the presence of *I*.

Could this then be the answer to the question of what lies beyond the boundary of the game and makes a game into a game? It must be the intent to play. The intent to play generates the subject that carries that intention into practice, forming the game that is played. One can find the subject only in the movement towards realization, for *I* is the song being sung of a potential being realized. After that and with realization, all becomes silence while, in some other place, chatter begins *about* the game, *about* how it is to be played, and *about* how it went.

The Disappearing Self

It is gradually becoming clear that *I* is the experience of being in relation—a relation with all that is taking form at any moment in the movement from potentiality to actualization. *I* points at a birthing process that brings forth meaning as an idea in the mind, as a sensation in the body, or as an observation or act attributed to the world. Simply put, what we call *I* is the experience of partaking in the activity that links intent to its outcome. This is ever an intimate process, inseparable from the subject that generates it. This, surely, is no surprise, for how could *I* not be subjective?

How is it, one might ask, that the function of *I* is relatively simple to describe and yet it is not widely recognized? What makes its presence and its abrupt disappearance barely noticeable? Three factors that mitigate the experience of self during the act of perception are noted in what follows.

Hardly Conscious

First, the experience of self that comes with the process of performing an action or producing a thought remains mostly out of consciousness. What we can notice of ourselves during the activity of bringing something to realization is fleeting and delicate and is easily erased and replaced by the presence of what is produced. The same happens when looking at something: the act of seeing goes unnoted, and the object seen engages our attention.

Inserting an Imposter

Second, there is the wish to prolong the fleeting experience of self, which leads us to insert an imposter to take the place of *I*. This is how it happens.

When perceiving something directly, there is the moment at which the experience of *I* ends. It seemed as if some *I* entity was present just before the process came to its end, and the sudden disappearance of this entity leaves us empty-handed, even bewildered. In the attempt to hold on to what was, we prolong the experience of that *I* by thinking of it consciously and turning what was an experience into a concept. We assume the experience of self just sensed was me and is me and continues to be me even though I no longer experience it. This is a subtle maneuver of thought that we enact over and over.

As an example of how this happens, imagine seeing a flash of lightning and hearing a sudden thunderclap. With this experience, waves of sensations pass through us, and these enliven the sensation of our own presence. They are formed through connections being made, for the most part out of consciousness, with other remembered or imagined experiences that relay the emotion—fear, elation, or whatever—we sense at that time. Immediately after the event, thinking over what happened (maybe with some emotion persisting), we formulate the experience in terms of *I*, as for example, "I was surprised" or "I recall what I experienced then." In this way duality enters and *I* becomes the supposed entity that had those experiences.

This shows how, as conceptual consciousness enters, there is a repositioning and one believes "it was I who experienced the perception." In other words, from the act of perceiving an object, one deduces the presence of self. However, in so doing, the word *I* has changed meaning and is employed to refer to something objective, to this entity (whatever it might be and typically imagined as being inside the body) that perceives something other. It is as if one object called *I* is observing another object. *I* is now a concept and has fallen from the position of experiencing subject to being just another object. Failure to notice this mutation leads easily to futile wrangling over the nature of *I* and the place of subjectivity. With humor, one might note here that *self-consciousness* is an oxymoron (*self-realization* too), for where there is consciousness (i.e., conceptual consciousness as described in the vocabulary key in the preface), no longer is there self. Self makes its exit the very moment that what is intended comes to realization as an object that occupies consciousness. To offer an analogy: Like a river upon reaching the ocean ceases to be a river and loses the features by which it is a river, so intent on attaining the intended goal ceases to be intent and loses all the qualities of intent. As is shown later, in the movement of intent towards its end, there is self.

It is surprising to note the extent to which the loss of self as a subjective experience, that is, its exit when an intent is realized, is ironed over by substituting an imposter, the object *I*, which is supposed to be the same as the subject.

The Flux That Is Self

A third reason for not registering the loss of self at the termination of acts of perception is because the actual loss is dissipated through the superposition of many different experiences of self. Any number of processes of self can be in progress at any moment so that the sense of self is a weave of superimposed realizations in progress. As one object enters consciousness, others are still forming: sights appearing before us, sounds being heard, feelings felt, and imaginations forming in the mind, and all of this together holds the sense of self vibrant. Each realization in its turn comes to a conclusion while those that have not yet gelled sustain an ongoing experience of self. Subjective experience is this interlaced sequence of many moments on their way to becoming conscious. There is no objective self, only the experience of the formation process that, like a background hum to which we have become accustomed, sustains the sense of being and of being present.

Sensing the Departure of Self

On occasion, we actually do have a fleeting sense of self's disappearance. For example, imagine working at an intricate miniature construction or being deeply absorbed either listening or reading when a sudden disturbance shakes you out of your concentration. There is a moment of disorientation, a kind of "where was I?" or "where am I?" Losing the net of connections that was the experience of self leaves one momentarily baffled until a new relationship is established for self within the new context. Experiencing self as connectivity means being without the concept self, and in being shocked out of that integrated experience of self, there is loss of the relationship that upheld the sense of I.

The concept "self" acts as a proxy for something that never enters consciousness.

In contrast to this kind of process, one can point to a second, very different, experience of loss of self that takes place when one enters a calm state in which thinking gradually subsides and the sequence of perceptive acts that animate thought ends. With the release of denotative intent comes release from the progression towards specific realizations that is the experience of self. In contrast to the first example of the rupture of the sense of self through a disturbance, this second case is the silent release of self that does not end with an object and does not activate the dichotomy of self and other.

Cooperation

The concept *self* acts as a proxy for something that never enters consciousness—something that is not mind and takes its form, instead, in intent. Conscious thought leads to the assumption that a leader, transcendental to the intent-carrying activity, is responsible for the presence of intent. This is so because thinking brings the paired duality of thinker and thought, of actor and act, of subject and object and requires a separate entity in the role of an independent intelligence that directs what is assumed to lack intelligence. How are we to escape conscious thinking and the need for a causal agent?

It is possible to consider this question without offering an explanation. For this, the image of an anthill can, once again, be of service. The queen ant does not direct the actions of individual ants, commanding what they should do from a blueprint she has of the anthill. In her presence, the functioning anthill simply happens and no one knows it is happening until you, with your thought, come along and conclude that there is form and purpose in the activity of the colony of ants. For the ants to perform successfully, there is apparently no need for this conscious view. Events relate to one another without the intervention of a conscious directing entity. This suggests that every event influences every other event, or to use a metaphor, that some binding viscosity transmits the influence of each act to the others. The intelligence of the anthill is this transmission. Interconnection happens without being known. Like fish or insects moving in formation, any single movement is transmitted through all and there is a group response. The process is blind because no one is watching, no one is interpreting, formulating, or commanding what happens. Unknown and unobjectified, it happens.

In contrast to this is the doctrine of classical science, in which inanimate matter is the foundation of the world. From this ensues the assumption that the world is accidental and, for that reason, thought and understanding are separate from matter. But to view thought as separate from matter overturns the dictum that all is fundamentally inanimate and that life is an accidental product of inanimate matter. Not surprisingly a further assumption that claims that thought and understanding are accidental by-products of complex living systems was added. In this way, the dichotomy of leader and led is upheld, and the duality it implies (but does not admit to) is folded back into some "not yet explained" function that directs inanimate matter—a hoped-for physical replacement for mind under the influence of intent. One contention has been that genes could fulfill this role. This is an example of tucking the unknown into the known and assuming an explanation will emerge. Today one can find leftovers of this same attitude in the search for the source of consciousness, of reason, and of the mind in nonclassical quantum exchanges within the living organism. If this search is for a separate functioning intelligence that directs what supposedly lacks such intelligence, then the motivation for this search, whether or not it achieves positive results, is part of the same mistaken quest.

For very long, the discipline of science, because of this founding doctrine, fought off views that suggest direct interrelation and it floundered at any suggestion of some inherent understanding and cooperation between events. Science and institutions that accepted the scientific belief structure thought that, without positing an outside intelligence (whether mind or god) to direct events, there is only randomness. But it appears that with such a criterion, most of what we observe in nature has been left out. Classical science explains marbles rolling down inclines and maybe carbon atoms oxidizing in a flame, but it does not explain the commonality of function we experience everywhere we look, not just flocks of birds in flight, schools of fish, the movement of swarms of insects, the rhythmic sounds of cicadas and of coyotes but, too, the branches of a tree that *know* not to run into each other, cells working together to allow for a functioning organ, and an untold number of processes like reproduction, digestion, and growth. Countless other less readily accepted examples await acknowledgment, such as a common accord between different species and between all forms of life, and even within aspects of inanimate nature, such as atoms or molecules adhering to one another in specific ways and forming specific structures apparently of their own accord.

Taken together, these thoughts reflect the attitude that the world may well be replete with interrelating phenomena. A study of such cooperation that pays attention to the presence of nonconceptual communion could lead to a very different understanding of the world and ourselves.

A Dynamic View of Self

Communion inherent in group action, as mentioned in the interlude above, illustrates intent becoming action without any role given to thought. Self is present but cannot be summed up in a picture or a word as a concept and has to be grasped as form unraveling through time. There is nothing new in this. For example, a story, too, has a form in time that cannot be encapsulated as a momentary object; and so too a song, a voyage, a disappointment, and so on. It is not really different from the earlier tale of the sculptor forming a work of art with separate actions coordinated over time. This *through time* view of self does not give satisfaction to the rational mind that requires a concept—something without duration in time. But this fact should not be troublesome because by now it is clear that the rational mind presents but a segment of what we are and what we know.

To satisfy the conceptual mind there must be a term or sign that refers to this particular unraveling thing, and the words just mentioned, *story, song, voyage*, and *disappointment*, serve this purpose. When named with specific words or signs, the experience has been extracted from time and formed as a concept. As such, it becomes a category to which the individual item belongs, and, in this way, the conscious mind gains access to what is extended through time. Even though concepts do not reflect the specific sequential content, they form objects to which consciousness can point. This process, one might note, serves as another example of how the expanded mind, hidden from conceptual grasp, is present and adds a wealth of meaning to what limited conceptual consciousness takes hold of. By employing concepts, consciousness erects a world of apparent objectivity that sustains the illusion of reality. On the other hand, it knows nothing of the experience of participation in the common accord that happens only where no independent objects exist and where no concepts are formed. It is here that we can find the unfurling of self. Whether forming a concept (self in the process of conceiving) or creating physical events (self in the process of doing), integration happens in the absence of consciousness.

Examples were given of coordinated effects in the natural world that do not require the insertion of a coordinator placed outside the system, neither as a separate intelligence nor as a set of natural laws. Multiple events uniting to produce a result form a self-contained process that is not divisible into subject and object. To recognize its presence demands a different way of understanding. It can be illustrated with a grammatical example. Although not explained as such in grammar books, this other way of understanding is the deep sense of the continuous form of the verb: to be + *verb*+ing, for example, *the sun is shining*. The continuous mode tells of activity without separation between the active agent (the subject) and the action performed. It expresses action without a cause; action that simply happens. It refers to a state of pure subjectivity. This is to say, a sentence with the verb in the continuous form refers to what was happening the moment before that sentence came to mind and the speaker took cognizance of what was happening. It refers to the experience of the single functioning unit that was directly experienced until the sentence intervened. (This explanation draws upon what was said in chapter 1, "The Temporal Present.")

Self is the unifying presence that comes to expression in coordinated activity and never becomes an object of consciousness. It manifests over time. It is the *coming together* that, when accomplished, forms the perception that monitors the fact that self *was* present. When this process is misunderstood, objects are imagined to already possess the concept by which they are known—a view that does not at all follow from what has been told in these chapters. The misunderstanding recedes when one realizes that the perceiver's intent is instrumental in generating perception and self is present in the coming together generated by intent.

What has been described here is the experience of *I*, of being oneself. Unity of action through coordinated activity is the expression of self. As such, self manifests duration. Unlike the self we refer to with the conscious mind and imagine to be a static timeless subject observing what is perceived, self-in-action is neither watched nor watching. It comes into being in the communion between events that, together, produce a specific outcome, and it disappears instantly when the purposeful action ends. Self engaged in any task, for example, self conceiving, is self-in-action and it cannot be objectified and extracted to become *the conceiver* or *the doer*. Self is the subjective experience of correlated activity in the process of forming a result.

Self emerges where events function in a coordinated manner, or to put it simply, self is the coordination within an ensemble of actions releasing a common purpose. This simple remark is, in fact, the answer to a pervasive enigma concerning self that comes to the fore repeatedly in philosophy, science, psychology, and the arts. It will be discussed further in the remaining sections of this chapter.

Taking the Definition Further

Self, the subject, can be understood as having no presence separate from the correlation of events. It arises together with the act of integration and disappears when it terminates. That no one is *there* is certainly strange: oneness is acting though no one is there. To say *no one is there* is an example of conceptual thinking that requires a presence within space and time; in contrast to this, oneness in progress has no spatial reference and is spread through time, uniting what happens in different places and at different moments. With no fixed presence, self, as process, is the becoming that manifests as acts that lead to the realization of a particular outcome. Thinking in these terms requires practice, for we are not inclined to release our grip on the concept of self as an object in order to perceive it as something that sprouts here, there, and everywhere whenever concepts form in the mind.

Given that self is to be found in the communion that integrates events, where then is the percipient subject? How does this self know what to do? The answer is very simple: it does *not* know! Knowing concerns the separated self: self conceived of as the organizer and not self in communion. But still, one may ask, what gives rise to coherence, what gives purpose and form to actions? The answer comes when we step back and take a wider view and see that communion is the basis of all existence and manifests wherever possible. The communion (or coherence) that manifests in actions of intent is a constituent part of the world. The relevant question, thus, is not "from where comes coherence?" which would be to ask why the world is the way it is but, rather, the more modest question of "how do things interrelate?"—a question that calls for a description of the coherence present in a given situation.

A Pause to Consolidate What Has Emerged So Far

Inherent in all is an impulse to interrelate and produce form. This could be described as an innate social function of existence, and its parallel is reflected in the mind's impulse to form meaning, for to make sense—as told in every chapter so far—is to have things interrelate. Our natural human impulse is part of a universal impulse; the world and our mind are not separate phenomena. Where self attains consciousness of an object, sense is realized through conception; where self produces events, sense is given in the correlation between actions. These are two views of the same thing. Self understood as the knower engages the physical support systems of the body as well as the expanded mind to generate objects of perception; self understood as the doer engages body and mind in coordinated action to produce an event. In both cases, the conceptual mind, limited by consciousness, imagines a separate intelligence as causal agent, something like the once proposed homunculus. However, there is no such entity where action and actor are one. In acts of integration, there is no separate thinker, no separate doer, no objects, no space, no time, no yours or mine.

Neither self-in-action nor self-in-thought has physical presence. Both come to expression when and wherever intelligence manifests in coordinated action that produces understanding or physical results. Self is an objectless state quite out of reach of the conscious mind and is active where nothing is finalized and nothing is named. The moment some *thing* emerges, the functioning self has already disappeared, leaving behind the impression of having been present. From the presence of the resulting object, we deduce the past presence of self that has been, and we assume that it is there all the time—but in any case, time only entered with the final act of integration. In broad terms, self is present in the integration of aspects that share in a common purpose. To have a common purpose has been described already as intent, and so self is the process of movement towards realization of an intention, movement from the unknown to the known under the influence of intent. Only with an understanding of the function of intent can the presence of self be described.

An Impersonal View of Self

Understood in this way, self is described as something totally impersonal. At first this sounds like a contradiction, but it is not, at least not to the extent we are able to let go the old version of self that was the attempt to stuff psychology and possessions into the emptiness of *little me*. One's self comes and goes. It is integration and, when stated as such, seems completely denuded of everything I feel I am. This is so, but beyond this dry technical description lies a reality that is very much me and mine and no one else's, for beyond *little me* is *greater me*, the intent pattern that is active whenever self arises.

This can be summarized as follows. Correlation, which is what self is, arises with the presence of intent. As established in chapter 5, there is no single origin of intent and to search for the source of intent leads out along multiple paths through the physical body, through the mind, and into all of time and space. This is so because the origin is out of the range of consciousness and out of range of sequenced time and differentiated space as conceived of in consciousness. In anonymity, the action of intent unites multiple sources across time and space, and in this anonymity can be found what we call self. Self, as the presence of correlation, is all inclusive yet is not present at any particular *when* or *where*. Once consciousness is roused, the unlimited range contained in the experience of self has to find a spatial and temporal origin. What was ubiquitous and unrestrained collapses into the self we commonly refer to and imagine as being time-referenced and space-referenced and present only in one place at one time. With this, it has become that which consciousness can point to and name *I* or *me*, and it *is* truly I and me, but only *little I*, the stand-in for the full *I* that was released. At the moment of saying *I*, all that was happening subliminally until that moment of consciousness becomes inaccessible and one assumes I was there all along running the show. Of course, I was not doing this! The coordination that brought about events happened in a world of intent that does not enter consciousness.

From Impersonal to Personal

Is it possible to identify with such a strange, seemingly impersonal view of self and claim: *that is who I am?* But maybe it is not so strange; the process itself is familiar. Intent is the tendency to manifest some particular thing, and it brings unity to the activity that produces everything we know. This, in part, is the same intent that repeatedly gives form to my character and guides my thoughts and actions.

We are everything together and nothing on its own.

To allow for this understanding of my self, any thought of who I am needs to be emptied of all that is incumbent in the idea of self as something positioned in time and space and anchored in the sentinel's box, one might call it, that was described as *little me*. What I actually identify as myself is the structure of intent on a much larger scale. I am able to sense the presence of myself through the relationship my actions have with intent—the little tugs and pushes that come of being part of an overall purpose or, as suggested, a nexus of such purposes. It may at first be difficult to accept self as form and not an object, as movement and not a permanence, but that is part of the letting go that allows for a view of self as both formed by all that is and giving form and purpose to all that is known. Self, as described here, arises in every formative process that moves towards a certain outcome. This is what we are: everything together and nothing on its own, the coming together of all that forms our world and nothing separate from it.

To Everything a Spirit

Self is described here as the process of integration and not as what is being integrated. While something is taking form, there is the presence of self. The formative function of intent and the presence of self can be understood only as a nonphysical presence. To see everything as a realization, as an object that forms through a process that necessitates the presence of self, resembles animistic views in which objects are inhabited by an extra something, a spirit of some kind. Perhaps such views refer to what is actually involved in the phenomenon of perception. To acknowledge the presence of divinity in a perceived object is to avoid the clumsy error we have made of imagining self to be part of the physical world. Impregnation by intent—yours, mine, anyone's—

draws upon far more than what is physically present at a particular instant. To form any thing is no small achievement and to recognize this achievement as something sacred is perhaps not that far removed from what a carefully thought through secular view can understand.

The Reign of Objectivity

Viewpoints that embrace mystery have receded, and particularly during the last two centuries, the world came to be interpreted in less ambiguous terms that were accepted as being more useful and more accurate. This view presented—and still does for many—a world formed of physical autonomous objects that interact through the forces they generate. Little distinction is admitted between what lives and what is inanimate, not because all is animate—a belief held by many through recorded history—but because all is taken to be fundamentally inanimate. The world was postulated as being objective, a fact no more open to question than was Euclid's postulate of parallel lines. To contradict this claim was all but unthinkable, and in accord with this, experience and research were systematically cleansed of subjective factors in order to present the perceiver as an unbiased recorder of objective occurrences. Feelings, sensations, emotions, and personal intuitions were not given a place in the postulates of reality and were deemed to be non-essentials that troubled the purity of the observation. The observer was understood as part of the world and had merely the incidental role of gathering information from the surrounding reality.

Paranormal phenomena, unnatural psychic abilities, ghosts, and such were denied a place in the world and were assumed to be misunderstandings that belong to beliefs held by people of lesser intelligence. In the final call, intelligence meant belief in the denotative rational worldview, and any person or culture that understood the world differently was thought to lack intelligence. In this way, the great spiritual, mystical, indigenous folk cultures of the world were viewed as expressions of a lesser intelligence. The world belonged to those who held the truth—scientists, academics, and elite of the scientific worldview—and not to those judged primitive. *Primitive* was a reference not just to intellect but also to values, and thus these peoples' behavior and understanding were deemed of no real value because they contradicted the truth. This attitude gave force to the eradication policies of what was, in essence, an undeclared occidental cultural revolution that eliminated traditions and artifacts within its national boundaries and throughout the world.

The accepted scientific approach, with its narrow-mindedness, led to procedural excesses, ridiculed in the now outdated comedies portraying *the mad scientist*. A commonly portrayed stereotype was of a man with a walking stick, a wooden leg, a monocle, and a partly paralyzed face, somatic twitches, and an interrupted speech pattern that has unnatural jumps in intonation. At the time, it was laughable, and only now, in retrospect, does the full meaning of this inadvertent metaphor emerge. The basis for such madness, unfortunately, was very real and, though hard to admit, was inherent in the scientific approach despite the fact that many of its attributes in themselves appear laudable. Systematically, scientific reports excluded the personal observer. The use of the words *I* and *me* was frowned upon, and writing in the passive form, which lacks an active subject, was encouraged. Reports on observations were described in a language that shows no emotions and no personal tendencies. Double-blinded experimentation and stilted abstracts for academic articles fit with this style. At the time, a phrase bandied about was *untouched by human hands*, meaning uncontaminated. Removing the personal subject had the further effect of absolving the researcher from moral implications. *All in the name of science* was a popular cry when the observer went through hardships as well as when the observed was killed and maimed. The scientific approach had a tremendous impact and was taken up in most disciplines of study. It spread through the world as the intelligent way to proceed, a view reinforced by the technical advances it produced. Very likely, it is in the underlying attitude of the scientific approach, especially in areas where this culture reached its height early last century, that one can find the beginnings of an explanation of the indifference with which those in highly sophisticated intellectual societies maligned ethnic groups, exterminated people, eradicated traditions, and destroyed nature.

Hidden at the base of this approach is a sinkhole formed by the loss of the sense of oneself. The loss of a place for personal sensitivity left a moral vacuity that brought the loss of personal responsibility and the loss of empathy towards all that lives. This madness has its roots in the denial of subjectivity and in the acceptance of objectivity not just as the basis of factual reality but also as a value.

For the past century, very gradually, the view that assumes matter to be the autonomous basis of reality is receding. This goes hand in hand with another, equally revolutionary change that has been slower to surface: the recognition that self, or *I*, is not a member of the same set as the rest of reality. The difficulty of accepting the view that the function of *I* lies outside physical reality may well be the factor that forestalled admittance of the quantum-demonstrated nonfundamental nature of all that is physical. Today, in all fields of interest, profound readjustment from former insensitive attitudes is taking place—though often not by the leading voices in the different fields—and we can finally become part of a change that offers respite from our tired history of destruction.

Self as Precursor to the World

When the personal subject is considered to be an added feature among all that is already in place as the world, a great error ensues. It suggests that self is an objective being occupying a place in the world and that, through acts of consciousness, it transforms an already present objective reality into subjective perception. In this view, the subject is anchored to a position in time and space. We then clothe that anchor point (little me) with attributes such as a body, a personality, possessions, and so forth. What is not taken into account is the fact that self, the correlation that unifies what is observed, is precursor to that world and was the presence that brought together everything that becomes intelligible. This greater action of self is forgotten the moment perception installs its object.

This situation can be summarized in a comic tale. Members of a dull-witted clan tried to verify whether they were all present, but each time someone counted how many they were, one person was missing. This is what results when those who do the counting forget to count themselves. Looking out at the world, we, too, acknowledge all it contains but are oblivious of the self-action that installed such a world. As for the clan, the solution they found was to put their noses in the mud and count the impressions. What will it take for us to realize our error?

To acknowledge that self is not part of the world and is the precondition for the presence of such a world brings a very different view. But to pronounce such a thought sounds preposterous, for, if self is not in the world, where else can it be? To this the answer is found in all that has been stated till now. Physical reality is only *part* of what is, and beyond the physical lies what is potential and engenders what becomes physical. Failure to accept the nonphysical and the attempt to tuck any suggestion of it into something called *mental* have turned the whole subject of self and subjectivity into a labyrinth. Self does not reside in the physical world but resides in intent. Without the dimension of intent, how can one speak of self?

Self is activity charged with a purpose—the coming together of all that forms what becomes perceptible. This dimension of living experience has been poorly recorded in our civilization, and this has led to strange notions about a world isolated in a present instance with no connection to the next moment in time, a world where every event is disunited from all that is, was, and will be. Missing from the description of such a disjunctive world is the integrated activity that has to be in order for any object to become present. Peel back the outer layer of physical reality and one finds the precondition of physical reality in the realm of intent where the coordination that is self is active. And what is self doing there? It is engaged in meaningful activity and, through interrelationship, is producing all that becomes known.

When We Say *I*

The word *I* spontaneously slips into our conversation when needed. Surely, it should be possible to describe in a simple way the specific experience that brings one to say *I*, that prompts the impulse we have to use this word. Setting aside the usual assumption of some *I*-entity physically existing here and now in my biology, what description is possible?

Saying *I* has to do with taking ownership of what is being stated. It shows that perception of the meaning of a statement (its content) is attributed to the person pronouncing that statement. This point needs to be emphasized, for it is a unique phenomenon in language. In employing the word *I*, two distinct *I*'s are simultaneously alluded to: one pronounces the statement (the speaker) and the other perceives the meaning (the experiencer of the content). To say "I feel sad" is to claim the presence of a single subject with a double function: making the statement (about the feeling) and sensing its content (experiencing sadness). The one word *I* integrates these separate functions and as such there is a fusion of two separate subjects into one person.

To take another example, "I cannot do it" identifies the subject who communicates this fact (the speaker) with the subject who experiences that inability (the content). The fusion of these two subjects is not the case with any other pronoun. For example, "you cannot do it" or "he feels sad" does not attribute the meaning content to the one pronouncing the statement.

To add a further example, imagine that, hearing a familiar sound, you realize it is raining. The object that comes to consciousness is rain, and you might employ the expression "it is raining." Saying this implies that there is a subject but does not create the experience of subjectivity. If, instead, you say, "I hear rain," there is *I*, the speaker pronouncing the statement, who, in the same moment, also claims to be the one experiencing the content of the statement (hearing the rain). Two separate roles are thus fused and this anchors the subjective moment.

By saying *I*, a particular thing happens: *what* I perceive and *that* I perceive is attributed to one being and integrated into a single experience. *What* I perceive is the content of a statement (the meaning). *That* I perceive is the speaker who pronounces the statement. Here are three parallel examples:

— To say "the silence at dawn is beautiful" is a statement of *what* is perceived but not *that* it is perceived. Only by deduction does it imply an observer.
— To say "you find the silence at dawn beautiful" states *what* is perceived and *that* it is perceived, but two separate subjects perform these two acts: there is the person mentioned as y*ou*, and there is the speaker pronouncing the statement who does not claim to have experienced the meaning of the statement and might well have been fast asleep in bed during those dawn hours.
— To say "I find the silence at dawn beautiful," thus including the *I*, brings a different situation. It combines two pieces of information: (1) that a speaker was making the statement, and (2) that the speaker making the statement also experiences the silence. While each bit of information on its own is a fact of how things are, their fusion necessitates a personal experience in which the speaker steps in and becomes implicated in the situation.

Witnessing *what* is perceived (a feeling, an understanding, an observation, etc.) and fusing this with the experience *that* it is being perceived call for a moment of personal identification with an event. This is the sensation we are familiar with when we use the words *I*, *me*, *myself*. It is an event that happens only when there is the experience of being present.

The word *I* encapsulates the fusion just described. It is enunciated at the moment when fusion ends in the same manner that a concept arises when the experience of all that comes together to form it ends. This personal identification with the ongoing experience of *I* happens in that moment of fusion. It can be thought of as a separate bubble of being that, as it drifts off, we refer to as *I*. By naming the experience *I*, we tend to anchor it to *little me*, a moment among the events that form the world. This is parallel to what was told of concept formation.

A statement with *I* always produces a situation in which one subject is both the speaker of what is told and the witness experiencing the content of what is told. The observation of the fusion of these two aspects is interesting in that it underscores the fact that employing the first person says nothing about what an *I* is. There is no claim that somebody is present, no claim of some independent entity. The only claim is that the perception of a certain meaning is attributed to the speaker, that is to say, the speaker and the perceiver imply one another. This is all. It says that whatever created the meaning of the statement is the same *whatever* that pronounces the statement. If this *whatever* is not a physical presence, what could it be? Well, this we know already because the previous chapter on intent described just this: it is the nexus of intent connections that forms all that is recognized as a particular being.

Placing the two claimants together, as the word *I* does, is a subtle move that inaugurates a worldview different from the one suggested by a statement where the speaker is not identified as the experiencer of the content of what is said. Statements without *I* suggest an environment made of independent events positioned in an objective world, whereas statements that include the word *I*, thus coalescing the two roles, fold that supposed objective world back upon the subject. It is the difference between a Cartesian coordinate system in which every event has its independent position in time and space and a concentric system centered on the one that pronounces the statement and experiences its meaning.

The fusion of the contrasting positions contained in the word *I* is, in fact, the resolution of a conundrum that troubled thinkers throughout the ages and, in our time, it has sustained a dualist view of reality. Within the expression *I*, incommensurables meet: knowing and experiencing, the cognitive and the sensory, the head and the heart. The pronouncement "I" dissolves the fundamental dichotomy between thought and being, outside and inside, carrier and content, objectivity and subjectivity—no small accomplishment, wouldn't you say?

Consciousness and Self-Consciousness

This context offers an opportunity to add a point of clarification concerning the two forms of relating to oneself. They correspond to what was mentioned, in the vocabulary key in the preface, about two distinct forms of consciousness.

The fusion of the two roles we call *I* (the speaker making the statement and the experiencer of the content) precipitates our intuitive sense of self. This is the awareness of self that does not register in consciousness (conceptual consciousness) but penetrates expanded consciousness, remaining ever subliminal. This experience is separate and distinct from the *conscious* experience of self, in which self takes the form of an object of consciousness and you find that you are consciously thinking of yourself. Employing the word *I* in conversation (*I say, I play, I like...*) requires only the intuitive sense of self that is experienced through expanded consciousness and not a conceptual, conscious grasp of self. Recognizing these two, mutually distinct manners of relating to self, one intuitive and the other explicit, is helpful in clarifying the distinction between consciousness and self-consciousness.

Multiple *I*'s

With the understanding reached about the function of *I*, it is possible to answer a question that is frequently debated. It concerns the fact that saying *I* can give rise to an infinite regression. In stating something about oneself, it is always a matter of one self having an opinion about another self. For example, saying "I am beautiful" leaves the question: which of the two is the true *I*, is it the speaker or the person spoken about?

One reason for believing there to be an infinite regression of one *I* within or behind another is that the moment of fusion is an experience not available to the logical, linear mind. As related in the previous sections, the subjective bubble of experience that identifies speaker and content is referred to after the fact, when the fusion that produced the sense and feeling of *I* is dismantled into two parts. The unity that produced the *I*-statement has come undone.

When one says *I*, rather than regression and a string of *I*'s competing for genuineness, each *I* presents a unified experience that does not depend on the others. These separate presences speak in the name of the absent source, and there can be any number of such presences. It has been noted that each time the word *I* is spoken, two claimant *I*'s are present. They can be described in a more general form as follows: *what is experienced* and *the acknowledgment of having that experience* are fused, producing a single living moment—a bubble of experience— that contains the intimacy that gives rise to the word *I*. Each call to *I* is such a bubble, and many different moments of *I* can interplay one with another. For example, I can think about what I feel, as well as argue with myself, doubt myself, deny myself, question myself, and so forth. Which, then, is the real *I*, the true myself? All are present as spokespersons for *greater me*, each with its own specific context, and none represents the individual that one recognizes as someone. As *little me*'s, all of them are equally true but are, in fact, quite empty without the presence of *greater me* in whose name they speak. Each *I* exemplifies something of the fullness of *greater me* set in a local context. When we say *I*, we hardly notice that we are merely spokespeople for something so grand that it is in no way confined by that momentary bubble of subjectivity. When we realize that *I* refers to the connection of all that makes us who we are in the world, then each consciousness bubble expresses much more than the fact that comes to consciousness at that moment and much more than can be known to the conscious mind.

Greater me is the background connectivity that is reflected in the connections formed at a specific moment. Actions and thoughts are shaped by a particular structure of intent that reaches far back into our culture and biology and influences every meaning we form. This, then, is what has come out of these reflections and it brings new possibilities of describing the nature of *I* and, too, new questions. In particular it prompts the question, could there be other deeper structures, deeper patterns of being yet unnamed, which influence attitudes and impulses that mold the person we are? For instance, can there be intent structures, emergent from tendencies inherent in all that is, that create the values with which we identify? Is there a more general basis, integrated into all that is, for what we sense as aesthetic values or moral values?

This question is about structures that form the manifestation of self in this world and this chapter is the correct place for such reflections. However, to enter this matter requires preliminary clarification of a different issue, for what could a sense of value signify without the possibility of choice? Creating a scale of values is only possible where choice from among a range of alternatives is feasible. For this reason, the discussion of value, and specifically of morality, is deferred until the final two sections of chapter 9 on freedom of choice.

The First of Two Summaries

All that has been told brings attention to what we refer to as self and points to its instrumental function in producing what is known. *I*, *me*, and *self* are employed interchangeably here, and each is the presence of the coherence that yields a meaningful object, either as a concept or as an act. Self is not an entity but an activity and is present solely when intent is actively engaged in the formation of some outcome. The moment the result is realized, the manifestation of self ceases. Being precursor to the arrival of an object, self is ever nothing, that is, no thing, no object. As long as the activity of interrelating lasts, there is the experience of subjectivity. It can be known only through participation, and it is to this participation in the purposeful activity of generating something meaningful that the word *I* refers. One could think of the plurality of interrelated factors coming together to produce the meaningful result as a sort of nondescript *we*, and, unified in purpose, it turns into *me*—graphically, *we* flips over to become *me*!

During the birthing process of an object or an act, self has the role of midwife.

Self is the enactment of the potential for something to be and, as potential, is not of the physical world. Where nothing is being accomplished, there is no movement from potentiality to actuality and no self is present. Seen from this angle, intent is the potential of nothing to become a particular thing, and self is the complicity of all that participates in its realization. To say the same otherwise, during the birthing process of an object or an act, self has the role of midwife. It brings forth the newborn meaning.

These lines, if read out of context, sound frightfully theoretical; however, having already described step by step the processes involved, what is told here is merely an all-too-concise summary. Let this be no worry, for the section that follows will unravel the tale one last time in a new and different format.

A Summary in Dialogue Form

Where is and what is self?

Q. *The proposition made so far is that the subjective I or self is spread through time and space, without being of time or of space or sustaining them. With no defined position within time or space, where then is self?*
A. It is off the grid.
Q. *And where does that put it?*
A. In some self-contained dimension not in the manifest world.
Q. *And where on Earth (not on Earth, rather) is that?*

A. In a dimension that relates to the material physical world but is not itself physical.
Q. *Is there such a dimension, a nonmanifest realm of the nonmaterial?*
A. Yes. It is well known and has various names. A simple way to refer to it is to call it form, in that the nonmaterial dimension of everything we know is its form. In this sense form is used to signal what is qualitative in an object. For example, what goes on when you think of an object? You hold the object in your mind. Actually, in placing it in your mind, the only part that has been left out is its material substance. What the mind grasps is its form, which includes its qualities and meaning.
Q. *So, the claim is that to think of an object, a piece of cloth, for instance, is to have grasped all that the cloth is except its material content.*
A. And so it is for everything we think of.
Q. *But where in this is the subjective self?*
A. Nowhere—and yet, there all the same. Integration of different aspects produces a recognizable object. Self is this integration by which objects become perceptible.
Q. *It's strange and even funny to think of it like this, as if to say: I am togetherness!*
A. That is it—the togetherness that forms a single coherent unit. It might be the participation of all aspects that form an observed object, or it could be that object's participation in all that is.
Q. *So then, I, or call it "self," is the coming together that forms whatever becomes perceptible to the mind: a piece of cloth, an elf, a fountain, a sense of humor…whatever!*
A. The words *integration, coming together, relationship, participation, togetherness, communion, correlation, whole*—they all mean the same thing in this context. Creating such an event is the expression of self. While it happens, there is self; when it is done, no self remains.
Q. *That would mean, then, that as soon as I become conscious of what is unified, I am no longer there. This sounds like a contradiction. It's like saying, when I am there to perceive an object, I am no longer present!*
A. Consciousness knows only the loss of self. Self is to be found in the process of awakening to the perception of an observed or imagined object, and it ends with the achievement of perception when the

activity of interrelating what became that object ceases. At that point, nothing of self remains—except for the tickle.
Q. *The tickle?*
A. The sense of loss. It is the tickle left by self that was experienced but, at that very moment, became absent. Self is recognized as a sense of absence, the loss of what had been present till that instant.
Q. *How do you know there is the tickle? I never noticed it.*
A. When you don't know what you're looking for, it is normal not to notice it.
Q. *That's too easy an answer! What proof is there of its presence?*
A. The present continuous tense.
Q. *I don't understand.*
A. Without the tickle, there could not be this grammatical form. The present continuous is a way of referring to nonconceptual experience. Saying, for instance, "we are listening" is how, in conceptual terms, we refer to this experience, to self in process. It includes a sense of duration that still echoes from the periphery of our perception. As such, it is a tickle we still sense from what had been ongoing, even though that ongoing experience terminated the moment it was recognized and spoken of. "We are listening" tells that until uttering these words, I was involved in a subjectless-objectless act. The present continuous form expresses the leftover effect (here nicknamed *the tickle*) of the experience of duration, an experience totally foreign to conceptual thinking.
Q. *This would mean that language gives expression to what is unknown and unknowable to conscious thought.*
A. An example of this was given already in chapter 4, where the significance of the word *mind* was shown to reach far beyond what we attribute to it consciously. The tickle of the experience of subjectivity is implicit in language, but once named *self*, it no longer is the experience of subjectivity.
Q. *If I ask where is the sense of self produced, I suppose you will give the same answer as above: "nowhere." But surely, it happens somewhere?*
A. To conceive of *somewhere* requires the conceptual mind, but this part of the mind is unable to know the fullness of self. What it knows is *little I*, the anchor point in time and space of *greater I*.

Q. *So, there is "little I," which is what consciousness knows of self, and there is the rest, "greater I." Where is the full self found and how do we sense it?*
A. So far, three domains have been mapped out: the conscious mind, the expanded mind, and intent. It cannot be in the first, for the conceptual mind only recognizes objective events, and, quite evidently, self is ever a subjective experience.
Q. *Is it in the expanded mind then?*
A. This would make a better fit, but it will not answer the question of how *the sense* of self is produced.
Q. *But if I sense self as a coming together of meaning, it must be in the expanded mind.*
A. The mind on its own would be formless and carry no meaning were it not impregnated by intent. Through the influence of intent, direction is given and there is the *coming together* of meaning. It is through such a formative process that self comes to expression.
Q. *I understand that to produce form there must be intent, so the question returns: How is the sense of self produced when it requires relating to more than the expanded mind?*
A. Although the question is the same as earlier, it is clearer now. What we are looking for is how we sense the effect of intent.
Q. *From chapter 6, it is clear that intent is not determined by thought but by a far more expansive level of being. Because this reaches beyond thought and consciousness, access to it must be some kind of experience.*
A. So it is. In intent, there is the sense of having a direction, of moving towards a particular meaning, and this, just like the physical sense of movement, becomes accessible to thought only after being turned into a concept. To feel the current of all that comes together to form a perception of meaning—of an object—is to sense preconceptual regions where the influence of intent is playing itself out.
Q. *With what do we access this realm?*
A. With all our being. Being senses intent.
Q. *But what exactly is it we experience? How can I tell when it is intent that I experience?*
A. What you are asking is, "How do I sense being?" In general, we cannot sense it any more than we sense the flow of a river when drifting downstream. Being becomes perceptible when there is in-

tent. In the presence of intent, there is cooperation of all that forms the movement towards meaning. This we can sense and with it we sense being.

Q. *Movement towards meaning also gives rise to self, so then there would be the experience of three in one: self, being, and intent. To sense being, to sense intent, and to sense oneself seem to go together.*

A. Self is experienced as participation in an intent, and participation in intent gives a sense of being.

Q. *Is the experience of any intent an experience of self?*

A. Yes. It brings the sense of self, but to feel what you sense as yourself is something more restrictive. It contains a component of familiarity and is the experience of a certain structure of intent.

Q. *So, one could then say, I sense myself when I feel the action of intent moving towards some meaning, but I sense myself as myself when this movement is a pattern I am familiar with.*

A. One detail is not accounted for in what you just said. Who is the *I* in the phrase: "I sense myself as myself"? It suggests there is yet another self.

Q. *That is the catch! There always seems to be a regression of selves, one referring to another.*

A. There is no limit to the number of selves we call *I* as soon as we free ourselves from the erroneous view of self being inside the physical body.

Q. *But if you want to say that self is present every time a meaning is forming, there will be selves popping up all over the place, coming and going, and they will surely not be "my" self?*

A. This would be so except that all the selves you know relate to things that come to have meaning for you. You are personally implicated in every meaning you perceive, and for this reason, experiencing the arising of meaning is sensing yourself.

Q. *Then each experience of self would come as a separate happening. Instead of being an infinite regression, each is a separate bubble of being.*

A. That is exactly what happens. Self is the sense one has of experiencing meaning, and each time this happens there is the experience of self. It is to this experience that the words *I*, *me*, and *myself* refer, or to put it the other way around, it is this experience that prompts the usage of these words.

Q. *Are you saying that self is the experience of experiencing?*
A. It is really very simple. Take, for example, the experience of listening. Absorbed in listening, you may have no sense of the presence of self. You are participating in *what* is being heard. In the opposite situation, to say "I am listening" could be to regard yourself from outside without personal experience of what is listened to and it would be equivalent to saying "someone—me, in this case—is listening." What you notice is only *that* you are listening. However, to sense as one single experience the content of *what* is listened to simultaneously with the fact *that* you are listening is necessarily a subjective experience and it brings a sense of self. As you just said, it is the experience of experiencing.
Q. *Then I am—and I always is—the experiencer of an experience. Very pleased to meet me! In that case, the experience I experience would be, I suppose, the common denominator of all experience and that is, as you described, the sense of something coming to be known.*
A. There are many words you could choose for this: *coming to be known, observed, perceived, grasped, seen, realized, recognized*. All of these words refer to what results from the process of integration that produces meaning through the influence of intent.
Q. *Can you say once again what intent is doing in this context?*
A. Intent is what guides the movement of mind towards a meaningful result. The general feature of this intent was described in chapter 1 as denotative intent. It generates the centripetal motion of aspects coming together to form a unit of meaning. This process is the ground for the experience of self.
Q. *To recapitulate: in the presence of intent, I experience being, and together with this comes the experience of self. Does this mean that self is what we experience when we feel the presence of intent?*
A. This is your suggestion, and it is certainly worth pursuing.
Q. *I only asked a little question about self and suddenly there are so many lines of thought to follow. It's intriguing—but a bit overwhelming.*
A. For now, it is well to stay with the initial question.
Q. *My question was "where is self?" The answer reached is that it is nowhere among the objects of the world. Instead, it is found where intent brings the formation of meaning, and it is lost again as soon as the meaning is formed. But I experience an incessant stream of meanings arising and disappearing so, while considering who I am, I*

must be born and die a million times over...and it doesn't even hurt! In fact, I hardly notice it at all.

A. While consciousness is given over to the resulting meanings, which are your perceptions and thoughts, there is an accompanying feeling of being alive, of being active, and of participating in life, and this is you sensing self. You might think you hardly notice it, yet, if ever it is taken from you, the change would be blatantly obvious.

Q. *All living beings share the feeling of being alive and in this we have a common sense of self. But what about my personal feelings when I say "myself" and refer to what I know as me personally?*

A. First, the experience of being alive is very much your experience even if it is an experience we share with all beings. In addition, in the general background sense of self that comes because we are engaged in a process of forming meaning, all moments are not equal. Some experiences reflect habitual ways of expressing ourselves, of understanding, and of doing things. These repeated patterns breed familiarity. You feel associated with them, and when they arise your sense of personal identity is awakened and strengthened.

Q. *Thinking about what you have said, it is as if self was a kind of binding material, a glue maybe, or better, a force field through which communion is established between all that comes together to form meaning. When the field of intent is active in a particular context of meaning, there is a sense of self and that sense of self can be augmented when the territory, the pattern of intent, is more familiar.*

A. The binding material or force field you speak of manifests in the mind—one could almost say it manifests *as* the mind. It is present when meaning is present and absent when no process of coming to meaning is in progress. When, as you said, you are in familiar territory with intentions you associate with and identify as your own way of being, the binding is more pronounced and the sense of self is more personal.

Q. *This self—myself—is not something and is not somewhere, yet it is not nowhere either. It arises out of what is beyond the physical world and beyond what I call reality. The only way this can be is if, somehow, who I am has its source in an activity that is not contained within what we commonly believe to be everything. I suppose that in order to understand self and intent and all that we have spoken of, I need to open my mind wider and admit what I never dreamed could* be. How strange it is that the quest to understand myself reaches beyond everything with which I am familiar.

A. Even stranger, perhaps, is the way people have held to the view of self as a thing, a kind of subjective object. To allow self to leave the physical world framed in time and space is to free ourselves finally of a burden that bent our attention on looking for what isn't and ignoring what is.

Q. *It becomes clear now. The mistake was to look for a material-based self that could be placed among all that is perceived as the world. While searching in the wrong direction, there was a failure to see the obvious fact that self is a subjective presence that arises in the integration that brings together every understanding and forms every object and event that comes to consciousness.*

[8]

Induction Contrasted with Causality

IN THIS WORK, intent is described as a process of induction rather than causation. The distinction between causality and induction is an important component in all that relates to intent. To understand this, we must go beyond the more general usage where *cause* refers to anything that produces outcomes and where induction can be included as a subcategory of causality. This usage obscures a finer level of distinction that reveals causation and induction to be two fundamentally separate modi operandi.

The definitions proposed here are nonstandard. A shift in thinking is necessary to overcome ambiguities in the standard viewpoint that obfuscate the clearly contrasted natures that induction and causality present. To make this shift demands readiness to reformulate the conventional view with which we may have become comfortable.

Conclusions That Will Be Reached in This Chapter

A single event can be viewed either as the process of induction or as a causal process, but not as both at the same time because they are mutually exclusive viewpoints that describe fundamentally different systems of interaction. Causation recognizes events as the result of single momentary impulses that do not communicate or share information with one another. Induction, on the other hand, recognizes an activator, an inductor, that is constituted through the integration of diverse factors that together give direction to events. Causation is constituted of characterless isolated moments; induction implies a formed whole that sustains an ongoing influence on events. These separate views reflect distinct ways of understanding phenomena.

Two Lexical Precisions

The first precision comes to limit the definition of causality and use it exclusively to refer to explanations of how effects are produced. This fits the classical view of causal action in a world where every event is the result of a sequence of prior causes. It points to the interaction by which events are produced. When the concept of causality is held to this understanding, other viewpoints can emerge, and it will then become apparent that induction has a different function and does not explain *how* things happen. Instead, it acknowledges *that* they happen and in a specific context. This remark will become clear in the discussion that follows but only to the extent that one adheres—just for this preliminary analysis—to the definition that restricts the sense of cause and causality to what is proposed here.

The second precision comes to clear induction from other processes with which it can be confused. There is a central fact that distinguishes induction from both generalization and inference. Although the subject's viewpoint determines whether an event is understood as induction or as causality, induction always brings an added factor: something *other* than the observer is present to generate a process of transformation. At times, one finds the word *induction* interchanged with the words *inference* and *generalization*. Both of these are the prerogative of the subject who draws the inference or makes the generalization, but induction is different in that some particular thing functions as inductor and holds the process in place. It can be an energy field that creates a particular physical response, or when applied to mind processes, it is a certain pattern of thinking, for example, a syllogism. Only with the recognition of a specific presence that lends direction to the process can one speak of induction, and it is this presence that serves as the reason for the transformation that takes place.

Even where *inference* and *induction* refer to the same situation, they express something different.

Having said that, a caveat needs to be included. In just one situation, the inductor is, in fact, identified with the subject: when the subject's intent becomes the inductor that generates events. This concerns an individual's freedom to choose and implement an action. How it relates to induction is elaborated towards the end of this chapter. Apart from this case, the subject's role is that of an observer recognizing events as induction, and in this, there has also to be recognition of an inductor.

Another way to view the distinction between induction and similar activities is to note that generalization and inference do not include a time factor. One makes inferences or makes generalizations, or one does not make them; the process itself does not imply duration, with something evolving over time. Induction, in contrast, cannot be momentary. It requires the presence of an inductor that, over time, influences events and produces a change. To attribute induction to a situation implies, necessarily, to allow for a time component.

Defining Causality and Induction

Causality has to do with *cause*, the word used to refer to what initiates an action. It reflects a worldview that supposes an action originates with an initial cause and proceeds through a chain of intermediary causes to arrive at a result. Causality, in its simplest form, suggests a single operator or many single operators that produce an effect: the bat that strikes the ball, the flame that heats the kettle, shouts that alert those who come to assist. In cases where the cause is constant over time, as in a flame heating water, it is understood as a sequence of momentary causes. Causes are individual, separate from one another, and momentary, and they do not interrelate to create a purposeful direction. This signifies that, together, they sustain no common relationship that implies the outcome.

Induction, on the other hand, is not concerned with the origin of actions but with transformation. It refers to the fact that there is a process by which change is enacted. Already in its etymology, induction signifies leading in a certain direction. There is no suggestion of *how* this happens, only *that* it happens. It signifies that there is a process by which transformation takes place, but the question of what makes it so is not raised. The absence of an explanatory chain of cause and effect gives way to a different vision of influence. It allows for the assumption that transformation is due to an overall tendency, a directionality implicit in whatever creates the change. It is the magnetic field creating current, the slope of the hill where the avalanche began, the presence of humor that triggers laughter. The presence of a state that embodies a tendency is possible because induction is a process sustained by divers factors that together impart a particular effect over time. Induction implies duration.

In causality, the assumption is of individual action–reaction events that are independent of one another. Any overall effect they produce is the accumulation of momentary events that have no relation to anything taking place elsewhere or at another moment in time. In the case of induction, the assumption is totally different. The overall process of change is the result of a single unified presence, such as the slope or the charged field. Instead of a collection of causes, what induces the result is understood as a single, meaningful, integral whole.

The inductive grasp of things, so distinctive in its effect, is quite vulnerable in our present intellectual climate. At any stage while considering induction, and that includes during this description, the causal, rational mind can perk up and break in to voice the objection that there is no binding force and that all can be explained in terms of individual random events whose combined effect requires nothing that the causal explanation does not account for and there is no need to speak of interrelationship, integration, purpose, and suchlike things. With this vociferation, the causal approach is able to build up enough commotion to strut off as vanquisher and sole champion of truth and common sense. But is this correct? Causality is as much the choice of a viewpoint as is induction. To choose induction demands a subtle shift in attitude that, on the whole, slips by unnoticed. Quite discreetly and unannounced comes the assumption that the collectivity makes sense. The collectivity carries meaning; it is purposeful; it is leading somewhere. While imbued with the integral view, one has entered a way of seeing that has far-reaching implications that determine how we understand the universe. It is strange to think this vision of reality remained implicit and has received so little attention—probably a result of the invasive power of the rational, analytical mind that upholds causality and steps in to dissect whatever enters the mind as an integral, self-contained whole.

The Integral Presence That Generates Induction

The formation of a whole was detailed in chapter 1. There, concept formation was described as a process of integration that takes place out of reach of consciousness and results in a meaningful whole—the unit meaning of which we become conscious. The same integration producing a unit of meaning is present wherever there is an allusion to induction. The unit meaning is the state that induces the process of induction: hunger producing the search for food, cold producing crystallization, a steep incline releasing an avalanche, and so forth. Induction always presents a meaningful state with a sustained effect. It is always a case of multiple factors that have fused and become a unitary thing. The distinguishing feature of induction is this attitude that enables one to recognize unity in multiplicity and claim the presence of some particular thing creating the effect. In this, induction is distinct from causation.

Causality has its roots in physics. When, repeatedly, x encountering y produces z, one infers that a law of nature is involved, and out of this causal mind-set, laws of nature are established. It is not possible to establish a system of laws from the inductive viewpoint; all one can conclude is that some particular thing or state produces the probability of a result. In this, induction is fundamentally different from causality.

Another aspect of the difference is that causality, in that it has established laws, imposes the result; induction cannot impose anything because it does not separate out intellect (in the form of laws) from phenomena. In the inductive view, tendencies rule because of the compliance of the individual components to the general effect and not because they are being directed.

Such an idea may at first seem preposterous, but through analogy, the strangeness can be allayed. In physics, there is a theory that says interactions take the easiest path possible, where easy is defined as the least costly in energy. It is the principle of least action and, if to stay within the causal viewpoint that separates the intellect (laws) from the physical, this view suggests that, in some unexplained manner, all the possible paths are known in advance so as to permit the choice of the optimal path. Pertinent to the present discussion is that, in such a world, we could imagine (though this is not how a physicist describes it) that each participating element finds what is right for it in accordance with the goal to be achieved. A coordinated movement, in this case, would be due to many participating elements responding to the same intended goal. Following on from this analogy, the integrated movement in processes of induction can be described as the coordinated behavior of participants, each responding to a preferable path. However, in the case of induction, the definition of *preferable path* is left wide open so as to accommodate unknown influences, even, for instance, effects from the future.

Can the influences that affect events in an inductive process be referred to as causes? Certainly they can; however, this would imply the wider sense of the word *cause* that was temporarily set aside at the outset of this chapter, in the section "Two Lexical Precisions." One can say an inclined slope *causes* an avalanche, but this does not mean through a process of causality. The incline determines the probability that snow begins to slip. Recognizing this, one already has acknowledged the presence of something recognized as an incline and, too, as snow, and from an inductive point of view, nothing more can be said. The potential present in the incline, together with whatever other potential the snow experiences, manifests as slipping snow. As observers, we might consider that a tipping point is reached when the snow begins to slide, but the snow is continuously on a preferable path that reflects its optimal way of being, and the action that takes place reflects the snow's participation in tendencies that are present.

If to make a distinction between the words *reason* and *cause*, one could say that induction supplies the reason and not the cause for results. To the causally oriented person, the two words are synonyms and reasons for anything are forcibly causes. But it is possible to pry apart two different significations that reflect two separate realities. If the word *reason* is not used to refer to cause–effect interaction but only to interactions that imply direction and possibly purpose, then where reason is present, each active component would have a significance of its own through which it relates meaningfully to whatever is present. In a world formed by reasons, everything relates to everything else. Meanings intermesh, forming further meanings, and this reflects the presence of a tendency to form meaning and suggests a world in which all has direction and events are not simply random outcomes. This is saying a great deal. It brings out the underlying significance of induction. Despite the fact that the manner by which direction is imparted is not told and even though it cannot be traced to a single causal source, a direction-giving process influences events and yields a comprehensive coordinated outcome.

A Closer Description of Causality and Induction

When seen from the viewpoint of causality, events spontaneously interact according to the laws of nature, and what they show, as noted in chapter 6, is the winding down of the universe in the sense of increasing entropy. On the other hand, seen as induction, relationships between meaningful wholes are recognizable objects that compose—not deconstruct—a world that is formed through the action of intent.

A closer look at the contrasting positions can illustrate what is involved. The causal view claims there is an explanation for all: a photon transfers kinetic energy to an atom, and this process, repeated many times, explains how it is possible for a flame to bring the kettle to boil. The chain of command from initial momentary cause to the result is assumed closed with all stations manned, so to speak. The chain of causes does not give the reason for the result, and this is because there is none. The causes produced the result of water that boils, but they had no reason to do so. In the causal view, there is no self-contained thing called *warmth* or *heat*, and these words are just a manner to refer to the effect produced through the movement of microscopic molecules that themselves are the result of other invisible events. As separate impulses, they have no integrated structure that could retain meaning. They manifest a chain reaction of noncoordinated responses.

The example of a flame heating water, given as an example of causal relationship, can be understood equally well as a process of induction. In this case there is no such causal chain, and what is recognized is the presence of heat that generates a constant influence that leads to the rising temperature of the water. The boiling water induced by heat is brought about by the inherent tendency of warmth, over time, to be transmitted to cooler bodies. The correspondence between all that unites to produce the continuing inductive effect is mysterious because there is no account of how individual factors correlate to produce the effect. An explanation may be supplied by a shift into causal thinking, but for induction, this solves nothing and is not an answer. With induction, the reason for the process is always contingent on a guiding principle, an inherent tendency, that is simply the expression of what things are. Nothing excludes a search for causal explanation, but to start down that path would be to shift registers and tear apart what is integral and was formed in the view that induction sustains. To do so would mean the loss of the very thing one wishes to explain.

The inductive view envisions a world with inherent tendencies in which nature, impregnated with inclinations, supplies not causes but reasons for events. The tendency of heat to dissipate into what is cooler, and vice versa, is an aspiration present in the natural world in the same manner that the desire for food and the desire for light are present in living organisms. Understood as the reason for meaningful transformation between states of being, they exemplify the process of induction.

Induction and Freedom from Determinism

The tendencies that manifest in induction are recognized through observation. They reflect the way things are. No law tells why things have to be this way; there is just the fact that that is how things turn out to be. Of course, the causal viewpoint typically slips in and fills the void with explanations, and we are left with what seems to be induction justified with a causal explanation. But that is just the causal view referring to what was understood as being induction and was grasped in the integrative moment that made induction independent of causes.

This last point may need repetition. The inductive view allows for the formation of a recognizable entity that has the tendency to produce a certain transformation. A process is associated with a particular entity such as warmth, a slope, and such. What in physics is called *fields* is such an entity, an integrated whole. It could also be called a *state*. When someone perceives the presence of induction, the concept of a particular state has necessarily formed in that person's mind. What the subject recognizes is a single nature that tends to produce particular effects. On one hand there is induction and on the other hand there is causality, a view that breaks any integral process into a chain of causes. One view does not deny the possibility of the other; rather, they are oblivious to one another.

As for the question of freedom and determinacy, the matter is very different in the two functions. Induction refers only to the presence of a transformation process and not to how the result is produced. As such, it does not refer to *a law* of transaction, and—have no doubt—determinism and necessity require laws! Induction can predict outcomes, but it cannot guarantee them; the outcome may be all but certain, yet there is no ground on which induction can underwrite the transaction. Results are expected and can be almost certain, yet multiple induction processes proceeding together leave place for new influences to come to bear on an intended result. With induction, nothing is reducible to what the rational mind comprehends to be single lines of cause and effect. Two reasons for this irreducibility are detailed in what follows. They are not new but implicit in what has already been told.

The simple reason is that induction does not explain the process by which the interaction takes place, the intermediary steps. It acknowledges only that the presence of the inductor produces a transformation. Instead of being explanatory and analytical, the inductive process is observational, acknowledging what is the situation, and from such a viewpoint one cannot speak of possibility or impossibility in events. A second reason goes somewhat deeper and has to do with recognizing wholes with inherent qualities. To grasp something integral is to attribute a way of being to it, that is, qualities that make it recognizable as what it is. In the case of a person, we might speak of character. There is something like this, an overall quality, that we attribute to every integral thing we recognize, and the way such a whole, an integrality, a character, interacts with the world is very different from how individual impulses interact. They retain their character in the exchange. Elm trees interact with their environment and what we observe are trees that differ greatly from one another yet all are elm trees. We describe growth as a process of *adaptation*, but what this word means is not fully understood, for somewhere adaptation includes rebalancing with itself as a whole entity. The tree, in adapting to its world, is transformed on many levels, branching out in different ways, and this it does in relationship to what it is, to its integral form-in-being. How this takes place is mysterious. The logical mind cannot follow interactions that involve a whole individual thing that retains a certain character (such as the species of tree). Here one encounters an inability to apply logical reasoning, and in this gap lies the indeterminacy of the inductive process.

From the viewpoint of induction, events are not bound by necessity, nor are alternatives excluded. When compared with closed causal sequences, this view is refreshing in that it leaves possibilities open and portrays an undetermined universe. What one observes is the way things tend to happen, that is all. Such a view offers no basis from which to argue in favor of determinism and neither does it support the opposite point of view, that of an indeterminate free-for-all. Defined and recognized by the transformation it produces, an inductive process tends to produce predictable results.

This discussion about induction is of interest in the context of contemporary science where causality is losing its absolute hold. If one wishes to know which photon impinges on a certain atom and at a certain moment, a causal explanatory plan is of little assistance. In classical physics it was assumed that, in principle, detailed prediction is feasible when one possesses a full description of the initial conditions; however, in today's physics, there is a fundamental limit in the degree to which an event can be predetermined. With the process of induction, no such reappraisal is required because, in induction, the transformation is due to a tendency inherent in the overall situation. Uncertainty about links in the chain of reactions is not an issue. The induced event is not understood as an alignment of independent punctual acts but as a directional influence of sustained duration.

Induction and the Ability to Choose

The inductive process is irreducible to a rational, causal understanding. This was shown to be the case with other systems of understanding considered in earlier chapters: the connotative contrasted with denotative, the activity of the expanded mind contrasted with the conceptual mind, the periphery activity of the physical senses, the self (referred to as *greater* self) in the identification of what is subjective, and, too, the function of intent as the source of reason everywhere that reason is found.

The presence of intent, it has been suggested, is ubiquitous and comes to expression in every realization, whether accomplished in the mind or in the world. Intent functions through induction and, for this reason, no causal chain of events is invoked, no laws of how things should be are stipulated, and there is no place for the imposition of necessity. Intent, understood as the creation of outcomes through induction, is necessarily free from determinism. The break with determinism is related to the unknown moment that allows for the binding of multiple elements into something integral (e.g., the elm tree). This brings a central point into focus. Does freedom from determinism imply freedom of choice? The answer to this question rests upon what is understood as the subject making choices. Freedom of choice implies a subject who is free and initiates actions. Without this, one would be led back to the conclusion that freedom of thought and freedom of action are illusory.

For an individual to have the ability to create change and influence outcomes, that individual needs be able to influence the tendencies that determine the direction her actions take. The presence of inherent tendencies is the potential called *intent*, and the generator of intent functions as an inductor—an object or state that produces a particular influence on events. This statement speaks of induction in the world without any reference to a personal subject and, as was noted already, induction does not issue from the subject who observes the situation and determines that there is induction. But, as already mentioned (the caveat in the section "Two Lexical Precisions"), there is one obvious exception: when the subject who acknowledges the intent also interacts with the world. In this case, the intent structure that gives expression to all that a person is acts upon the world and, through that person's presence, becomes the inductor that brings a certain set of influences to the world. Freedom to choose one's actions is then linked to the possibility of readjusting the inductor, thus bringing a change in one's personal intent structure.

The statements of this next paragraph will be given in summary form. They were already discussed in detail in chapter 7 and will be developed further in chapter 9.

This personal intent structure is both the identity of the subject and the source of the subject's influence on events. A subject making choices is necessarily an *intent being*, that is to say, not a physical entity and not detectable in the limited world we typically refer to as reality, and yet, through the physical body, the intent being can manifest in the world. Freedom to choose signifies the ability to reformulate intent, and since intent structure gives form to self, freedom of choice entails transforming who we are. The freedom implicit in the inductive action of intent is the prerogative to become other, to manifest otherwise, not simply by performing otherwise but by *being* otherwise. To give a simple example: in the rain, a passing bike splashes mud on our clothes. The range of possible responses is large and each—from anger to indif-

Freedom of choice entails transforming who we are.

ference to forgiveness—gives a different expression to who we are at that moment. Even though deeper, more constant trends in our individual structures of intent are present, to enact a particular response already signifies giving form to a certain pattern of being that, in turn, influences events. The ability to reformulate our personal intent structure or identity lies at the source of our freedom to act and to make choices. It is not by intervening directly on events in the world that we exercise our freedom to choose. This is the outcome. The source of our freedom is in the ability to change our personal engagement in life, that is, to modulate the intent that forms our presence in the world. How this is accomplished will be detailed in the next chapter.

With an understanding of the nature of intent, we see that freedom is inextricably linked to being. Rather than an exterior force that intervenes in a given situation, as in the view of causality, the subject generating intent participates in the overall formative process that integrates all movement towards realization. To enact change is to transform the intent that impregnates events. This intent is bound up with the identity of self, and the subject expressing this intent necessarily takes part in the change that is enacted. A change of intent is a change of being, and this is what freedom of choice entails.

Understanding the inductive process as distinct from causality completes what has been presented throughout this work on the dual functions of mind and the influence of intent. Issues relating to freedom of choice are particularly cumbersome in our culture because we are immersed in a causal point of view that, more often than not, regards induction as if it were an appendage of causality. It is hoped that this discussion rebalances the matter somewhat by pointing to what is independent in the inductive process and characteristic of it. This subject brings further precision to the presentation of intent and of self and offers a less obvious vantage point from which to consider nondeterminism and the presence of freedom of choice—the theme of the following chapter.

[9]
Freedom of Choice

Freedom and Intent

To what extent do we exercise freedom over our actions? Central in any understanding of free choice are three factors: consciousness, nonconsciousness, and intent. With an understanding of the way they interact, it is possible to measure to what degree our spontaneous sense of free will is an actual fact.

Crucial to an understanding of intent, as shown in chapter 5, is that intent does not stem from consciousness; it is generated elsewhere. Whenever we become conscious of a particular intent, it is merely the recognition of an already formed intent. This fact was important in the description of self and, in this chapter, proves important for an understanding of individual freedom.

Conscious intent implies that a person is conscious that an outcome, not yet achieved, will become reality. As noted earlier, *having* such an intent (which is more than just thinking of the result or referring to it) includes a sense of freedom in that there is the feeling that one can affect events. It includes the implication that the intended result is not purely the outcome of random events but reflects coordinated activity generated by a subject. The same fact is evident also where intent is denied and one says, "Sorry, I didn't intend to do it." This signifies that the act perpetrated was not my choice. Choice is implicit in every experience we have of a conscious intentional act.

Nonconscious intent presents a very different situation in that here, a person performs actions that lead to a specific outcome without consciously thinking of the acts being performed or, very possibly, of the outcome. The influence of intent, whose origin is rooted in one's state of being and even in the state of the world, enters events without any participation on the part of consciousness. The following example should make this clear.

Putting your hands out in front of your body during a fall is certainly done with the intent to lessen the shock of the fall and protect the body, but the intent driving this act does not wait for consciousness to license it, never mind formulate it. The act results from an appraisal, largely unconscious, of the situation and also involves one's skill to handle all that is incumbent at that moment. But then, is there any choice in the matter or is it a case of autonomous systems doing what they have learned to do? Added precision on what exactly the question is may be helpful. Neurological information about, for instance, the amygdala and its ability to bypass rational systems is irrelevant here as the question is more fundamental. It does not concern the route that choice takes within the sensory motor system but the origin of the initiative to act. This includes, on one hand, the source from which the action stems and, on the other hand, whether some*one* generates the choice and if so, how this *one* relates to our sense of self.

Returning to the question of reaching out to break a fall, is this an act of choice or an involuntary response? For example, could you choose *not* to put your hands out in front? The answer is *yes*. Holding something very precious in your arms could make your reaction very different. Alternative courses of action are possible. To say that all is automatic and determined by the givens in the situation would stretch the rational argument to its breaking point because *automatic* would then need to include the value judgment made about what you are holding in your arms. In any case, a debate over this is not necessary as the question lies elsewhere. Instead of asking if I choose my course of action and debating where yes and where no, the determining question is: Do unconscious actions reflect choice and constitute an expression of freedom, and if they do, is there someone making the choice?

With these reflections, the question of choice can be expressed as follows: Is intent designed into the situation or is there a free individual who chooses to have certain intentions?

As long as consciousness is taken as the basis for independent self-driven action, choice is excluded where actions are not produced consciously. That is, if making *conscious* choices is the definition for freedom of action, obviously no expression of personal freedom is possible in actions made without consciousness. However, a completely different option opens where consciousness is taken to be no more than a passing moment at which an individual integrates the understanding of that moment and grasps one particular limited display of what is known. This is the view that has been entertained throughout this work. Consciousness is one moment embedded within a wider expanded consciousness, and with this understanding, personal choice in a context of freedom has not been encroached upon by loss of consciousness. The full unperceived dimension of self in action is to be found in expanded consciousness. For example, the change in one's fall that takes place when holding something precious in one's arms is due to a sense of values inherent in the attitudes and feelings of that person, that is, in values developed by the subject in the course of a lifetime and beyond, including cultural traits and even traits common to the human species and to living beings. Thus, although one's performance during the fall largely results from what is out of consciousness, recognizing this as the presence of expanded consciousness allows the action taken to be the result of the intent and desires embodied by the individual.

All this seems plain enough, but the implications are many and could prove disconcerting both to a person who imagines self to be something contained within the physical body and to a person who tries to do away with self altogether. Can an action generated by nonconscious influences be an act of choice? Can effects that come from beyond my present body, from earlier times and from across the universe, be included in what I sense as my self? With these questions, the kernel of the matter is reached. The key to an answer seems to be the question whether these effects are separate events independent of one another or whether they are, in some way, unified so as to be an expression of some*one*, of a single subject who intends the outcome.

It is already clear that such an individual subject must be far greater than anything we initially would have ventured to imagine ourselves to be. That others can be part of me as well as events that took place in times and places my body never entered certainly goes far beyond anything considered when it was thought that self terminates within the confines of the body or, in some views, within the confines of the central nervous system. But this sudden expansion of self is of no pivotal consequence and just means that the commonly assumed presence that was given to *me* is a minimized, reduced model of what everyone is. This view will become more settled as the discussion on individual freedom progresses.

What It Means That Some-*one* Is Choosing

With every gesture we make and every action we take in thought and in the world, we draw upon sources that go far beyond what we know consciously and give expression to our expanded self, to *greater me*, made of all the structures and relationships that promote what we understand as self. Acts result from an amalgam made of experiences, abilities, feelings, qualities, both innate and acquired, and, while performing an act, the subject *I* arises as the coherent tendency of all to produce a certain outcome. This was described more specifically in chapter 7.

With this understanding it is possible to recognize that the intent that forms an action is personal and individual yet is not under the control of rational thought. Each person is involved in acting out patterns of behavior that are an expression of this greater self, the expanded me that has been referred to as greater me. But then—and here comes a crucial question—if this act is not under my immediate control, how can it be an act of choice? In what way can it be an expression of freedom? To this there is an answer and to perceive it clearly a shift in position is needed for someone still holding to the idea that *oneself* is inside the body. Actions are certainly under my control, only the word *me* now means very much more than what was assumed when, in its reduced version, it was merely the conscious actor. Now it includes a vast array of undefined participating factors. Any one factor, if defined, would need to include the function of all the others. This whole interrelated matrix available throughout the system makes up the personality of the individual, of the being that guides the choice of actions taken at any one moment. The array of participating influences *is* my self—me and nothing other than me!

If this is so, then where does freedom come into such a vast program already set forth in all that I am? The answer comes as a surprise because it is what, intuitively, we have always believed. When I am conscious and understand what is before me, I can choose, to some degree, the way I relate to it.

In this context, it may be well to respond to those who have concluded that we are a product of psychological and physical systems and that our actions are really only reactions, biological preprogrammed patterns of behavior. This work does not come to argue with such a position; its purpose is not to present the correct version of reality. Instead, it offers those wishing to reflect on an alternative version an account that includes intent and shows how conscious influence in a program that is largely not conscious is possible.

What will be described is how it transpires that, on a very simple level, there is a degree of choice, never complete perhaps, but enough so you can tell the waiter *I would like the chocolate one, please*, choosing to choose the flavor you like or maybe choosing to choose a flavor you do not like. Consciousness is not at all irrelevant, as might appear from what was said up till here, and has a very definite role in choice even though it engages but a minute part of who we are. But there appears to be a catch to this, for, even though I can choose the flavor I prefer or not choose it, the choice seemingly ends there. Liking or not liking that flavor appears beyond my power of choice. In actual fact, it is not beyond my power, only the trail that leads to influencing what I like is indirect and far less immediate.

The Contribution of Consciousness

Intentions form from countless factors that never enter our conscious thought, and so it is evident that this influence on our actions and thoughts is not directed by consciousness. Were this all there is to say about the influence of intent, the question of freedom of choice would end here. But there is more to say! Consciousness, the timeless happening that creates a fictive subject that identifies a momentary object (chapter 1), brings about a new situation and, although it *does* nothing, it changes everything, and with it, the whole story of living in the world needs to be retold.

Although consciousness does nothing, it changes everything.

That consciousness is the ability to consider possibilities is evident, but how does this happen? Consciousness offers a suspended moment in which possibilities are considered and no action is taken. The implications of this are great. The view developed throughout this work is that everything carries intent, and it can now be seen that the experience of consciousness is related to this. It serves to neutralize the intent charge of a particular item, relieving it of its active role in events. Consciousness creates a free zone in which a possibility can be extracted from the purposeful activity that is inherent in all events. For that moment, as an object of thought, it is withheld from the flux of interpenetrating effects and is singled out so as to become a still-frame presentation of the flux that animates all from beyond consciousness. We are well familiar with this state, for it is what is called *reflection*.

A common view of the act of reflection is to imagine it as a thinker thinking about things. Implicit in this is the view that mind activity is directed from the intellect. But, with the fact that neither what directs the sequence of thoughts that enter the mind nor what formulates decisions is produced through conscious thought, this simplistic view is distanced. How, then, can reflection—thinking and not doing—lead to new outcomes?

With the following example, a wider view of the act of reflection is proposed. Imagine that I want to scold a child for a particular behavior, but I stop and reflect on this intention. This means my action is suspended and possible actions and thoughts that relate to this episode come to mind. These fill the space of possibilities opened by consciousness whose function can be seen as disengaging thought from action and from the specific intent that is carried by that thought. Let us say that, at that moment, the attention I give the matter brings forward a memory of something I realized before, for instance, the importance of meeting a child's own sense of justice and respecting it. The impulsive response I might have had is tempered by this reflection or is completely changed. Allowing a place in the mind for this new influence somehow brings about a change. It is as if within the space of nonaction offered by consciousness, the presence of this added factor (the thought I recalled) brings new influences to bear on all that powers my response. The response still issues from intent (not from thought) and for this reason one can conclude that the new factor taken up by thought must insert itself into all that forms the pattern of intent that generates the action I take. In short, by allowing a place for factors that were not initially present or not fully present to enter the mind, it is possible to change the constellation of intent that forms my response.

Reflection opens the possibility of readjustment whereby, through some manner of resonant exchange, specific factors taken into consciousness affect the overall pattern of intent that determines one's action. This exchange is mysterious, and this writer has no understanding of it, but there is little doubt that factors that cohere to produce an action interrelate in some way. To suggest what kind of steps are involved, a rough sketch is offered in the next paragraph.

An intended action, by entering consciousness as a thought, is short-circuited. What happens is that its potential to produce an intended result is realized in thought instead of in action. For that moment, its potential to produce an effect in the world has been neutralized. Reflection makes for delayed or canceled action, and with this, it opens the possibility for the mind to accommodate other influences, some that relate to the items that enter consciousness as thoughts and others that play into the expanded mind and do not register in consciousness. This flux of influences produces constantly changing levels of pertinence in the formation of intent. For example, momentary effects playing into intent blend with deeper, more constant strands of one's intent being, and together they generate the action one takes at a moment. In this way, reflection offers the possibility of reaching more deeply into the intent being we are (*greater me*), thus giving a fuller expression of who we are or, in opposite cases such as during emotional turmoil, giving expression to a less integral self.

To summarize: Consciousness, without initiating or deciding on actions to be taken, promotes a reorganization of factors that influence the course of events. The change is in the structure of intent relevant to the situation and, given that I am to some degree that intent structure, it is me that changes. My engagement with what defines my present situation undergoes transformation.

Self in Transformation

As just stated, fluctuation in one's intent is fluctuation in who one is. Two key aspects discussed in earlier chapters are important here. One is that self can be understood as the coordination present in the movement of realizing intent, and the second is that consciousness is the moment when this coordinated movement achieves it purpose. To realize a different purpose would then imply a change in the movement of intent that is being realized, which amounts to a change or transformation of self.

Freedom of choice is thus freedom to become other and to impact otherwise all that is subject to intent. To be free to enact a change in self is where logic breaks down because it seems senseless to say that self produces a change in itself. This would require duplication of self, with one self creating a change in another self, but this view leads back to the erroneous view of self in infinite regression that was amended in chapter 7. The logical impossibility arises because cause and effect have been separated on a time line and, though less obvious here, because intelligent cause, or, call it purpose-carrying cause, has been separated from the effect it produces through an implied dualism of mind and body. Such views have no place once intent is recognized. To enact change in oneself—in who I am—does not require separate parts, one affecting another. Self that arises with the process of intent coming into being is neither the cause nor the effect but the process that unifies cause and effect. Self comes to expression when a future goal acts upon a present situation.

How strange this manner of nondualistic thinking sounds at first. The presence of self is found in intentioned action, and the future it implies is the direction implicit in present actions. Another way to state this is that self both carries the message of change and at the same time enacts that change. This statement is an echo of what was told in chapter 7 about how the word I fuses the subject pronouncing a statement with the subject experiencing its content, a blending of thinking and experiencing. Any change in performance necessarily implies a change in self. It is transformation of the manifestation of who we are.

Choosing

Key factors involving acts of choice have been delineated, but one might still ask, has the issue of *the chocolate one, please* been substantiated? The next paragraph details how a simple act of choice is enacted.

When accosted by the waiter who wants to know what your choice is, there is an interruption of the flow of intent passing into actuality relative to this matter. In consciousness, an option, the possibility of alternative action, arises. At that moment, as movement of intent being realized as action is arrested, reflection occurs and this brings new factors to play upon intent. Some are conscious and seemingly related to the choice being made, and others, unconscious, are never realized in consciousness yet are able, all the same, to influence the immediate structure of intent that pertains to the choice of action taken. On the background of one's full intent being, one chooses, and the choice reflects the specific pertinent aspects of intent that have been activated in that situation. It is very definitely my choice because I am the movement of intent that produces the outcome.

Promoting a Way of Being

With this in place, an earlier question resurfaces: How can a person have the freedom to influence decisions rooted in impulses that are inaccessible to consciousness, as, for example, the flavor I like or do not like?

There is such a thing as cultivating taste and developing, for instance, pleasure in something for which, initially, one had no affinity. The presence of choice is introduced in a conscious pause. Although we are not conscious of countless influences that weigh upon our likes and dislikes, we can arrest their immediate effect on our actions and, through the conscious or semiconscious pause, call in certain influences that will affect the balance of effects that are present. Some are conscious, such as a memory or a new thought, and others never condense into specific thoughts. It could be, for instance, that a moment's thought brought forward the possibility of undertaking a training program and maintaining it for some time. No matter how trivial the degree of freedom that is opened by that new option, it leads to the development of qualities and abilities that become integrated into the intentioned being one is and which, in turn, influence one's thoughts and actions. Cultivating sensitivity can intensify certain experiences, and impairment of sensitivity can limit the available range of experiences. (This is the subject of the interlude in chapter 6, "Intent and the Cultivation of Values.")

The power of indirect action, gained through the ability of conscious thought to disengage from intent, can be formidable. One moment's reflection can influence the path of actions of an individual throughout a lifetime. The consideration one gives to the qualities and abilities one wishes to manifest augments their influence within one's personal intent and can promote one's commitment to repeat and develop certain ways of being, and this, very definitely, influences how one relates to others and to the world. Behavior patterns, sociability, morality, aesthetic values—or to spell it out in more specific terms: kindness, likes, dislikes, respect, wonder, friendliness, love, and laughter and ever so much more—are influenced by conscious consideration of options that present themselves at different moments in our lives.

This view of life, it should be noted, is foreign to the mechanistic model that is repeated ad nauseam in textbooks, articles, and the media. The effect of the reductionist view of life is deafening and makes it difficult to hear the messages coming from our personal experience. One example of this is the constant barrage of objective terms thrown at us and yet the terms refer to what is not at all objective. The implication that comes with this is that the subject is dispensable. This happens frequently with such expressions as *the brain sees, it decides, it wants, it sends a message,* and so forth, when, instead, one should elucidate who and what is this action-initiating *it*. We might hear, in answer, that it is instinct or genes, but far too rare is the response "I have no idea." This is because an underlying attitude assumes there is reason for all phenomena, and this encourages hypotheses that obscure deeper reflection with simplistic answers. In this, the phenomenon of intent brings a fundamental change, for with it we recognize ourselves as being an intractable part of a world that takes form through the complicity that generates purposeful action.

Direction within the Flux of Events

Repeatedly, in this work, the idea that all events have direction and relay purpose suggests itself. The source of such a movement is implicit in all that is the world, and it can be described as a tendency to manifest certain qualities or values. Values constitute inherent potential and navigate evolution and events towards states that express these values. At first this might sound strange, but actually it is not different from what science teaches: events in the physical world happen as they do because of an inner guidance system known as the laws of nature, and because of these inherent principles, nature performs in an organized manner. A mysterious inner guidance system is requisite in whichever way one interprets the world. In science it is not usually viewed in this manner, but its curious nature does surface at times as, for example, in terms of the recurrent metaphysical question, why do physical events correlate with mathematical calculations? But what if this mysterious inherent movement of the universe is not an imposed structure of physical laws formulated by the conscious mind but, instead, the goal-oriented process of intent producing outcomes, as with the earlier example of the anthill? When the idea of inherent guidance is juxtaposed with the equally strange scientific view of natural laws, its strangeness subsides. Whether expressed as mathematical formulae or as values, the guiding component is mysterious. It is true that, presented as formulae, they constitute statements that stake claims, and this fits well with the scientific method. Values are not statements but the expression of forms of being. Formulae profess objectivity, values express a subjective view, and yet the two viewpoints are not so different since everything objective is grounded in subjectivity and every act of perception stems from the integration of qualities transformed by a subject into concepts that denote what we observe. Perception begins with qualities, and this implies value judgments, and these lie at the basis of all we observe as reality. This, in turn, suggests that all we perceive reflects the tendency to become intelligible and that intent, in this context, can be understood as the tendency to be.

To open to a wider view, one could say that what we call reality has many forms. The form we recognize as our universe presents combinations of effects that unite in a way that enables us to perceive what we perceive. Whether the thing we perceive is square, soft, bright, discordant, or harmonious, this reflects the perception of qualities that show relationships. Our ability to recognize certain qualities determines what we recognize as the world. The tapestry of reality is built through the prodigious abilities of discernment with which we are gifted, and, though the world we call reality may seem all there is, there is no basis for such a claim. How could we tell what other forms of discernment are possible and, with them, what other unrealized realities can be revealed?

Values

What was mentioned, in the previous section and earlier, about promoting capacities that affect the values one chooses to develop leads straight to a further issue. It concerns the sense of one's varied engagements and, eventually, one's purpose and commitment in life. But first of all, a word of justification is needed to show that this topic has a place in a discussion of how freedom is enacted. One might argue that personal evolution is a private affair and the values one lives by have to do with personal predilections and beliefs, that is, with sociology and not with philosophy. When today a person is faced with the authoritarian imposition of moral structures, a healthy response is "don't tell me what to do." There is no lack of examples of people who identify with a set of beliefs on good, better, best, and employ them to hoist themselves into a position of command. It's the old trap of a moralist wishing to insert a personal viewpoint into what is presented as being universal.

Seeing through this confusion and perceiving the inherent place of value in life clarify who we are as living beings. It is a simple matter and depends on recognizing that the goal we share is not some abstract idea of development or progress. It is something very different and has to do with expanding our potential in a direction that enables us to recognize ourselves, that is, to be the person with whom we can fully identify. When we recognize the power of reflection and realize that it issues from the free zone held in place by consciousness, it becomes evident that we are personal agents in our own realization and in producing a quality of life that is profoundly personal and expresses a quality of being with which each one of us happily identifies.

In studying the function of intent, it becomes evident that much of what we thought to be invented by thought is actually present in our experience of the world. Morality, for instance, is not created separately in the conceptual mind and subsequently applied to living in the world. It is present independently of mind in the movement of nature and in the structure of our sensitivities. For this reason, what we tend to accomplish in the world, individually and collectively, is not some medley of disparate impulsive desires and ideologies but reflects underlying structure that carries the imprint of personal and collective purpose. This thought returns in the final section of this chapter.

Free to Be Me

It is curious how consciousness is generally accepted as being the director of intent when in fact its role is the very opposite, that of enabling disengagement from intent. Out of this error came the erroneous view that freedom of action is impossible because we have no control over matters. Control, control, and again control—now you have it, then you lose it, and this sports-commentator view of the world worked its way into our understanding. Consciousness controls nothing! It entertains influences that affect the balance of all that enters the world through intent. Intent, too, does not control anything in the sense of *making* something happen; rather, it allows things to happen. This was alluded to when intent was described not as a causal agent but as an inductive field. A clear grasp of what this signifies is basic to an understanding of this work, and this is why a full discussion of induction was included in the previous chapter.

Redressing the matter of control leaves space for refining our understanding of freedom. Lack of a rational controlling entity is no reason to find ourselves cornered into an interpretation that reduces individual freedom to nothing or almost nothing. This negating view results from misunderstanding the role of intent and the manner in which consciousness affects behavior. By disconnecting from intent through the nonaction of consciousness, our structure of intent—the unespied self that sets our trajectory in life—becomes permeable to new influences. It is plain that cultivation of thoughts and actions has less to do with answering requirements imposed from without than with experiencing oneself as the person one feels oneself to be—a person attuned to what personally one finds beautiful, just, and good. It is a case of being true to oneself. Personal freedom is the ability to expand the influences that produce what was referred to as our *greater self*. This is much more than individual whims and notions and has to do with a deep-rooted intent that reaches beyond our individual selves. The aim we share is to find a way to be the person with whom we are ready and happy to identify; this identity has structure, and it is the motive that determines the quality of all involvement in life. It is a kind of isotach that holds its influence even though the turbulence of psychological crosscurrents may trouble and reroute some of its force, at least for a time, until we become free of contradictions and disturbances and reintegrate our whole self. And who can this whole self be other than the uncomplicated person we feel well with, the self we embrace and love to be?

It sounds right to say it this way. Yet, can I claim that there is such an individual presence exercising intent, a *you* and an *I*, who match this description? Very definitely there is, as the next section shows.

Character and Uniqueness

The experience of self includes a further aspect not yet fully considered. We repeatedly recognize ourselves as being the author of our thoughts and actions. One aspect that leads us to this conclusion is the fact that it is within our power to alter and interrupt a course of action or a thought sequence. This has to do with the ability of consciousness to suspend action and disengage the intent that leads our mind and body into action. This was already discussed.

A second aspect of identifying ourselves with the actions we take has to do with recognizing ourselves. For each person, there is the sense that the thoughts one has and the actions one takes are *in character* and reflect the way one tends to be. This is the sense of uniqueness we carry around with us—the sense that whatever I am physically, emotionally, psychologically, and so forth is me alone and distinct from anyone else. One feels one occupies a unique here and now that is the anchor point of *little me*, but there is more to individuality than this. I sense I have a presence that is unique to me. Presence is the subjective experience of relating, and presence of self has to do with the way I feel myself to be in relation to all else. This leads to a sense of identity, of something that finds repeated expression in my experience of life. One way to refer to what is unique in a person is to call it character. Despite all that escapes definition in character, the process that creates character is not difficult to describe.

A person's specific character includes many factors that form an ensemble with or without contradictions. Psychology and other disciplines study this dimension of the individual. The present interest is to consider only what relates to philosophy and this includes the relationship between character and intention, and in this context, a person's intention is understood as a general pattern of engagement in life and the world. What a person finds meaningful and worthwhile in life is a reflection of a personal structure of intent. Intentions become apparent in one's attitudes and in the sense of mission (conscious or unconscious) that prompts one's actions. Stating that an individual carries a mission was once totally repudiated by those who rationally rejected any such idea, believing it to be pure nonsense. However, psychological tools that have become available today give voice to unconscious motivation and clearly demonstrate that it is common for people to have a sense of purpose and sense a connection to a specific guiding impulse that brings meaning to their lives. An encompassing sense of values of every sort influences the way one positions oneself in life, one's initiatives, and one's reactions—what seems right, what seems beautiful, what seems meaningful and what seems useful. Intuitions like these make up what is pleasurable and what is disturbing, what is interesting and what

Intentions give form to a person's character.

is boring, and together constitute the intentions with which an individual is aligned. Whether conscious or nonconscious, whether part of our physical state, our emotional attitudes or whatever, intentions give form to a person's character.

The intent pattern that gives the structure of character is, in return, influenced by our way of being. This is a reference to the degree of freedom, described earlier, that arises through the ability of consciousness to disengage from action and bring to the fore possibilities that influence one's overall intent. Through reflection comes the ability to influence intentions that influence actions. Our daily occupations and our style of life no doubt influence the extent to which we leave an opening for diverse thoughts and feelings, for memories, imagination, curiosity, gratitude, and the many ways of being that determine the degree of freedom our actions have from characteristic intent patterns. In short, conscious activity, though it does not trigger our actions, can affect them in more ways than one might at first realize.

The potential for personal choice is greatly reduced if we are indifferent to the fact that we have this possibility of affecting what we think about and, too, of choosing to exit from thoughts. To the extent we ignore the fact that we have the option of cultivating the form of our expression in the world and our personal character, we remain largely disempowered from our true potential. Associating *exclusively* with *little me* in the belief that I lead my life with conscious intentions is to be caught in a trap of ignorance because it reduces self to consciousness, that is, to only a minute part of the overall form of self, of *greater me*, that ultimately is the only me there is. How strange and wonderful it is to return to our deeper intuitive sense of how things are and realize that this personal me can set the direction for much of what I do in my life and holds the power to mold the intent being I am that is formed out of connections linking me to all that is the world.

A Moral Dimension to Self

Before closing this work, another subject—a mere sketch can suffice—needs mentioning so as to allow the return of a banished dimension of living experience. Wherever a position of scientific objectivity was embraced, the criteria allowing phenomena to be accepted as real excluded structures of experience that were based on intent and the intensity of engagement of an individual. These were relegated to the position of add-ons for which, if mentioned at all, some utilitarian function in the natural world was proffered. For example, the idea of serving some purpose was remodeled as the fervent belief that evolution in nature is driven by the (unexplained) need for self-preservation. Everything suggesting the presence of meaning and value, even altruism, was seen as illusory and, in this gargantuan oversight, the generic presence of aesthetics and morality in everything known was passed over. There is no need, just here, to develop this subject beyond what is necessary to allow areas of knowledge that were wrongly exiled to return to the fold.

The ability we have to influence the unconscious flow of intent and to remodel our inheritance comes to expression during the rich spiritual journey of life that includes our activities, experiences, reflections, learning, sensitivities, and behaviors—everything that promotes our direction in life and, in more specific terms, that develops our sense of values and our ability to embody them. In this context, the moral nature of being becomes obvious. The form we have in life, as an individual and in our commonality, is that of a moral being. It issues from *greater me* and is expressed through the intentioned being that forms our character. Consciously, I recognize values I wish to embody in my life and these values are what I accept as me when I am unperturbed and fully absorbed in enacting mentally and physically those things with which I feel right. Our sense of value is a form of intent that influences how we are and how we act and, as already noted, can itself be influenced by options that arise in consciousness.

The implication of this is that values and morality rise from a deeper level than the conscious mind and are a constitutive part of all that integrates self and world. Our personal way of being expresses a commitment we uphold with all that is. Its form is that of a moral imperative we create for ourselves—*we* meaning the whole unlimited nature of self as an intentioned being. The philosophy of self is about this being, its commitments and the freedom it has to influence the position it takes up in the world. Here philosophy, psychology, and science can meet to recognize that character, freedom, individuality, and morality and values in general are constitutive parts of what we know as life and the world.

In the feeling we have of being ourselves, there is much to understand. Although thought may be misled and form very false ideas of what we imagine ourselves to be, giving place to experience and to our intuitive sense of self rebalances this, and we then can see self as the intent pattern we carry into the world through our thoughts and actions. The awe-inspiring part is that this structure is not within our physical being but is formed by the totality of all that is. Its source is everywhere and, as an individual, I am the expression of all that there is. I am everything that has bearing upon the world I inhabit, and everyone else is the very same—an expression of all that is the world each inhabits. To the extent that their world and my world are the same world, we are the same. I differ from them in my bearing, in the arrangement of intent that is my character, but to follow that intent to its source and to sense its all-embracing origin, which is my origin, is to blend with all that everyone is and with the structure of intent that forms this world.

To open an understanding of the subjective dimension present in all we perceive has been a central purpose of this work and, with this, to present intent not as fictive function of the mind but as an independent feature of the universe that is as real as any other constituent we might name. Intent brings an understanding of what we call self and of the interrelationship that unites personal experience with all that we assume to be objective. Presented in these pages is one view of our experience in this world, and it is no more than a primary tutor on ways we relate to intent. As a primer, even if not fully fledged, its time has come to leave my notebook and set out into the world.

Epilogue: A Personal Viewpoint

SO, IS THAT IT? Is that what mind is, what world is, what we are, what is real, and what lies beyond reality? Have riddles been solved? Has some deeper truth come out? It would be quaint to say this is the path to unraveling the universe, but that is not how it goes.

Truth does not reside in an explanation. It is not found in any particular way of apprehending things. Everything that at one moment creates understanding can, at another moment, disintegrate in countless new mysteries that defy the knowledge that was carefully amassed.

Was it not always like this? There is reticence to accept the loss of the foundations of one's knowledge and allow for the possibility that what was painstakingly amassed is totally changed. Many scientists and thinkers argue in favor of progress and repeat the tired formula that new developments are refinements of general truths discovered earlier, as if rough truths are polished to become ever more exact and ever more universally applicable. A typical example of this is the claim that earlier scientific theories, say those of Newton, were a refinement of previous ones and that physics in the twentieth century refines these further. This is part of a simplistic view of a grand progression of knowledge and of our place at the top of what has been accomplished—the lineage of the chosen who were graced to lead the understanding of all humanity. Granted, for a limited spell within a given truth paradigm, there may be some justification for claiming progress and refinement occurred; however, the error is to take this to be an objective fact that holds beyond the flux of changing viewpoints.

How cozy this progression towards truth sounds until one asks how old this whole enterprise is. It has been propounded for maybe five hundred years—that is all—and in this time has managed to educate one way of understanding that is noted for its denial of the validity of other civilizations both ancient and present. This approach, it well appears, has functioned as an undeclared inquisition on all who carry another understanding only to arrive, in our time, at a point where the whole edifice of Western ideas in all fields of knowledge is coming apart. What is plain, though apparently difficult to accept, is the fact that the emerging understanding of life, nature, and the world does not at all arise through a refinement of what was previously established and does not belong to the same framework. This suggests that progression towards truth is an illusion. No single truth is independent of the perceiver. It runs its time and eventually unravels and loses its truth kernel and becomes irrelevant and irretrievable. A view of science or knowledge as something bouncing from head to head, from one genius to the next, where each perfects and furthers the knowledge established previously is to ignore the wisdom that sustains the venture of life in which everyone, through accumulation of life experience, is an equal participant.

A person observing a lifetime of events in the home gathers a treasure of wisdom as valid as any other, and as with all understanding, this wisdom is made of different levels of truth. One level has to do with the wisdom of life that accrues through observation and reflection; another is the hidden depths whereby concerns not formulated consciously are part of the mysteries of the time and culture. In sensing these underlying enigmas, the person at home is on a par with everyone—scholar, laborer, whomever. These deeper truths have a time of validity that is limited and will, in due course, lose their attraction. Strange as it may sound, their appeal recedes and later they will no longer be the vibrant personal expression they were when their time was ripe. This is not to deny that deep understanding of life and the world can arise and the context in which it is set can remain vibrant over very long periods. Yet even here perspectives and emphases change and the initial understanding submits to readjustments and new questions. These changes reflect changing truths rather than progress to a single truth.

We may expect that development in disciplines of study is the result of eliminating hypotheses and reaching solutions, but this is uncommon. It would be to consider understanding in the way one considers technological development. Such a view can have certain relevance in the case of an individual researcher who advances through the resolution of problems, as might an engineer, historian, mathematician, or artist. Shakespeare, for example, sets out a knot of existential issues that are worked through in a play, and subsequent plays go beyond those issues and set further and different challenges. But currents of thought are unlikely to change direction because the hypothesis worked on has been exhausted. A particular line of thinking can lose its pertinence without having answered the questions it came to answer, and this, simply because the quest for understanding changed orientation. The reason for change is usually not apparent at the time. The animating tendency of a period is sensed on a deep and subtle level and comes to expression spontaneously in all that is produced in that period. This deeper pertinence is an undercurrent that animates what is known consciously and, in general, becomes recognizable only after that particular period is over.

Different peoples of the world hold different truths. Who can claim to be in a position to contrast and evaluate them? Deep and far-reaching knowledge, past and present, held by individuals and cultures that are not part of Western ideas has been eclipsed by one short-lived tradition—yes, ours—and this attitude has probably much to do with the mentality of the period leading up to the present, which is characterized by individuals relinquishing any claim to personal understanding. Individually, we ceased to consider what makes good sense to us personally; we ceased to consider what we understand as being true, having turned our personal power of discretion over to the priests of modern knowledge. We elected those priests to preach the truths by which we live. Reticent to take a stand of our own, we follow these authoritarian figures: economists, doctors, archaeologists, astronomers, educators, biologists, psychologists, physicists, historians, as if they had an extra window on truth—of course, they do not.

One might question what doctors know of approaches to healing, what archaeologists know about the mystery traditions of ancient cultures, what economists know about social values not linked to supply and demand, what psychologists and psychoanalysts understand about powers of the mind, what teachers know about learning and every student's capacity to be brilliant, what scientists know about what is unreasonable, biologists, about life? To continue, philosophers, more often than not, take their cue from the statements of scientists, relinquishing philosophy's independence and its role as a source of understanding to which science must bend. The litany goes on. What do politicians know about creating peace and harmony, and what do those making military decisions understand of the sacredness of all life forms? Do we need to give these people authority? How did we turn dimensions of unfathomable richness over to such priests who hold the authority to know? How did we impoverish our state of understanding to such a degree? These elected figures study their separate disciplines and know what they know. Their knowledge can be profound and extensive, but that has nothing to do with approaching what is true, right, respectful, kind, just, and beautiful.

The compendium of knowledge that has been studied and assembled by scholars can be of interest when coming to personal understandings, yet, when gleaning from the knowledge they amassed, we often come to realize that their conclusions have little to do with the way we understand and experience the world. Every individual has a personal, intuitive way of reaching ever more fully into the experience of being. This cannot be turned over to another to exercise in our place. If we give it away, it dies. No one can have these insights in our place.

Just how personal every understanding is can be far from obvious. For instance, the statement *oxygen and hydrogen form water* is an opinion and not pure fact. We easily forget that it is couched in a personal view. Sure, it is a fact that physical experiments show that hydrogen and oxygen can combine to form water and that water can be separated into these elements, but this does not necessarily tell what water is. Defining water in this way excludes many variables, some to do with water—flow patterns and snowflakes, for example—and others that reach into the nature of the world, such as the role of the observer, the effect of the quantity of matter in the universe on the chemical reaction, and, why not, the participation of nonmaterial beings, say, legendary nymphs such as undines, and whatever more in the observed event. Every claimed fact is encased in certain personal viewpoints. To consider water to be conclusively defined by the chemical molecule H_2O makes it very easy not to take other aspects into consideration, such as phenomena that suggest water molecules organize themselves to retain electrical charges that supply the body's meridians or, for instance, that the structure of water molecules carries very specific meanings such as those we identify as emotional states.

To determine what is objective and factual is not achieved through naïve statements about the outcome of reactions because context, environment, and attitude are part of any objective fact. Descriptions and explanations we attribute to phenomena typically state far more and far less than what an observation implies, and as a result, our endorsement of scientific-style observation may imply views of life and the world that we have not consciously chosen to accept as true. It is through a subjective viewpoint that life comes alive. Our ability to experience is not determined by the quantity of things we have learned but by our identification with qualities of being, and this has to do with our implication in the meaning we create. Realizing this, we can take the cloaks off the priests we anointed. We can appreciate them for who they are while knowing that what makes sense to me is personal and distinct and it comes to me from a different wisdom path than theirs.

All this leads in the direction of an answer to what makes a quest vibrant, makes life real, truth true, and meaning meaningful. To this, there is just one answer: *I* does. As shown in this book, a living connection of all is needed to create meaning. Without this connectivity, nothing arises—no concepts, no objects, no meaning, nothing to understand, and no one to understand it. The advent of integration happens through intent, an intent that is intimately bound with the structure of self. Only with the presence of self do facts and meaning arise; only then does truth arise as well as everything that makes truth true, beauty beautiful, and goodness good.

And what precisely does the *I* bring to make something take on meaning? What could the magic power unique to self be? It is the power that holds together all that is at any moment. When a verb is introduced into a string of words, they become a unified, meaningful whole, a sentence, and when *I* enters any given context, it brings a unifying effect similar to that of the verb. That effect has a name: what self brings is intensity. Intensity is the condition needed to integrate aspects into wholes. For a series of notes to become a melody, one needs to bring an intensity of listening. It cannot be achieved when one is feeling weak and low in energy, especially if the melody is lengthy and complex and heard for the first time. Just as holding notes together to form a melody requires an intensity of being, so with everything that produces a perceivable object: a string of words that form a thought, thoughts that form a meaningful narrative, a scattering of stars that form a constellation, colors that give the quality of a sunrise, and trees that become a forest. Different meanings require the presence of different degrees of intensity, whether to hold a picture together so as to recognize what it represents or to hold a dance performance together so its overall meaning becomes apparent. The intensity present in the subjective observer brings forth meaning in what we experience. An intensity of engagement brings life, beauty, elegance, and all that becomes meaningful in everything we imagine, observe, think, and do, and this same intensity of self brings the sense of rightness we feel when something is true (see chapter 1, "The Nature of Truth"). Truth holds for as long as the intensity that actively binds what we observe into a whole is present. When that intensity is no longer active, the capacity to hold that particular form of truth is lost. It is not that truth has changed, but simply that a truth faded away and has become irrelevant because the intensity of self that animated that structure of intent passed on and now engages a different intent.

Self, thus, has intensity. It has an intensity of being that powers all that is drawn together to produce the world of which we become aware. But remember, self is the activity of an intent structure whose source reaches into all the world and into all time and that intent structure—you, me, everyone—is what gives rise to our world and gives it the form that makes it what it is. The intent that forms self is the intent that gives form to everything. From the world arises the self that creates that world! So you see, pulling ourselves up by our bootstraps is not at all beyond what is possible, and we even seem quite adept at it. But who is doing the pulling, is it us or is it the world? You can take your choice. Either will do as an answer because neither we nor the world is autonomous. Both stem from the subjective act of reaching for intelligibility. But can it be that the physical world is as insubstantial as self was shown to be? The apparent permanence of the world and all that we call real is bound together with our collective ability to sustain the intent that forms a common viewpoint. This thought, however, leads beyond the scope of this work and into a nowhere-land that is off the game board. The adventure trails followed

From the world arises the self that creates that world.

Epilogue: A Personal Viewpoint | 249

in this book keep to what is generally familiar though often not well understood.

If truth does not hold through time and meaning is transitory, one might ask, what is the point of all that has been written in this little book? The reply is that it serves, like any careful study, to sharpen our senses and refine our understanding of a viewpoint. The way we understand mind, self, and world has an impact on our personal life and on the society we create. What results from this study is not objective truth and not part of such a truth and not even progress towards this truth but is a way of formulating what makes sense to us at the present time. If carefully crafted, such a study serves to blend together what we know of subjectivity and objectivity and of the physical and the nonphysical in a way that helps enter more fully into the experience of life that is ours. To the extent the connections drawn are valid, the account will have a ring of truth to it—truth in our time that relates to the queries that animate a personal search for expression and understanding. All important is that it is my truth; it may well be ours should our viewpoints coincide. Understanding carries with it the pleasure of finding myself integrated in a wholesome manner into all I know and, too, of sensing closeness with what is intimated yet remains unknown.

Index

Adaptation	126, 221
Animals	78, 157, 182, 184
Anthill	152, 189-90, 235
Audition (Hearing)	56-67, 71, 73, 74, 80, 83, 84
Awareness	**xv**, 27, 30, 65, 75, 105, 110-12, 117, 119, 121-2, 158-9, 202
Beauty (Aesthetics)	42, 69, 74, 77, 158, 160, 165, 174, 204, 247-8
Bohm, David	30
Bridge (Passage, Transfer) between	
Feeling-Concept	55, 65, 85
Potential-Actual	58, 62, 84, 183, 186
Expansive-Limited	35-6, 83
Fovea-Periphery	55, 85
Calculus	80, 150
Causality (Cause)	34, 131-2, 144, 146, 157, 163-4, 168-9, 172, 232
vs. induction	**213-224**
Centrifugal	22, 25-6, 30
Centripetal	xi, 22, 25-6, 30, 57, 210
Character	115, 183, 221, 237-241
Choice	43, 106, 117-8, 125, 141, 144, 204, 223-4, **225-41**
Cognition	16, 25-6, 35, 39, 75, 115
Coherence (Communion)	36, 103, 174, 191-4, 204, 231
Color	67, 73, **87-102**
Coming together (as a unit)	22, 36, 38, 43, 76, 82-3, 162, 185, 192, 196, 199, 206-10
Complicity	111, 137, 157, 205, 234
Concepts	4, **7-46**, 51-53, 56-7, 64, 67, 76, 82, 97, 119-20, 154-5, 166, 175, 180-2, 187-8, 191-2, 208, 235
Connotation (Connotative)	8, **12-14**, 15-16, 21, 31-2, 35, 180
Consciousness	**xiii-xv**, and otherwise throughout the book
Continuity (Discontinuity)	30, 40, 44, 51-2, 126
Contradiction	**87-98**, 112, 156, 178
Correlation	29, 83, 151, 156, 165, 168, 193-5, 206

252 | *Making Sense*

Creatures (Living Beings)	181–182, 211, 236
Cupid	150
Definitions	13, 23, 99–101, 103, 213
de La Garanderie	53, 148–150
Denotation (Denotative)	8, 12–17, 22, 28, 31, 37, 50, 52, 55, 74, 83, 145, 180, 197
Depth	91–2, 95–8
Dimensionality: 1st, 2nd, 3rd	87–98
Dunstable, John	23
Duration	28–9, 38–41, 76, 82–3, 85, 119, 146, 180, 191–2, 207, 215–16, 222
Entropy	161–5, 219
Evolution	158, 172, **173–4**, 234, 240
Existentialism	44
Expanded consciousness	xiv–xv, 13, 55, 65, 69, 80, 119, 121, 159, 203, 227
Eyck, Jan van	23
Facial recognition	17
Feelings	27–9, 32, 43, 61, 65, 85, 97, 158, **159**, 166, 170, 240
Form	9, 16–7, 28–30, 35, 67, 74–6, 100, 135, 144–8, 152–7, 166, 182, 184, 186, 191, 193–196, 206, 224, 235, 239–40, 248
Fovea	48–58, 64–5, 70–1, 76–8, 79–82, 84–5
Freedom (of choice)	24, 117, 119, 120, 138, 163, 220–4, **225–41**
Gestion Mentale, la	**148–50**
Grammar	103, 137, 170, 192
Greater Me (Greater *I*)	178–81, 195, 204, 207, 228, 231, 239, 240
Hearing *see* audition	
Humanism	45
I	5, 8, 36, 88, 98–9, 102, 107, 114–17, 143, 154, **177–211**, 232, 237–9, 241, 247
Ibex	167
Imagination	34, 62–3
Induction	156, 173, **213–24**
Information	2, 16–17, 35, 65, 66, 93, 131–132, 154, 161–2
Integration	35–6, 42, 67–9, 83–4, 97, 99–101, 132, 156–8, 163, 170–1, 192, 193–6, 206, 210, 212, 214, 247

Index | 253

Intelligence	35, 69, 75, 134, 166, 189–90, 194, 197
Intensity	93, 247–8
Intent (Intention)	xii–xiii, 4, 11, 23, 45, 50–1, 71, 73, 90–1, 96, 98, 106, 112, **125–50, 151–76**, 178, 181–3, 186, 188, 191–6, 204–5, 208–11, 219, 223–24, 230–41
Interference	74–5, 85, 100
Intermingling (Blending)	55, 62–3, 65, 85, 184, 232
Intuition (Intuitive)	xiii, 16, 24, 28, 42, 44, 67, 77, 100, 171, 182, 202–3, 239, 241, 246
Joy	5, 33, 78, 120, 123, 130
Laws (of nature)	24, 132, 157, 163, 165, 179, 217, 219, 220, 234–35
Letting go	14, 17, 19, 77, 81
Learning *see* school	
Limits (Limitless)	35, 39–40, 55–6, 62, 85, 162, 167, 178, 195, 222
Little Me (Little *I*)	122, 178–80, 195, 196, 199, 201, 204, 207, 238, 239
Masaccio	23
Maxwell's demon	162
Material (Materialist)	17, 25, 34, 45, 65, 67–8, 119–20, 126, 143, 147, 152–7, 171–2, 184, 206, 212
Meaning	xi, 2, 4–6, 7–46, 49–51, 57–8, 64, 67, 69, 73–9, 85, 91, 100, 103, 158, 160–5, 166, 168–75, 180–81, 186, 194, 204, 205–11, 216–20, 238, 240, 247–8
Melody (Tune)	4–5, 58–9, 61, 96, 153, 247–8
Mind	2–6, **7–44**, 50–85, 92, 96, **103–23**, 141, 146, 148–9, 155, 165–6, 175, 180, 186, 189–90, 191, 194, 208, 216, 222, 230, 235–6
Conceptual Mind (Rational, Logical, Analytical Mind)	
	14–16, 35, 43, 55, 59, 60, 67, 80, 122, 172 191, 216, 221, 236
Expanded Mind	4, 18, 27–8, 30, 34, 36, 40, 41–3, 69–70, 76, 83–5, 92, 120–2, 171, 191, 194, 231
Morals	45, 160, 197–8, 204, 235–6, **239–40**, 246
Multiconsciousness	4, 30, 85
Narcissus	81

254 | *Making Sense*

Negentropy	164
Nonconscious(-ness)	xi, **xiv,** xv, 2, 4, 7–31, 38, 40, 43, 63–5, 76, 84, 225–7
Noncontinuity	29–30, 39, 44
Nonmaterial	22, 147, 153, 157, 166, 184, 206
Nonphysical	80, 147, 155, 156, 171, 196, 199, 249
Now	**37–41**, 45, 56, 59–60, 75, 79–81, 84, 101, 178–80, 238
Objective	15, 23–5, 34, 36, 42–3, 48, 55–6, 64–5, 69, 73, 80, 82, 98–9, 101–2, 109, 115, 119, 145, 156, 161–2, 165, 187–8, 197–8, 202, 234, 241, 244, 247
Objectivity	5, 13, 23, 32, 44–6, 48, 57–8, 63, 84, 145, 170, 191, 197–8, 239
Perception	**xiii, xv**, 11–12, 16, 26, 32–45, 47–85, 87–90, 100, 119, 146, 159, 162, 165, 171, 192, 196, 199, 235
Periphery	48–85
Perspective	23, 54, 101–2, 126
Pleasure	2, 120–123, 249
Potential	43, 58, 83–4, 105–7, 112, 118, 178, 186, 199, 205, 223, 231, 234
Presence, degrees of	xiii, 14–16, 26, 39–40, 54–66, 79, 84, 89, 91, 99–100, 158–9, 186, 192–6, 199, 214, 238, 248
Present, the	37–41, 56, 59–62, 73–4, 80, **82–4**, 91, 168–71, 199
Purpose (Purposeful)	3–5, 44–6, 130, 142, 154, 163–8, 171–2, 179, 182, 194, 196, 199, 205, 230, 231–2, 235–8
Quality	8, 15–16, 28, 48, 76, 94–7, 100, 145–6, 163, 221, 236–7
Random	110, 152, 161, 164, 190, 216, 218
Reality	15, 23–4, 34, 44, 48, 51, 54, 62, 65, 73–74, 80, 119–20, 135, 145–7, 169–71, 185–6, 191, 197–9, 202, 235
Regression, infinite	64, 203, 209, 232
Relationship	23–5, 45, 61, 83–4, 91–100, 131, 157, 161, 166, 174, 181–4, 235
Renaissance	23–5, 126

Index | 255

Romanticism	171–2
Scale	51, 54, 69–70, 75, 83–4, 93, 99–100
School (Learning)	19, 77, 130, 134, 148–50, 245
Science (Scientific)	5, 25, 36, 44–5, 56, 131, 146, 157–8, 163, 165, 168, 171, 179, 190, 197–8, 222, 234–5, 243, 246
Sculptor	153–4
Self	4, 24–7, 42, 44–6, 58, 79–81, 102, 111–16, 119, 154–5, 160, **177–212**, 223–4, 226–32, 237–41, 247–8
Self-consciousness	26, 188, **202–3**
Senses, the	27, 33, 51, 61, 70–1, 110–12, 153, 158
Sight (Seeing)	18, 39–40, **47–85**, **87–102**
Space	13, 23, 44, 65, 79, 80, 90, 96–7, 98, 100, 126, 135, 146, 149–50, 161–2, 178–9, 202
Spatial	52–3, 63, 67, 74, 79–81, 84, 95–7, 149–50, 175, 195
Subjectivity	23, 36, 43, 44, 65, 71–3, 98, 135, 188, 192, 198–207, 235
Subliminal	xiv, 63, 67–69, 72, 153, 195, 203
Surrealism	57–58
Temporal	23, 39–41, 56, 58–9, 62–3, 66, 74, 78–84, 88–9, 95–7, 101, 149–50, 175
Theater of the absurd	45
Thinking (Thought)	xi–xiv, 1–5, 7–31, 33–46, 48, 50, 51, 55, 57, 63–5, 81, 85, 100, 105–7, 111–12, 118–23, 130, 139–42, 158, 170–5, 179, 182–3, 187, 189–90, 193, 202, 204, 207–8, 214, 219, 228–33, 237–41
Time and Space	13, 35, 44, 55, 57, 79, 135, 145–7, 159, 174, 178–9, 193, 195–6, 199
Tinctoris, Johannes	24
Transformation (Transfer)	23–5, 28, 35–6, 38, 42, 53–4, 68–70, 83, 84, 94, 131, 154, 214–6, 220–2, 231–2
Truth	**42–4**, 74, 197, 216, 243–9
Unity	10, 15, 43, 49, 55, 64, 79, 82, 87–9, 98, 154, 161, 181, 192, 196, 203, 217

Unknown, the	xv, 12, 21, 34, 36, 41, 43, 81, 83, 95, 138–9, 141, 152, 186, 190, 194, 207, 249
Universality (Universal)	51, 58, 132, 157, 194, 243
Values	25, 42–3, 45, 122, 160, 181, 197–8, 204, 226–7, 233–5, **235–6**, 238, 240
Vasari, Giorgio	24
Virtual	26
Visual field	49, 55, 59, 75, 79, 89, 99, 100
Wholes	12, 42, 44–5, 50, 51, 59, 64–5, 67, 69, 74–9, 82, 85, 126, 144, 152, 162–3, 170, 172, 214, 216–21, 237, 247–8
Will, the	19, 117, 133–4, 138, 148, 154
Zebra	100–1
Zen archery	139–41

ABOUT THE AUTHOR

Peter Moddel was born in Ireland and lives in Fribourg, Switzerland. Experiences gathered from studies in various disciplines, from visiting different cultures, and from periods of personal retreat have found their way into this work. Philosophy holds a central place among the author's interests, which also include astronomy, music, hiking, and an active concern for life, beauty and the environment.

Lightning Source UK Ltd.
Milton Keynes UK
UKOW03f1459310317
298024UK00002B/47/P